WEST HAM
IN MY DAY

To Trevor

Be lucky

WEST HAM
IN MY DAY

By Terry Roper & Tony McDonald

FootballWorld

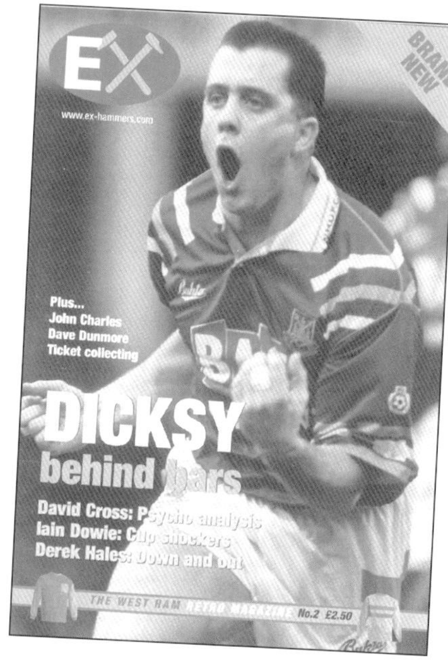

First published in England in November 2008 by

FootballWorld
Tel: 01708 744 333
www.ex-hammers.com

Printed by Biddles Ltd, King's Lynn, Norfolk

Distributed by Football World
103 Douglas Road, Hornchurch, Essex, RM11 1AW, England
Email: editorial@footballworld.co.uk

Set in Times Roman

ISBN 978-0-9559340-1-8

EX
www.ex-hammers.com
100% UNOFFICIAL MONTHLY
BEST of times
EXCLUSIVE!
Big Clyde talks from Bermuda
Plus...
Julian Dicks: part 2
'64 Hero Ronnie Boyce
Alan Curbishley
Keith McPherson
Hit Men
EX
www.ex-hammers.com
10th Anniversary SPECIAL
BOBBY
We'll never
Plus...
Mooro Memorabilia
Billy Bonds
EX
www.ex-hammers.com
In respect of those who have worn the shirt
MAD DOG
Unleashed
EXCLUSIVE
Martin Allen on madcap memories and kicking Glenn Roeder
Plus...
Bobby
Innocent
Dudley Tyler
George Cowie
Ernie Gregory
Lee Boylan
Maine Road
EX
www.ex-hammers.com
For people who know their West Ham history
BROOKING
The real Trevor and why he must quit the top job
Plus...
John Bond
Ade Coker
Tommy Taylor
Redknapp's Pompey Party
Joe Gallagher
Moore cards
Loan deals
Books
THE WEST HAM RETRO MAGAZINE No.6 £2.50
EX
www.ex-hammers.com
Forget the present...The past just gets better!
Plus...
Di Canio & Brooking go Head-to-Head
Cole blow
Marshy & Bish
Frank O'Farrell
Memorabilia
There's only one McAVENNIE
THE BLOND BOMBSHELL IS BACK WITH HIS BRAND NEW BOOK. EXTRACT AND EXCLUSIVE INTERVIEW WITH FRANK INSIDE...
THE WEST HAM RETRO MAGAZINE NO.7 £2.50
EX
www.ex-hammers.com
No.1 for Exclusives with former West Ham players
INSIDE...
Clive Charles
His last interview
Neil Ruddock
Kenny Brown
Mal Musgrove
Memorabilia
ALVIN ADMITS:
'I want to be manager'
PARDEW CONFIRMED BOSS...AS EX-HAMMERS MISS OUT
THE WEST HAM RETRO MAGAZINE No.8 £2.50

www.ex-hammers.com
Plus..STUART SLATER, ALLEN McKNIGHT, STUART PEARSON, BOYS OF '86
EX
The life of
BRIAN
BRIAN DEAR ON WHAT REALLY HAPPENED AT

www.ex-hammers.com
Plus..BOBBY HOWE and TREVOR HARTLEY, KEITH COLEMAN, TREVOR DAWKINS
EX
AVCO
Top
MARK
WINGER WARDIE REFLECTS ON HIS ROLE IN '86 AND PREPARES

www.ex-hammers.com
Plus..BILLY JENNINGS, ALAN DICKENS, MEMORABILIA
EX
Eddie
BOV
Midfield
Iron Man's

www.ex-hammers.com
Plus..VIC KEEBLE & JOHN DICK, KEVIN KEEN, MEMORABILIA
EX
BONZO
Exclusive with our

www.ex-hammers.com
Plus...MARK ROBSON, COLIN MACKLEWORTH, MEMORABILIA and much more...
EX
"I NEVER ENJOYED MANAGEMENT"
Part 2 of our Billy Bonds special
BONZO
Exclusive with our former boss
THE WEST HAM RETRO MAGAZINE No.13 £2.50

www.ex-hammers.com
Plus...PAT HOLLAND, PAUL ALLEN, MEMORABILIA and much more...
EX
The Auction of the Year
LUDO
Exclusive with our big Czech mate
THE WEST HAM RETRO MAGAZINE No.14 £2.50

CONTENTS

ACKNOWLEDGEMENTS

A sincere thank you to all the following for making this book possible:

Dave Alexander, Tim Crane, Terry Connelly, Danny Francis, Steve Blowers, Neale Harvey, Nicola Lagzdins, Tony Hogg, Susie Muir, Lucien Gover and Anne Walker.

A big thanks to the former West Ham United players who kindly gave up their time for the interviews that appeared in *EX* and have been edited for inclusion in this book. Their co-operation is very much appreciated.

And for their help with photographs: Steve Bacon, Arthur Griffiths, Richard Austin and John Helliar.

www.ex-hammers.com
Plus...ROGER CROSS, MATTIE HOLMES, YOUR MEMORIES and much more...
EX
EXCLUSIVE!
JOHN LYALL
Part two: The Management Years
NEW! Memorabilia auction inside

www.ex-hammers.com
Plus...STEVE POTTS, LEROY ROSENIOR, MEMORABILIA and much more...
EX
LEROY!
EXCLUSIVE!
'POP' ROBSON
The 70s striker reflects on his two spells at Upton Park

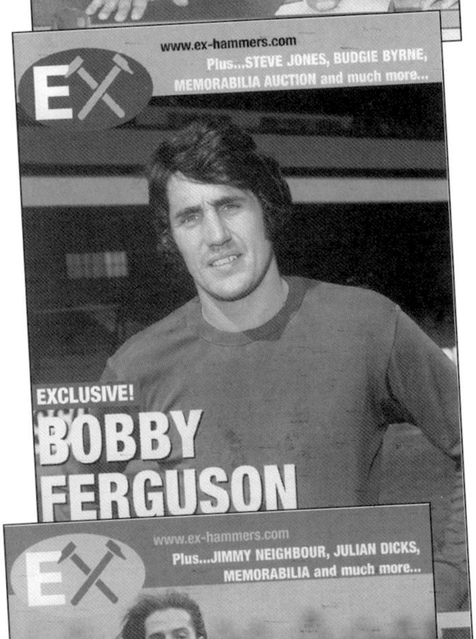
www.ex-hammers.com
Plus...STEVE JONES, BUDGIE BYRNE, MEMORABILIA AUCTION and much more...
EX
EXCLUSIVE!
BOBBY FERGUSON

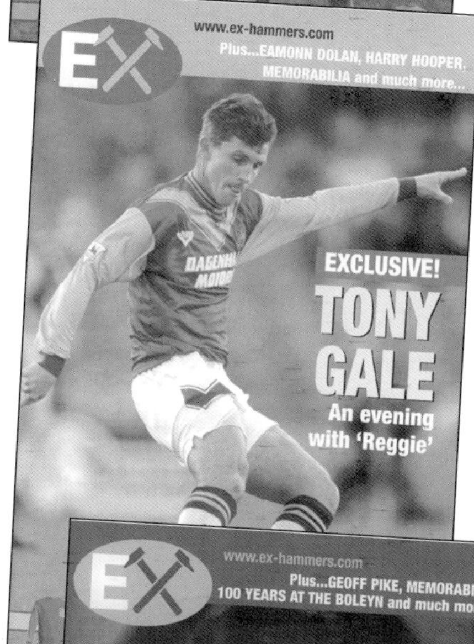
www.ex-hammers.com
Plus...EAMONN DOLAN, HARRY HOOPER, MEMORABILIA and much more...
EX
EXCLUSIVE!
TONY GALE
An evening with 'Reggie'

www.ex-hammers.com
Plus...JIMMY NEIGHBOUR, JULIAN DICKS, MEMORABILIA and much more...
EX
DAGENHAM MOTORS
EXCLUSIVE!
BISH
"Fans don't realise how they can affect players"
Di Canio goes wild!
Pictures from Italy
THE WEST HAM RETRO MAGAZINE No.21 £3.00

www.ex-hammers.com
Plus...GEOFF PIKE, MEMORABILIA, 100 YEARS AT THE BOLEYN and much more...
EX
MAJOR EXCLUSIVE!
LOU MACARI
'My BIG Regret'
THE WEST HAM RETRO MAGAZINE No.22 £3.00

www.ex-hammers.com
Plus...TIM BREACKER, JOE COLE, 100 YEARS AT THE BOLEYN and much more...
60s Cup winners reunion dinner details inside
PENALTY! Hits and misses
RAY
on the spot again
www.ex-hammers.com
Plus...PETER BRABROOK, ROB JENKINS, MORDECHAI SPIEGLER and much more...
60s Cup winners Reunion Dinner Tickets still available
EXCLUSIVE
TC
www.ex-hammers.com
JOHN SISSONS & JIM STANDE
Exclusives with two Wembley heroe
40th Anniversary Specia
Euro Kings
Our greatest achievement
www.ex-hammers.com
64-65 CUP WINNERS' DINNER REVIEW
Plus...Roger Hugo, memorabilia and comps
ANOTHER MAJOR EXCLUSIVE!
PAOLO
www.ex-hammers.com
JOHN MONCUR, HAT-TRICK HEROES
Plus...When We Were Young, memorabilia
NOEL
Tributes to Cantwell
THE WEST HAM RETRO MAGAZINE No.27 £3.00
www.ex-hammers.com
1975 & '80 CUP WINNERS' DINNER
Plus...Noel Cantwell, Mark Ward, Bill Kitchener
FREE BOOK when you subscribe!
NIGHTMARE ON GREEN STREET
LIAM
Brady signed off in style
THE WEST HAM RETRO MAGAZINE No.28 £3.00

10

INTRODUCTION

IF you don't care too much for the excesses of modern football and the way the game is now poisoned by self-interest and driven by the relentless pursuit of money by players not fit to lace the boots of their much more accomplished predecessors, then *IN MY DAY* should be right up your street.

Those of you who bought *IMD* Volume One a year or so ago, many thanks and we trust you enjoyed it otherwise you wouldn't be reading this now. You will already know what the book is all about. For those who didn't, shame on you! *IMD* is a compilation of some 24 exclusive interviews conducted with former West Ham United players whose careers spanned five decades, from the late 1950s to the 90s.

The interviews are effectively extracts from previous issues of *EX* magazine, which we launched in November 2002 and is now approaching its 50th edition. The copy has been edited and updated for the purpose of this book and there is also new material. In most cases, new pictures of the subjects – many rare or previously unseen images – have been included.

IMD is, we believe, an entertaining way of providing a fascinating insight into the history of West Ham and how the club has evolved over the past half-century – the fascinating characters who have come and gone through the claret-and-blue gates and the atmosphere, both buoyant and gloomy, that has existed within the Hammers camp at various times. *IMD* is also in itself a reflection of how drastically football has changed over the same period – mainly for the worst, it has to be said.

For us it continues to be an absolute pleasure to sit down with so many former West Ham favourites, many of them big names in their day, and recall the good times and the bad they experienced at Upton Park and after leaving the club. By virtue of the fact that they are ex-players, the people interviewed on the following pages have been able to speak very freely and candidly about their careers, the players they played with and the managers they played under, without fear of upsetting their old employers. At times their honesty is compelling.

And the fact that *EX* is published independently of the club means we don't have to tow the party line either! As far as we know, it's the only retro publication of its kind covering a Premier League club.

Many of you reading this won't have heard of *EX* and have therefore not yet sampled this nostalgic delight. Where have you been for the past six years? Most back issues are still in stock, so you can catch up with all that you've missed while taking out a subscription to ensure you don't miss a single issue from now on.

Here's to some more happy memories!

Tony McDonald & Terry Roper
EX magazine, October 2008

Chapter 1

BILL LANSDOWNE

"Those were the days of the maximum wage – we earned only £8 a week during the season and £5 a week in the summer. All the players used to do other jobs during the summer months to earn some extra money and I remember working with Ken Brown at Ilford golf club, where we used to cut the grass. Also, I worked in a plaster factory in Dagenham with John Lyall for a short while"

THE names of Barratt, Brown, Lampard and Lansdowne form a unique part of Hammers history. They are the only father and son partnerships to play for West Ham United in league football. Curiously, each of the sons has the same christian name as his respective father.

'Big' Jim Barratt was West Ham's legendary centre-half between the two world wars, playing a total of 442 league games. Jim holds the unenviable record for the shortest international career of any player starting a match for England. He was carried off in the eighth minute of his debut against Ireland in 1928 – which England won 2-1 – and was never selected again.

'Young' Jim Barratt was a more than decent midfielder who played 85 league games for the Hammers in the 50s before moving on to Nottingham Forest and Birmingham City. In later years, Jim returned to Upton Park and became an important member of manager Ron Greenwood's coaching staff.

Ken Brown's career at West Ham bore a remarkable similarity to that of 'Big' Jim Barratt. Also a centre-half, Ken was another legend, playing 386 league games and also gaining one England cap against Ireland – in 1959, which England again won 2-1. While at Upton Park, Ken won a second division championship medal plus winners' medals in the FA Cup and European Cup Winners' Cup.

Kenny Brown, junior, played 63 league games in the early 90s as a midfielder and right-back. He attained immortality with West Ham's fans for scoring the goal that denied Alex Ferguson's Manchester United the first division title in 1992.

Undoubtedly, the most famous of the father and son quartet are the Lampards. Frank, senior – another legend – played 551 league games having made his league debut in 1967. Frank gained two FA Cup winners' medals and a second division championship medal, plus two England caps during his distinguished career.

'Young' Frank made 147 league appearances before transferring to Chelsea in 2001 where he has won two Premier League championship medals and become England's most prolific goalscoring midfielder.

Conversely, the least well known of the quartet are the Lansdownes – Bill, senior,

Bill Lansdowne (left) training with John Dick and John Bond.

who played 60 league and cup games, and Billy, junior, who made 14 league and cup appearances.

For older West Ham fans, the second division promotion season of 1957-58 remains a special time and the players who were part of that success more than 50 years ago are still held in high esteem. Bill Lansdowne played 17 league games that season, enough to gain a championship medal at the end of the campaign.

These days, Bill – now 72 – is retired and lives with his wife Pat at their comfortable home in Barkingside, near Ilford, in Essex. Bill has fond memories of that season and points out: "It was the first time that a West Ham team had actually won anything."

Up until that point, the club's sole claim to fame was playing in the first Wembley cup final against Bolton Wanderers in 1923, which they lost 0-2.

West Ham had a very settled side during their promotion season. Ernie Gregory was an excellent goalkeeper and had gained an England 'B' cap. John Bond – another England 'B' international – and captain Noel Cantwell, who also skippered the Republic of Ireland, were as good as any full-back pairing in the Football League. Ken Brown was very strong and powerful at centre-half and dominant in the air.

In midfield, Andy Malcolm was as hard as nails and young John Smith was a great prospect. Mike Grice and Malcolm Musgrove were fast raiding wingers and they were a perfect foil for the strike partnership of Vic Keeble and John Dick. Bill tended to share the number six position with Malcolm Pyke.

Bill says: "We had a disappointing start to the season and we were in mid-table, but the turning point was the signing of Vic Keeble from Newcastle United in October. Vic was a real star, having won a FA Cup winners' medal with them and he was a prolific goalscorer for the Geordies. After joining West Ham, he struck up a fantastic understanding with John Dick."

In fact, Keeble and Dick scored 40 goals in the promotion campaign. West Ham scored a total of 101 goals in 42 league games and had some big wins at Upton Park – against Huddersfield Town (5-2), Stoke City (5-0), Bristol Rovers (6-1), Swansea Town (6-2) and Rotherham United (8-0). They also won 6-1 away to Lincoln City and 4-1 at Leyton Orient.

Bill recalls: "We ended up as champions, one point ahead of Blackburn Rovers who were promoted with us. I still have my second division championship medal. It's a wonderful memento of a great season."

Bill Lansdowne was born on November 9, 1935 in Shoreditch, East London, where he lived with his parents, Bert and Annie, and his five sisters and two brothers. However, the second world war broke out when Bill was only four-years-old and shortly afterwards, due to the heavy bombing in London, he was evacuated to Wales with one of his sisters: "We were the two youngest of the family," he says.

"When you look back, it was a horrible situation for young kids who were sent away from their families. When we arrived in Wales, all the kids – dozens of us – from London were lined up and the families who were going to look after us went along the lines choosing the kids that they wanted to take in. I was hanging on to my sister's arm when this woman came along and said: 'I'll only take the girl', so we were split up. It was awful.

"Fortunately, we both ended up staying with families in the same village, so I saw quite a bit of my sister. When the bombing eased off in London after 18 months or so, we went back home and just carried on with life. It's very strange looking back on it. We must have been very adaptable."

In fact, Bill's family moved to Debden, Essex soon after the war and his dad started a thriving business delivering fruit and vegetables around Debden Estate. Bill says: "I sometimes helped my dad on his rounds. The post-war years were a time of great austerity – food was rationed for a long time – but I recall they were very happy days."

As Bill was growing up, he was beginning to take a big interest in football and would watch Arsenal and Spurs on alternate Saturday's. "My big hero was Leslie Compton, who played for Arsenal and England and also cricket for Middlesex."

Bill's own prowess as a footballer was beginning to be noted and he played for Hackney boys and also for the excellent Loughton Town Boys FC. It was when Bill was playing for the latter that he first came to the attention of West Ham's legendary chief scout Wally St. Pier. Bill's progress was monitored by St. Pier but West Ham's plans to sign him as a professional had to be put on hold in 1953, when Bill was called up to do his National Service at the age of 18.

"I joined the RAF and I was stationed at Oxford, but I was allowed each weekend off during the season to play as an amateur for West Ham in the Eastern Counties League. I used to meet up with John Lyall and we'd travel to the games together. Sometimes, I had to get up at the crack of dawn to travel across country to arrive in time for a 3.00pm kick-off.

"I worked as a telephonist in the RAF and I had to make a lot of calls via the Oxford telephone exchange. I always seemed to end up speaking to the same girl and I started chatting her up. I discovered that her name was Pat and she lived in Oxford. I asked her out and we met up. It was almost like a blind date, despite the fact that we'd spoken over the telephone. It must have been fate, because we ended up getting married in 1958 and have been together ever since."

Bill continues: "On the day that I finished my National Service in 1955, I left the RAF base in Oxford and went straight to Upton Park and signed professional forms for West Ham. I wasn't taking any chances in case they changed their minds. After that, I went home!"

In 1955-56, Bill's first season as a pro footballer, he made good progress and became a regular in the reserves. He was given his league debut in the penultimate match of the season, against Lincoln City at Upton Park. He recalls: "West Ham were in the second division at the time and down in the lower half of the table. I wore the number six shirt and we lost 2-4."

West Ham's goals were scored by John Dick and Billy Dare and Bill kept his place for the last game of the season, against Bristol City – again at Upton Park – which was won 3-0. Alan Blackburn and Dave Sexton (2) scored the goals.

Bill says: "Dave was a deep thinker about the game and it didn't surprise me that he became such a successful manager with Chelsea, Manchester United and QPR.

West Ham's captain at that time was Malcolm Allison and, as Bill confirmed: "He was a huge influence on everyone at the club. I remember that manager Ted Fenton would give us a team-talk in the dressing room before the game and after he had left, Malcolm would say: 'OK lads, this is what we are going to do . . .'

"Sadly, Malcolm's career came to a tragic end a couple of years later when he was diagnosed with tuberculosis and he had part of a lung removed. It says a great deal about the man that he was able to recover from such a set-back and became a very successful manager and coach in later years, particularly with Manchester City.

"Those were the days of the maximum wage – we earned only £8 a week during the season and £5 a week in the summer. All the players used to do other jobs during the summer months to earn some extra money and I remember working with Ken Brown at Ilford golf club, where we used to cut the grass. Also, I worked in a plaster factory in Dagenham with John Lyall for a short while.

"I wasn't in the first team for the first few matches at the start of the 1956-57 season, but then Frank O'Farrell – who usually wore the six shirt – was transferred to Preston North End and I became a regular."

Bill played 26 league games that season, including a fourth round FA Cup tie against first division Everton at Goodison Park which drew an attendance of more than 55,000. He says: "I'd never played in front of such a big crowd. We were a bit unlucky and lost 2-1."

Proud Bill with his second division championship winners' medal.

Manager Ted Fenton was very innovative with his training methods and Bill recalls that West Ham were one of the first clubs to begin using weights as part of their training programme. Fenton arranged for a trampoline to be brought into the Upton Park gymnasium to aid agility. It must have done some good because West Ham were crowned second division champions in April 1958.

Bill says: "On our return to the first division, we won 2-1 at Portsmouth on the opening day of the 1958-59 season. There was a big crowd at Fratton Park – but it was our fans who made most noise."

However, it was the game on the following Monday evening that was special for West Ham supporters. They had waited for 26 years to see their team back in the first division and the visitors to Upton Park were Wolverhampton Wanderers – the reigning champions and one of the most formidable teams of the post-war era. Wolves were managed by the legendary Stan Cullis and had an array of England internationals, such as Bill Slater, Ron Flowers, Norman Deeley, Peter Broadbent and captain Billy Wright, the first man to gain 100 caps for England.

Those were the days before it was possible to purchase match tickets in advance – it was 'first come, first served.' Some fans arrived at Upton Park at 2.30pm – five hours before kick-off – to find hundreds of people queuing around the Boleyn Ground. Eventually, 37,500 packed into Upton Park with thousands locked out as the kick-off approached.

The atmosphere was electrifying and the roar that greeted Bill and his team-mates as they ran on to the pitch reverberated around the whole of East London. Bill says: "It was the greatest night of my career. The noise was unbelievable and we won 2-0." John Dick scored just before half-time and John Smith wrapped it up for West Ham with a goal 15 minutes from time.

Five days later, Hammers' fans were in ecstasy as Aston Villa were crushed 7-2 at Upton Park, with Bill scoring a rare goal. "We started the season really well but in mid-September, we lost 4-1 against Manchester United at Old Trafford and I had a nightmare. Ernie Taylor gave me the run around and although I didn't know it at the time, it would be my last appearance in West Ham's league side for 18 months.

"I was dropped after the Manchester United defeat but the real problem was that there was fierce competition for the number six shirt. Andy Nelson briefly took over from me and John Smith had a spell in that position. Then, a youngster called Bobby Moore established himself. After that, what chance did I have?"

During Bill's spell in the reserves, he had the opportunity to join Colchester United. He explained: "They were managed by Ted Fenton's brother, Benny, but I wasn't interested. I stayed at Upton Park."

It was April 1960 before Bill was recalled to the side, against Luton Town at Kenilworth Road. He continued "I was anxious to do well but I ended up scoring an own goal early on when I lobbed the ball over our keeper Brian Rhodes. What a disaster! We lost 3-1 and I spent another two years in the reserves."

By the time Bill played in West Ham's first team again, Ted Fenton had been sacked by the club and Ron Greenwood had taken over as manager. After a 3-0 defeat at Everton in April 1962, Greenwood made five changes for the next game, against Cardiff City at Upton Park on Good Friday morning, including a recall for

Billy Lansdowne junior (far left) and jubilant team-mates after he had scored the winner in the 2-1 home win against Burnley in September 1979. Alan Devonshire (11) is first to congratulate young Billy, with league debutant Paul Allen, Ray Stewart (our other scorer that day) and David Cross also in the picture.

Bill at centre-half. He says: "It was good to be back and we won 4-1."

It was a memorable game. Not only was it the first time that Moore had captained West Ham's league side, it was also Martin Peters' league debut. Bill played alongside Moore and Peters throughout the rest of the season, including a 3-3 draw against Arsenal at Upton Park when goalkeeper Lawrie Leslie was injured and ended up playing on the wing and Bill scored the equaliser.

"I played in the opening match of the 1962-63 season but we lost 3-1 at Aston Villa and I was left out again. It was my last appearance in league football. I started to have a lot of problems with an old hip injury and although I continued to play in the reserves, I really began to get involved in coaching. I started taking the juniors on a Tuesday and Thursday evening at Upton Park and I got my FA coaching badge at Lilleshall.

"In 1965, I retired from playing and took over as full-time manager of the junior team at Ron Greenwood's request. I enjoyed it, but I left West Ham a year later to become manager of non-league Eastbourne United. It was a good experience and I stayed there for two years.

"But in the summer of 1968, West Ham contacted me and asked me to go back –

there had been some changes on the coaching staff. I readily agreed and became manager of the youth and colts teams. By 1974, I'd become manager of the reserves."

Greenwood left to manage England in 1977, although John Lyall had already taken over as team manager at Upton Park some three years earlier. Following Hammers' relegation in May 1978, Lyall decided that some changes were going to be made.

Bill explained: "In September 1979, John called me into his office and said that I was being given immediate notice to leave the club. I was shocked. It was completely out of the blue and I had no prior knowledge. John said that I'd been a loyal servant to the club and that I had done absolutely nothing wrong, but he was changing the training structure.

"I'd been at Upton Park for a long time – it was a sad way to end my association with the club. I never saw John again after that.

"After I left West Ham, I worked for a few weeks in a garage in Ilford High Road, but I had to decide what I was going to do. My brother was a curtain fitter and Pat, my wife, was a curtain maker – so we set up a little family business. It was quite successful, mainly local work and in the end, everything we did was based on recommendations. It earned us a decent living until we retired five years ago.

"My only other contact with football was in the early 80s, when my ex-West Ham team-mate Eddie Presland asked me to join him at Dagenham. Eddie was the manager, he was setting up a youth team and he wanted me to take the training on Tuesday and Thursday evenings – just as I used to do at Upton Park. I was there for a couple of years and enjoyed it, but when Eddie left the club I was not long in following him."

These days, Bill and Pat continue to enjoy life. They have four children – Billy, Michael, Deborah and Greg, plus six grandchildren – Billy, Joe, Tom, Ben, George and Charlotte.

Striker Billy Lansdowne (junior) spent six years at Upton Park as an amateur, semi-professional and fully fledged pro, but his 14 league and cup appearances all came within a seven-month spell in 1979. Billy – now 49 – has lived in the coastal town of Kalmar, in south-east Sweden, since 1983. It was there that he set up his own company selling leisure and corporate clothing.

Bill (senior) and his son Greg are season ticket holders at Arsenal and Bill enthuses about the Emirates Stadium. "It's fantastic," says Bill, who explains that Greg has been an Arsenal supporter since he was six-years-old. It's ironic that Bill is now watching one of the teams that he followed as a young boy.

Nevertheless, Bill admits that he will always have a soft spot for West Ham. "I spent almost 25 years there as a player and coach. I have some wonderful memories of my time at Upton Park."

Chapter 2

KEN**BROWN**

"From a skill factor, I couldn't do a lot of things that Ron Greenwood wanted me to do. I couldn't pull a ball down and play it out the way Bobby did, so that's why I never felt that I was ever good enough for the manager"

IT says everything about the typical modesty of the man that former centre-half Ken Brown never felt he was quite good enough for Ron Greenwood, the manager who inspired Hammers to their greatest ever victories.

Ken believes he owes Greenwood a debt of gratitude for developing into the player who picked up FA Cup and European Cup Winners' Cup winners' medals in consecutive seasons during the mid-60s.

Ken and his wife Elaine were holidaying in Jamaica, to celebrate their birthdays, in February 2006 when he heard the news that Greenwood had died of Alzheimer's Disease.

As soon as he was back home in Norwich, Ken phoned the *EX* magazine office to pay tribute to the man who did so much to make him the player he once was. Ken said: "I was watching television in Jamaica when Ron's face suddenly appeared on screen. The channel didn't broadcast in English, so I wasn't even sure if he had died until it was confirmed later. I'm so sorry to have missed his funeral, because I would have wanted to pay my last respects to a special man.

"If anybody owes anything to Ron, then it's me," he added.

Anyone who knows the amiable Ken – a promotion winner with Hammers in 1958 – would not be at all surprised at the honesty of the big man, one of football's genuine nice guys.

Of the FA Cup-winning team of 1964, Brown and John Bond were the oldest, most experienced players in an otherwise young and vibrant team that was still evolving under Greenwood. It had been three years since Ron took over from Ted Fenton and no-one noted the change in management style more acutely than Ken, one of numerous star products from the famous Dagenham football factory in the late 50s.

"Ted was a fitness fanatic and, under him, we were a very, very fit side, although we didn't know it at the time.

"Malcolm Allison and Noel Cantwell came in and laid the foundations for our future success with their bright ideas and coaching methods, but it was Ron who took that on to the next level. From Day One, he wanted to change our style of play and everything we did was geared to going forward."

While Fenton was never a 'tracksuit manager', Greenwood was among the best of a new breed of football academics who belonged on the training field, developing

Ron Greenwood and his players gathered together at Chadwell Heath in August 1963. Left to right: John Bond, Ron Boyce, Jack Burkett, Lawrie Leslie, Joe Kirkup, Alan Sealey, Tony Scott, John Lyall, Eddie Bovington, Bobby Moore and Ron. Front row: Martin Peters, Peter Brabrook, Geoff Hurst, Ken Brown and Johnny Byrne.

the skills and broadening the horizons of his players.

But the fundamentals of Ken's no-thrills style were based on strength and stamina. He would defend his penalty area for his life but he is the first to admit that he was no Franz Beckenbaur. He did his job and preferred to leave the clever stuff to his more talented team-mates. And why not? After all, he played alongside no less a legend than Bobby Moore, the most accomplished English defender in the history of the game.

With admirable candour that you will not heard expressed by players of the modern era, Ken admitted: "I never thought I was good enough for Ron.

"I had nothing but admiration for the fella but I never felt that I'd given enough to him from a physical point of view. Ron seemed to think that the usual pre-season training was all we really needed in terms of building up the right level of fitness but I always wanted to do more myself after the season got underway. After training had finished, I'd run around the field on my own to improve my fitness.

"But we were all keen to learn from Ron's original coaching ideas.

"From a skill factor, I couldn't do a lot of things that Ron wanted me to do. I couldn't pull a ball down and play it out the way Bobby did, so that's why I never felt that I was ever good enough for the manager.

"I don't remember receiving too much praise from him and I don't think he was particularly happy with me, although maybe that was his way of spurring me on. I was simply an out and out defender – not a ball player – who just wanted to clear the ball away from the danger area as quickly as possible.

"I felt I was quite good in the air – perhaps I was the only one in the back four who could head a ball well?

"But I heard it said that Ron would like to have signed the Leicester City centre-half – I can't remember his name – because he really *could* play."

For all his humility, this gentle giant should never underestimate his value to West Ham. Signed from the Dagenham-based Neville United FC in 1951, he made his first team debut under Ted Fenton in 1952-53 and went on to play 455 league and cup matches in the claret-and-blue.

In November 1959, Ken made his one and only senior England appearance against Northern Ireland at Wembley – and many felt he was unlucky not to be given more chances to become the long-term successor to Billy Wright.

And, of course, Ken featured in the club's biggest achievements, winning FA Cup and European Cup Winners' Cup medals in 1964 and '65 respectively. He played in all nine ECWC matches and remains proud of his part in the 1964-65 campaign that led to our epic 2-0 final victory over TSV Munich 1860 at Wembley.

"We were a very well balanced side, including left-footed players such as Johnny Sissons, Brian Dear and Jackie Burkett, plus people like Bobby, Geoff Hurst and Martin Peters who could kick very well with both feet.

"People should watch the video or DVD of the European final time and again, to see how the game used to be played and the spirit it should be played in. When I look at matches today, at the way players dive around and cheat and try to get their fellow pro's booked or sent off, I think, 'look at that game from 1965 and learn how football should be played'.

"The Munich team were great to us. We played against them again soon after the Wembley final, in a tournament staged in New York, and this time the match was much closer. Afterwards, their players invited us to a German beer garden and it spoke volumes for the good time we had together that night that neither team won another game in that tournament!"

Not that West Ham's second round trip to the old Czechoslovakia did much for

Ken and Martin Peters help Jim Standen snuff out this TSV Munich attack in that epic European final.

Ken's or football's image as a game for battle-hardened pro's. Recalling a surreal experience in the Czech capital, Ken says: "Bobby was injured and missed the game against Spartak in Prague, so I stood in as skipper. Just as I was about to lead the team out, I had an enormous bunch of flowers presented to me by our hosts. It was enormous and it would have done any lavish wedding proud. For a man to receive a huge bunch of flowers like that 40 years ago . . . well, I didn't know if they were taking the mickey or what!"

During Ken Brown's 15-year career at the Boleyn Ground, he faced some of the most famous names in the game and also some of the toughest centre-forwards of all-time. The list is endless and includes such legendary strikers as Nat Lofthouse (Bolton), Bobby Smith (Spurs), Dave Hickson (Everton), Brian Clough (Middlesbrough), Derek Dougan (Blackburn), Ray Pointer (Burnley), Denis Law (Manchester United), Wyn Davies (Newcastle), Jeff Astle (WBA), Gerry Hitchens (Aston Villa), Tony Hateley (Aston Villa), Mel Charles (Arsenal), John Radford (Arsenal), Ray Crawford (Ipswich), Andy Lochhead (Burnley), Joe Baker (Arsenal), Alan Gilzean (Spurs), Ian St John (Liverpool), Fred Pickering (Everton) and Alex Dawson (Preston).

Anyone who was present at the 1964 FA Cup final at Wembley, when West Ham beat Preston North End 3-2, will remember Ken's tremendous physical battle with the bustling Alex Dawson.

Ken says: "I had some real battles with Alex that started way back when he was with Manchester United. He was a really tough opponent who would give as good as he got. A lot of the centre-forwards in those days were 95 per cent physical and you knew that you had a real battle on your hands virtually every week."

In the early years, Ken used to prepare himself for such encounters with the help of team-mates John Bond and Noel Cantwell during extra training stints long after the other players had gone home. Ken reveals: "I used to get Bondy or Noel to whack over dozens of crosses into the penalty area while the other challenged me in the air using every dodgy tactic possible."

Clearly, it was a form of preparation that played off handsomely as Ken proceeded to nullify the threat of numerous dangerous opponents – with one notable exception.

He admits: "I thought I did OK against them all, but the one who caused me the most problems was Alex Young of Everton. He wasn't particularly tall and he wasn't the bustling type of centre-forward, but he had the ability to 'hang' in the air and I could never get to grips with him. Alex was sharp and his timing was terrific and I couldn't get near him a lot of the time. He caused me more problems than any other

Happy Hammers – Ken having fun with Eddie Bovington after the 1964 FA Cup final.

It's April 1962 as Ken and Bobby Moore take care of Everton's aerial threat while Geoff Hurst (4) looks on.

centre-forward that I faced in my career."

Ken also acknowledges that he never got involved in any 'verbals' with opposing centre-forwards. He says: "I just concentrated on doing my job and trying to stop my opponent from scoring." However, Ken concedes that there was an occasion when one opponent seriously upset him together with team-mate Andy Malcolm and, with just cause, they decided that retribution was in order.

The player in question was Blackburn Rover's Irish international striker Derek Dougan, who scored four goals in his team's 6-2 victory against West Ham at Ewood Park on December 12, 1959.

Ken says: "It wasn't the fact that Derek scored four against us but, later that night, Andy and I saw the goals on television and we realised that each time Derek was celebrating, he was 'taking the mickey' out of us behind our backs. We decided there and then that one of us would need to sort him out when we next played against him."

As things turned out, the opportunity for revenge fell to hard-man Andy Malcolm when Dougan faced Hammers at Upton Park some months later.

Ken recalls: "Derek went to the bye-line and was about to cross with his left foot when Andy went straight through him and Derek ended up against the boards around the edge of the pitch."

Nearly fifty years later, Ken still winces at the ferocity of that challenge. In any walk of life, it is an undeniable fact that revenge is always sweet.

With almost a permanent smile stretching from ear to ear and his endearing personality, Ken deservedly remained a popular figure with the West Ham crowd.

He says: "It was strange the way they were towards me. Although I wasn't skilful, the crowd still loved me. In their eyes, I think if I'd scored three own-goals in a match, it still wouldn't have been my fault!"

In May 1967, 14,695 turned out on a Monday night at Upton Park for the Ken Brown Testimonial match, the game in which Billy Bonds made his Hammers debut against a Select XI following his transfer from Charlton.

Ken says: "I left West Ham that summer on a free transfer. I was 33-years-old at the time and I'd had my day. I had no complaints but I still felt that I had some football left in me, though, so I signed for Torquay United. It was like a West Ham old boys team – John Bond, Tony Scott and John Smith were all playing there and Frank O'Farrell was our manager.

"I think I played about 40 matches for them and then I had a season in the old Southern League playing for Hereford United. It was great and I really enjoyed it. Our player-manager was the legendary John Charles, who had played for Leeds, Juventus and Wales. He used to pick me up in his car from the station when I turned up for matches. I got on really well with John.

Despite his move to Torquay, Ken maintained his links with the Hammers by running the club's pools commercial operation and he also continued to train with his former Upton Park team-mates.

"Ron Greenwood was good to me. Even after we'd left to sign for Torquay, he continued to allow me and Bondy to train as usual with the other West Ham players. He didn't isolate us from the others. He made us welcome and didn't forget us or what we'd done for the club," says a grateful Ken.

John Cushley and Alan Stephenson tried to fill Brown's number five shirt in the late-60s, before Tommy Taylor and Kevin Lock formed a successful new central defensive partnership after Bobby Moore was sold to Fulham in 1974. But it's probably fair to say that West Ham didn't find another powerful centre-back, who could head the ball as effectively as Ken, until the emergence of youth team product Alvin Martin in the late-70s.

"I packed up playing in 1970 and then I teamed up with John Bond again. He'd taken over as manager at Bournemouth and I joined him as his assistant. We built a good side and were very successful."

Greenwood's influence as an inspirational coach remained with Ken, as it did many others, long after he'd left Upton Park. Brown's teams always set out to play in an attractive and entertaining way that mirrored Greenwood's own adventurous style. Ken says: "The training we did with Bondy at Bournemouth, in my first coaching job, was very much based on Ron's ideas and what we'd learned from him at West Ham in the early-60s."

Ironically, it was during his time as assistant manger at Bournemouth that Ken suffered the most serious injury of his career. He says: "I managed to stay fairly injury-free during my time as a player but the Bournemouth team were coming back from a game at Scunthorpe and our team coach was involved in a smash-up on the way home. Believe it or not, I ended up breaking my thigh in the accident!"

Ken continues: "Bondy and I were at Bournemouth for about three years and then we had the chance to take over at Norwich. We got on great with the chairman Sir

Arthur South and, again, we did well.

"A few years later, around 1980, Bondy had an offer to manage Manchester City, which he accepted. I was a bit surprised that he didn't take me with him but it gave me the chance to take over as manager at Norwich.

"I was manager there for seven years and we won the 1985 Milk Cup final by beating Sunderland 1-0 at Wembley and we won the second division championship the following year. I signed some good players such as Martin O'Neill, Dave Watson, Steve Bruce, Chris Woods, Keith Bertschin, Mike Channon and Asa Hartford.

"I created a good youth set-up at Carrow Road and players like Robert Rosario, Jeremy Goss, Louie Donowa and (future Hammer) Dale Gordon all progressed to the first team."

Ken says: "The problem was that a new chairman, Robert Chase, took over and we just didn't get on. In the end, we fell out over my contract and I left Norwich in 1987. I was very sad to leave. It was my worst day in football."

The situation was made even more difficult for Ken because, sadly, his first wife, Joan, had been diagnosed with cancer just a few months earlier.

Ken recalls: "Soon after I left Norwich, I had the chance to become manager of Shrewsbury Town but, at the time, it just didn't feel right and I turned it down. Anyway, the following year, Plymouth Argyle asked me to take over as their manager. Joan and I had always liked the West Country and I had two years in charge there."

Unfortunately, it was the beginning of a desperately sad time in Ken's life as he was sacked as Plymouth's manager in 1990 and, two years later, Joan tragically lost her battle against cancer.

Ken worked for some while as sports co-ordinator at Lakenham Leisure Centre, near Norwich, in which he retained an interest for many years thereafter. In 1994, Terry Venables took over as England manager and immediately asked Ken to become one of his scouts – an appointment that merely confirmed Ken's immense standing from within the professional game.

He says: "In the end, I was an England scout under four successive managers – Terry Venables, Glen Hoddle, Kevin Keegan and Sven-Goran Eriksson. It meant travelling mainly in Europe watching England's future opponents and when I got home from each trip, I would submit my report to the FA who would hold it on file until the manager needed it."

It was a position that Ken held for over 10 years and which included a trip to Japan and South Korea for the 2002 World Cup where, incidentally, he lost a stone in weight in the stifling Asian heat and humidity.

He says: "I didn't mind travelling on my own and I really enjoyed the whole experience working for England. But when Steve McClaren took over as manager, it signalled the end of my scouting role."

Ken is now fully retired and, happily, life has gone full circle for him as he re-married in 1999. He says: "Elaine and I are very happy together and we enjoy plenty of holidays. We particularly like the Algarve but we've done a lot of travelling." However, their most regular destination is Spain, where Ken's son – former Hammer

Ken with his wife Elaine (left) and Janet Bond (John's wife), at the official opening of the Bobby Moore statue at Wembley in 2007.

Kenny, junior, who played 75 times for the club between 1990 and 1995 – is following in his father's footsteps by taking charge at Spanish club Javier.

The sporting prowess of Ken's children is not just restricted to Kenny junior, since Ken's daughter Amanda was once an outstanding tennis player. These days, Amanda has long since retired from the professional tennis circuit and lives with her family at Langdon Hills in Essex.

However, Ken says: "Amanda was number three in England at the age of 18 and played all over the world, including the European circuit as well as Australia and the USA. When she played at Wimbledon and I watched her walk out on to number one court, I've never been so bloody nervous!"

Quite rightly, Ken remains justifiably proud of the sporting achievements of both of his children. However, so far as football is concerned, Ken says: "I miss it up to a point, but I still go to watch most of Norwich's home games and I sometimes go to West Ham, so I still keep in touch with people.

"I'm a great believer in the old saying, 'Whatever will be, will be.' I had no real disappointments in my football career. It was great. I enjoyed every minute of it."

Chapter 3

LAWRIE**LESLIE**

"At my mother's insistence, they decided to operate and in the end, they were able to save the leg and I made a full recovery, although I had to spend six months in hospital"

FEW West Ham players can rightfully claim to have become a cult hero during their time with the club. It takes a special breed of player – such as 'Mad Dog' Martin Allen or the indomitable Julian Dicks – to attain such iconic status with the Upton Park faithful.

In 1961, Scottish international goalkeeper Lawrie Leslie joined West Ham from Airdrieonians for £14,000 – a considerable fee in those days – and quickly established himself as Upton Park's cult hero of that period with a series of spectacular and astonishingly brave performances.

West Ham's fans took Lawrie to their hearts and, fittingly, he was voted Hammer-of-the-Year in his first season at the Boleyn.

Sadly, Lawrie's bravery resulted in a number of injuries which ultimately curtailed his Hammers career. Lawrie made just 61 league and cup appearances before moving on to Stoke City, Millwall and Southend United. Even so, during his two years at Upton Park, he made an indelible impression on the West Ham fans of that era.

These days, Lawrie lives in happy retirement with Janette, his wife of 50 years, at Bexley in Kent. Lawrie's broad Scottish accent remains completely unaffected despite having lived south of the border for 47 years.

"I was Ron Greenwood's first signing for West Ham," he recalls. "I signed in June 1961, just two months after Ron had joined West Ham from Arsenal where he had been assistant manager. A couple of days later, he signed Ian Crawford from Hearts, so it was good to have a fellow Scot around the place. Most of the West Ham players at that time were London boys."

Lawrie says: "It was a good move for me. West Ham had some tremendous players – John Bond, Ken Brown and Phil Woosnam. Also, the likes of Bobby Moore, Geoff Hurst and Martin Peters were beginning to emerge. I had a great rapport with the fans and I remember they used to sway in time as they sang their *Bubbles* song."

Lawrence Grant Leslie was born in Edinburgh on March 17, 1935. It was a harsh economic period but Lawrie talks fondly of his parents, George and Georgina, and his upbringing with his brother and two sisters. Lawrie took a strong interest in football from an early age and supported Hearts.

He was four-years-old when the second world war broke out. "My main

August 1961 – New signing Lawrie demonstrates his acrobatic skills at the old Grange Farm training ground at Chigwell. In My Day co-author Terry Roper is pictured (far left) with his father Bob up on the grass banking.

recollection of the war years is that it was the only time I ever saw my father in tears. Honestly, he cried when the Germans bombed the local distillery! We had whiskey running in the gutters and men were lying down trying to drink it!" says Lawrie with a laugh.

At the age of 10, Lawrie's resilience and determination to overcome adversity – which would later stand him in good stead in his career as a professional footballer – were put to the sternest test when he was knocked down by a lorry and badly injured. Apart from serious injuries to his face and neck, Lawrie's right leg was broken in several places . . . but the most serious injury was to his left leg, which doctors feared would have to be amputated.

He explains: "At my mother's insistence, they decided to operate and in the end, they were able to save the leg and I made a full recovery, although I had to spend six months in hospital." Today, the scars high on Lawrie's left thigh bear testimony to the injuries sustained in that appalling accident in 1945.

"In my later years at school, I started playing in goal because I couldn't run very well for some while after my accident. I left school at 15 and became an apprentice plumber. I was beginning to make a name for myself as a goalkeeper and I joined Newtongrange Star, who were a semi-professional club and the equivalent of a team in the present day Conference league.

"There was still National Service in those days but since I was an apprentice, my call up papers were deferred until I was 20 and I was allowed to finish my apprenticeship. When I went into the army, I joined the artillery and I was stationed at Oswestry in Shropshire. I played in goal for the command team and among my team mates were Manchester United legends Duncan Edwards and also Bobby Charlton.

October 1961 – Braveheart Lawrie diving at the feet of Burnley's Jimmy McIlroy while Bobby Moore covers.

"Jock Buchan, an influential Hibernian player, was also in the army at the time and when we went home on leave, he suggested that I joined him in the training at Easter Road. At the end of the week, I was invited to play in a trial against Falkirk reserves.

"I must have done OK, because I was then asked to play in a first team friendly at home against Liverpool – who were then in the second division. We lost 1-2 and Billy Liddell scored both of their goals. I managed to split my ear open during the game – the shape of things to come! After that, it was back to the army, although I was allowed to travel home most weekends and play in the reserves."

Astonishingly, such was Lawrie's progress, that by the end of the season he had made his league debut for Hibernian and retained his place for the rest of the campaign – even though he was still in the army!

"I finished my National Service at the age of 22 and became a full-time professional with Hibernian." It was around this time that Lawrie met Janette – a fervent Hibernian fan – and ironically, they were introduced by a mutual friend, the Motherwell goalkeeper Alan Wylie.

"We were married in April 1958," says Lawrie, "just two days before I played in the Scottish Cup semi-final against Rangers at Hampden Park. We beat them after a replay and four weeks later, I played for Hibernian in the Scottish Cup final against Clyde at Hampden. After beating Rangers, we were confident of lifting the trophy, but we ended up losing 1-0 through an own goal. It was a bitter disappointment.

"The following summer, I went on tour with Hibernian to Spain, but I didn't play well and I injured my elbow. At the beginning of the new season, I was out of contention and after making around 80 appearances for Hibs, I was transferred to

Lawrie diving in West ham's 3-2 defeat at Molineux in August 1961, watched by Wolves' Jimmy Murray, Ken Brown and Joe Kirkup. The unhappy keeper later received a ticking off from a policeman!

Airdrieonians in November 1959 for £4,470. Surprisingly, I was immediately made captain. In those days it was very unusual for a goalkeeper to be made skipper of a team but I relished the challenge."

Clearly, the Airdrieonians management at that time were fully aware of Lawrie's commanding and powerful presence. It was an inspired decision. With Lawrie at his spectacular best, unfashionable Airdrieonians reached the semi-final of the Scottish Cup before losing to Celtic and finished a highly creditable fifth place in the league. It was an astonishing achievement for a club of their stature. In later years, Lawrie's heroics would be rewarded with a place in Airdrieonians 'Hall of Fame'.

"Without doubt, the 1960-61 season was my best in terms of recognition," says Lawrie. "During that season, I made my international debut for Scotland, appearing in five of the six internationals." His first appearance was in a 2-0 defeat to Wales in Cardiff on October 22, 1960. Then came three victories – 5-2 v Northern Ireland at Hampden Park, 4-1 v Republic of Ireland in a World Cup qualifier at Hampden and 3-0 against the Republic in the return in Dublin four days later. His fifth, and ultimately last, cap came in the Scots' 4-0 World Cup qualifying defeat against Czechoslovakia in Bratislava on May 14 1961.

He also played for the Scottish League that season and they won all three matches – 2-1 v the Irish League in Belfast, 5-1 v the League of Ireland at Celtic Park and 3-2 v the English League at Ibrox.

However, the one international match that Lawrie missed that season, on April 15, 1961, proved to be the biggest disappointment of his career. He explains: "I was selected to play for Scotland against England at Wembley but the previous week – typically – I sustained an injury playing for Airdrieonians and was forced to pull out."

Celtic's Frank Haffey deputised for Lawrie but it was a game that will go down as the blackest in Scotland's football history. England slaughtered the Scots 9-3 in the

Above: Lawrie with Ian Crawford, who joined Hammers at the same time. Right: Chairman Reg Pratt addresses the Upton Park crowd as Lawrie (far left) presents some match tickets to a young fan.

Wembley sunshine and the hapless Haffey was ultimately forced to emigrate to Australia to escape the wrath of Scottish fans.

Some 47 years later, Lawrie still rues the injury that caused him to miss the biggest game of his career against the 'Auld Enemy'. It's a defeat that still rankles with Lawrie: "One thing's for sure, there is no way that England would have scored nine goals against me!" he says in typically determined fashion.

Lawrie played with some of the greatest Scottish players during that period, including Denis Law, Pat Crerand, Billy McNeil and Dave Mackay, but – perhaps surprisingly – Lawrie says that Tottenham's John White was the greatest of them all. "John had wonderful ability," says Lawrie who fondly remembers his former Scottish international team-mate who would later die in tragic circumstances when he was struck by lightning while playing a round of golf.

Lawrie continues: "By this time, I had been at Airdrieonians for approximately 18 months and I had played around 50 league and cup games for them. I suddenly got a call from a reporter on the *Daily Express* who told me that West Ham United were about to sign me. It was the first that I had heard about it and I knew nothing about West Ham – not even the name of their manager! Even so, I was happy to go with the flow and try my luck in English football. I met Ron Greenwood and signed almost straight away. It all happened so quickly."

Lawrie remembers: "We moved into a club house in Clayhall Avenue, near Barkingside, and Ian Crawford – who had just been signed from Hearts – lived close by. In fact, quite a few West Ham players lived in the area, including John Dick, Malcolm Musgrove and Ken Brown."

He settled in very quickly and made his debut on August 19, 1961 against Manchester United at Upton Park. "We drew 1-1 but I can't recall much about the game," admits Lawrie. However, those Hammers fans who were present will recall that despite being beaten by an early Nobby Stiles goal, Lawrie made several spectacular saves and seemed to relish diving at the feet of onrushing forwards!

The following week, West Ham lost 2-3 at Wolverhampton and Lawrie was particularly upset at Wolves' third goal, scored by Norman Deeley, which took a freakish deflection. He recalls pounding the turf with his fist in anguish and letting out a string of obscenities before realising that a policeman was standing by the goalpost. The copper told Lawrie sternly: "We'll have less of that language, son!"

On September 16, 1961, Lawrie received a serious head injury against Chelsea at Upton Park. He was knocked unconscious and carried off with blood pouring from a gash on his forehead which required 12 stitches. With no substitutes in those days, young Bobby Moore took over in goal and 10-man Hammers held on to win 2-1 in a memorable match. Today, Lawrie's forehead still bears the scar of that injury.

Within two weeks, Lawrie was back against Leicester City at Upton Park and – in typically daring fashion – he was forced to dive at the feet of an onrushing Leicester player in the very first minute. That save exemplified Lawrie's bravery during his time at Upton Park.

Lawrie's injury against Chelsea forced him to miss the next Scotland international match and Tottenham's Bill Brown – an excellent goalkeeper in his own right – took the opportunity to establish himself as Scotland's No.1 choice.

Nevertheless, Lawrie's form for West Ham throughout the 1961-62 season was remarkable and it came to a memorable climax on Easter Saturday, when West Ham played Arsenal at Upton Park. He remembers: "Early in the second-half and with the scores level at 1-1, I dived at the feet of Arsenal's Geoff Strong and broke a finger. I went off to have it strapped up and John Lyall took over from me in goal."

In Lawrie's absence, 10-man West Ham quickly conceded two more goals and were 3-1 down with 20 minutes to go. At that moment, Upton Park roared its approval as Lawrie reappeared from the players' tunnel like a latter day 'Braveheart', wearing a numberless claret-and-blue shirt, black shorts and a strapping on his damaged hand. "I couldn't go back in goal," says Lawrie, "so Ron Greenwood just told me to play on the right wing and try and make a nuisance of myself."

He did more than that. In fact, Lawrie produced a series of dazzling runs that tormented Arsenal's Irish International left-back Billy McCullough. Inspired by Lawrie's astonishing performance, which included an audacious overhead kick, West Ham fought back and reduced the arrears when Martin Peters crossed for John Dick to head home.

In the dying minutes, Lawrie took off on another mazy run which forced McCullough to concede a corner. From the resultant flag-kick, there was a scramble in the Arsenal goalmouth and amid near hysteria on the Upton Park terraces, Bill Lansdowne stabbed home the equaliser from close range. The game ended in an amazing 3-3 draw and Lawrie left the field to a thunderous ovation from the West Ham fans.

Lawrie says: "It was a great comeback and we nearly nicked a winner right at the end as well! I couldn't play in the last three matches of the season but the hand healed during the summer and I was fit and raring to go when the new season began the following August."

Unfortunately, on November 3, 1962, disaster struck when Lawrie sustained the

October 1962 – Lawrie (right, sat on ball) listens to another Ron Greenwood coaching lesson, along with team-mates Johnny Byrne, Joe Kirkup, Phil Woosnam, Eddie Bovington, Bobby Moore and John Bond.

most serious injury of his career. West Ham met Bolton Wanderers at Upton Park and Lawrie broke his right leg in a 2-1 defeat. Martin Peters took over in goal and, once again, Lawrie was carried from the field and taken to hospital.

"It was the third time in 14 months that I'd been taken into the same hospital and each time I saw the same nurse," laughs Lawrie. "When I was taken in following the injury against Bolton, she said: 'Oh, no Lawrie – not again! We are going to have to stop meeting like this. My husband is getting suspicious!'"

In Lawrie's absence, West Ham signed Jim Standen from Luton Town and Lawrie acknowledges that Standen was a first class goalkeeper with superb reflexes and positional sense. In fact, Standen proceeded to make the goalkeeping spot his own with a series of assured performances.

"I defied the odds and got myself fit again. I even managed to play in the last four matches of the season," recalls Lawrie, "but it was clear that Jim had effectively taken over from me."

Lawrie's last game for West Ham came on the final day of the 1962-63 season, when West Ham beat already relegated Manchester City 6-1 at Upton Park. When the new season began, Lawrie found himself back in the reserves and with Standen playing consistently well, Lawrie decided to leave Upton Park.

"In October 1963, Stoke City – who were in the first division at the time – made an offer for me of £15,000, which West Ham accepted and I decided to move on.

Left: Lawrie in full Scottish regalia while clutching a pint. Right: Pictured in 2006 with the goalie's shirt he wore on international duty.

As it turned out, it was a great move and Stoke had some fine players including the legendary Stanley Matthews who was coming to the end of his career. Stan was a lovely man. Sometimes, he stayed in the same hotel as me and I always remember that he wore lead inserts in his shoes. They were heavy and he kept them in all week.

"The reasoning was that when he put his football boots on before a game, the boots – minus the lead inserts – would feel that much lighter! It's a strange story, but it's true," says Lawrie. "Stan played league football until he was 51-years-old, so it must have done him some good!

"During my time with Stoke, we reached the League Cup final, but lost 4-3 on aggregate to Leicester City. I was at Stoke for just under three years and I played in nearly 100 league and cup matches for them.

"In the summer of 1966, I was injured – again – and with the up and coming John Farmer coming through the ranks, Stoke decided that I was surplus to requirements.

"I joined Millwall in July 1966 and stayed there for exactly two years. I played 67 games for them and thoroughly enjoyed my time at The Den. I know the Millwall fans have got a bad name over the years but I thought they were great – they were real diehards. Ex-Hammers Harry Cripps and Dennis Burnett were at Millwall at the same time as me."

Lawrie continues: "Again, another young goalkeeper – this time Bryan King – was coming through the ranks and in July 1968 I went to Southend United. I played 13 games in the 1968-69 season but I got another – and final – injury at Peterborough. I also knew that my reflexes were not as sharp as they should have been. While I was at Southend, I got involved in some coaching with the youngsters and one of my protégés was Peter Taylor, who later went on to play for Crystal Palace and England and who has just been named as the new manager at Selhurst Park.

"I was at Southend for a couple of years and then I had the opportunity to go back to Millwall as a coach. I did OK, but manager Benny Fenton – brother of ex-West

Ham manager Ted – was sacked and when the new manager, Gordon Jago, came in, he brought his own backroom staff with him and I was given the elbow."

Lawrie admits: "It was a worrying time. I had a family and a mortgage and suddenly I was out of work. A friend asked if I fancied doing a spot of coaching during the summer holidays for school kids in Holloway. I was only supposed to work there for six weeks until the kids went back to school, but it led to an ongoing part-time job coaching more kids in Holloway and Highbury as well.

"After that, I was approached by the Cardinal Pole School in Hackney to work there full-time as a sports teacher – and I ended up staying for 25 years until I retired at the age of 65. During that time, I became a fully qualified teacher and even taught maths and English on occasions!"

These days, Lawrie and Janette live in contented retirement in their comfortable home which backs onto Bexley golf course. Lawrie says: "I play golf most days – it's my daily exercise. Also, I pretend to do a few jobs around the house. Janette and I see a lot of our family and that is the greatest joy of all."

Lawrie and Janette are extremely proud of their three children – Grant, who is a civil engineer, Guy, an RAF pilot, and Jennifer, who used to work in the City in the banking industry. Also, Lawrie and Janette are doting grandparents to Stephen, Becky, Jodie, Tom and Louise and look forward to the birth of their sixth grandchild in November.

Lawrie says: "I watch football on TV and I have also started watching Gillingham, our local team, with the family. We are all season ticket holders."

Lawrie remains a charismatic figure and is philosophical about the injuries which, at times, hindered his career. When told that he had played almost 400 Scottish and English league and cup games, he laughed and said: "I am amazed, I thought I was always in hospital!"

At various times in his career, Lawrie played alongside some of the greatest legends in the game – Duncan Edwards, Bobby Charlton, Denis Law, Stanley Matthews and the West Ham triumvirate of Bobby Moore, Geoff Hurst and Martin Peters. Not bad for a boy who they said would never walk again.

There is an amazing sequel to Lawrie's road accident and his subsequent football career, which he reveals: "A few years ago, I went for a full medical check-up at the hospital which included various x-rays. I was given a clean bill of health but when the doctor held up the x-rays, there was a long shadow down the length of my left thigh. It transpired that it was a metal rod that had been bolted into the shattered leg to hold it together following my accident when I was 10-years-old.

"I had no idea that it was in my leg and it is amazing to think that I played all those games – including reaching international level – without knowing it was there. I don't know who carried out the operation, but he must have been one hell of a surgeon."

Chapter 4

JOE KIRKUP

"That was seriously hard work since I had to get up at 4.00am every morning and sort out the deliveries for the paper boys"

JOE Kirkup will go down in West Ham folklore as one of that select band of players who took part in the greatest night in the club's history. The date was May 19, 1965, when West Ham beat the German cup holders TSV Munich 1860 by 2-0 to win the European Cup Winners' Cup at Wembley in front of 100,000 spectators and an estimated 30 million television viewers throughout the UK and the rest of Europe.

In those days, the ECWC was second only in importance to the European Cup. In the modern era, it would be the equivalent of West Ham winning the UEFA Cup with the final being played at the new Wembley.

Quiet man Joe was West Ham's stylish right-back on that memorable night. He spent 10 years at Upton Park before moving on to Chelsea and Southampton. These days, he is retired and living contentedly near Marseilles in the south of France with his wife Jill.

Joe told *EX*: "I played nearly 500 league and cup games in my career but the years at Upton Park were simply the best. They were a great bunch of lads and most of us grew up together. That's what made it so special. Apart from Bobby Moore, Geoff Hurst and Martin Peters who went onto somewhat bigger things with England the following year, that night at Wembley was the highlight of our careers for the rest of us."

Most of Joe's team-mates came from the London area but Joe was one of the exceptions having been born in Sunderland on December 17, 1939. Even today, there are still traces of Joe's North-East accent.

Joe recalls: "As a kid, my greatest hero was Len Shackleton and I followed Sunderland and Newcastle because 'Shack' played for both teams. I was a good all rounder and represented Northumberland boys at rugby and football."

Joe was also outstanding academically and gained nine 'O' Levels. "I wanted to join the RAF and become a pilot," he says, "but a chance meeting on a bus literally changed my life."

Joe had just played a game for Northumberland boys. His dad had been at the game and was travelling home on the bus when he began talking to another passenger. It transpired that the other man was a West Ham scout who had also been at the match and had been impressed by Joe's performance. "That's my son!" exclaimed Joe's dad.

Joe, Jack Burkett and Ron Boyce with trainer Albert Walker.

As a result of that meeting, West Ham invited Joe down for pre-season training. He says: "I later learned that Burnley and Sunderland were also watching me but West Ham were the ones who made the first move. For the next 12 months I spent the school holidays training with West Ham. It was perfect, because my sister Joyce had got married and was living in Dagenham, so I just stayed with her. I was never homesick."

Clearly, West Ham liked what they saw because in the summer of 1957, Joe was offered professional terms. "My signing-on fee was £10," recalls Joe, "and West Ham's manager Ted Fenton shook hands with me and wished me good luck."

Sadly, Joe's dad died in November 1957. "My mum moved down soon afterwards and the club set us up in a flat in Canning Town," explains Joe. "West Ham were such a friendly club and George Wright, a full-back who played over 100 games for the Hammers, took me under his wing. My best mates in those early days were John Smith, Andy Smillie, Harry Cripps and John Lyall."

Joe recalls his first game for West Ham's youth team, against Chelsea. "I played at right-half and the little fellow I was marking scored both goals in West Ham's two-nil defeat. His name was Jimmy Greaves," says Joe with a rueful smile.

The climax to Joe's first season was West Ham reaching the FA Youth Cup final against Manchester United but it was an unhappy ending, United winning 8-2 on aggregate.

Joe also gained an England youth cap that season, against Ireland at Leyton Orient's Brisbane Road ground. "We won 6-2," says Joe, "but I had a poor game and I was never selected again.

"In my second full season, I began to progress through the ranks to the reserves and I became great friends with another youngster called Bobby Moore. I would sometimes stay at Bobby's house in Waverley Gardens, Barking at weekends. Bobby's parents were lovely people. Bobby was just one of the lads and he never changed, even when he became England's World Cup-winning captain."

Joe remembers that around this time club captain Malcolm Allison had been struck down with tuberculosis and Noel Cantwell had taken over the captaincy. "Noel was another who had a big influence on my career," says Joe. "I owe him a lot." Indeed, Cantwell led West Ham to the Second Division championship in 1957-58 and the fans were fanatical in their support for the newly-promoted Hammers who were back in the First Division after an absence of 26 long years.

After a series of impressive appearances in the reserves, Ted Fenton gave Joe his league debut against Manchester City at Maine Road on December 13, 1958, just four days before his 19th birthday.

"I wasn't nervous," says Joe, "and I really enjoyed the game. I thought I did OK, although we lost 1-3."

Both Joe and Bobby Moore made their league debuts that season and it says much for Joe's ability that he had made a total of 11 appearances to Mooro's five outings by the end of the campaign. Joe particularly recalls the game at Newcastle on Easter Monday, because he was forced to take over in goal from the injured Noel Dwyer (no substitutes in those days).

"We were 1-3 down when I took over in goal," says Joe, "and that was the final score, so I managed to keep a clean sheet. I must be the only goalkeeper in West Ham's history never to concede a goal!"

It was around this time that West Ham players would often meet in Cassettari's café, near the ground in Barking Road, and Joe noticed an attractive young girl who was often in there. Joe discovered that her name was Jill Eggleton and that she worked in a chemist opposite the café. Joe and Jill started going out together, although their first date had to be postponed due to the fact that Joe had collided with the West Ham goalkeeper Brian Rhodes in a reserve match at Bournemouth the previous day. Joe left his two front teeth embedded in Rhodes' shoulder and had 20 stitches in his mouth. "Jill's dad was a big West Ham fan, so I couldn't go wrong," says Joe.

Joe's progression continued in the 1959-60 season with a further 16 appearances. Early in the 1960-61 campaign, he found himself in opposition to the legendary Stanley Matthews when Blackpool visited Upton Park and fought out a thrilling 3-3 draw. Joe recalls: "Stan was the most famous footballer in the world at the time but he tended to play out wide on Blackpool's right wing and Bobby Moore had to mark him. Bobby had a good game against the old maestro."

With West Ham languishing in the lower half of the table, Fenton left the club in March 1961. "I was sad at Fenton's departure because he had given me my chance," says Joe, "but these things happen in football."

On Easter Monday 1961, Joe scored his first goal in league football against Leicester City at Filbert Street. "It was a cracker!" he recalls. "I raced through the middle and latched onto a long ball from John Bond and fired it past Gordon Banks. Unfortunately, we lost 1-5, so it didn't make a great deal of difference."

Joe lines up for England Under-23s (next to manager Billy Wright), with Bobby Moore (other end) in 1961-62.

Shortly afterwards, Ron Greenwood was announced as West Ham's new manager. Greenwood had been the assistant manager at Arsenal and came to Upton Park with a glowing reputation. "Ron was a fantastic coach," says Joe. "He made an immediate impact. Ron would spot things during a game and have a few quiet words with the team and individuals at half-time. He never lost his temper in front of the team and was always in control."

Under Greenwood's influence, 1961-62 was Joe's best-ever season as he made 41 league appearances and gained three England under-23 caps. Among his team-mates in those England games were fellow Hammers Bobby Moore and Johnny Byrne.

At the end of the season, Joe and Bobby played for Young England against England at Highbury and both gave impressive performances. In those days, the England manager was Walter Winterbottom but the FA selection committee picked the team on Winterbottom's behalf. After the Young England game, the committee had to choose the 22 players who would represent England at the 1962 World Cup finals in Chile.

Joe reveals: "I later learnt that the committee were prepared to allow one of the young, uncapped players to go to the World Cup and that it was a toss up between Bobby Moore and myself. In the end, they chose Bobby and as the saying goes, the rest is history."

However, there was consolation for Joe in missing the 1962 World Cup tournament, since he and Jill were married on June 9, 1962. Joe's best man was his former West Ham team-mate Andy Nelson and the happy couple moved into their new house at Abridge, Essex.

Joe helps out Jim Standen as the keeper dives at the feet of Everton's Roy Vernon at Goodison Park in April 1962.

Joe was a permanent fixture in the side until October 1963 when he lost his place to John Bond after a 0-3 defeat at Sheffield Wednesday. It was the beginning of the lowest point in Joe's career. In fact, he was out of the side for nearly 18 months, only getting occasional outings when Bond was injured. Joe's absence from the side coincided with West Ham's FA Cup run which ended with the Hammers beating Preston North End, 3-2 at Wembley in the FA Cup final.

Recalling the disappointment, Joe says: "I sat next to Martin Peters who had also lost his place earlier in the season to Eddie Bovington. I was pleased for the lads because they were my mates, but I was gutted for myself."

As the Hammers paraded the FA Cup on the lap of honour, Joe and Martin Peters began walking back towards the Wembley tunnel, but not before Ron Greenwood tried to console them. "Ron said to us that now that West Ham had qualified for the European Cup Winners' Cup, then perhaps we would get our chance if the team reached the final in a year's time. It was an amazing statement and, of course, it came true."

Joe and Martin Peters had become great friends and Joe was best man at Martin and Kathy's wedding later that summer.

In December 1964, and with still no sign of a first team recall, Joe went to see Greenwood and asked for a transfer – but the West Ham manager turned it down. In fact, it was the turning point for Joe. Within two months, he regained the right-back berth from Bond and retained his place for the rest of the season. It was perfect timing, since West Ham had reached the quarter-finals of the European Cup Winners' Cup and Joe played in both legs against Lausanne of Switzerland. The Hammers won 6-4 on aggregate and were drawn against the dangerous Real

November 1962 – Joe looks on as Martin Peters battles with John Fantham at Sheffield Wednesday.

Zaragoza of Spain in the semi-final.

"We won the first leg, 2-1 at Upton Park, and in the second leg in Spain, they absolutely battered us for 89 minutes. The Zaragoza forward line were all internationals and were nicknamed the 'Magnificent Five' and it was real backs-to-the-wall stuff. We drew 1-1 on the night and went through 3-2 on aggregate. It was a great defensive performance and as usual, Bobby Moore was superb."

Joe has an interesting theory about Moore. He says:"I always thought that Bobby was a good player for West Ham but that he was a truly great player for England."

And so it came to pass that Greenwood's prophesy had come true. Both Joe and Martin Peters had regained their places and West Ham had indeed reached the final of the European Cup Winners' Cup. By the most delicious irony, UEFA had decided that the game would be played at Wembley.

West Ham warmed up for the final with a 3-1 win against Shamrock Rovers in a friendly match in Ireland. Joe recalls: "The build up to the final was very low key. We were able to watch our opponents TSV Munich1860 in their semi-final play-off victory over Torino of Italy. They were a good side, very skilful and well organised, just what you would expect of a German team. Their two stars were the Yugoslav international goalkeeper Peter Radenkovic and their captain and centre-forward Rudi Brunnenmeier, who had played for Germany earlier in the season.

"We stayed at the Hendon Hall Hotel on the night before the final and then travelled to Wembley by coach. The excitement really began to build as the coach edged along Wembley Way and we saw the thousands of Hammers fans. I was keyed up, but I wasn't nervous. The dressing room at Wembley was very quiet. It was difficult to hear any noise from the crowd and Ron spoke to each of the players in turn, reminding us of what was required.

"The signal came for us to leave the dressing room and we lined up in the tunnel and I can remember seeing daylight at the far end. As we walked up the slope and out of the tunnel into the evening sunshine, the stadium erupted. It was the proverbial wall of sound. I will never forget it."

The match was a classic with skilful and inventive football being played by both teams and it is still regarded as one of the greatest matches ever played at the old stadium. Joe recalls that the first half was very even, although Brian Dear had a goal disallowed for offside. The Germans played neat one-twos around the West Ham penalty area but Moore marshalled his defence superbly. There were no goals at half time and the mood in the West Ham dressing room was upbeat.

Joe says: "I knew I was playing well and so were the rest of the lads. We felt we were more than capable of going on to lift the trophy.

Alan Sealey's two second half goals ensured a place in Hammers' history for the 11 who graced the Wembley turf on that momentous night.

"We were well on top by the end and could have scored four or five. John Sissons hit the post and crossbar and we were worthy winners."

West Ham may have been Kings of Europe but their league form was poor at the beginning of the 1965-66 season. Indeed, they were leaking goals at an alarming rate and at one point, they conceded 15 in three games. After a 1-2 defeat at Newcastle on January 8, 1966, Joe was dropped in favour of the promising Dennis Burnett. Although Joe did not realise it at the time, it would be his last game for West Ham.

"I was very disillusioned," admits Joe, "and a couple of months later Steve Richards, who was a newspaper reporter and good friend of mine, told me that Chelsea manager Tommy Docherty was interested in signing me. Steve asked me if I wanted him to print it and I said 'yes'.

"When Ron Greenwood saw it in the paper, he called me into his office and went ballistic. He ended up by shouting: 'You put that in the paper. If you want to go to Chelsea, then just go. You and Docherty deserve one another.'

"Obviously, Ron didn't think much of me and he thought even less of Tommy Docherty. It was the only time I ever saw Ron lose his temper.

"I'm sorry it ended like that. Ron knew more about football than anyone else I have ever met but his man-management skills left a bit to be desired at times. We had a few run-ins over the years.

"Anyway, I signed for Chelsea and spent two years at Stamford Bridge. I played in an FA Cup semi-final, when we lost 2-0 to Sheffield Wednesday at Villa Park, and an Inter-Cities Fairs Cup semi-final, when we were beaten 5-0 by Barcelona in the Nou Camp. When Chelsea reached the 1967 FA Cup final against Spurs at Wembley, I was named as substitute. Chelsea lost 2-1 and I got a FA Cup runners-up medal, although I didn't get on during the game.

"In February 1968, Southampton made an offer for me and I signed for them, with

David Webb going in the opposite direction," explains Joe. "It was a good move and I spent six years at The Dell. I was a first team regular and the manager, Ted Bates, was a lovely man. Also, my sons Anthony and Nick were born while I was with Southampton, so it was a very happy time for me."

Joe's final Football League appearance came for Southampton in a 0-2 defeat at Norwich in August 1973.

He says: "Early in 1974, I had the opportunity to succeed Johnny Byrne as player-manager of Durban City in South Africa and I went out there with Jill and the boys. It didn't really work out, though. I had a lot of problems with the chairman, who kept meddling in team affairs, and we ended up having a major row in front of all of the players. It was the beginning of the end and we headed back to England in 1976.

"I didn't have any trouble adapting to life after football. I knew it would end some time. One of the Chelsea directors, George Thompson, got me a job with Byfleet Machine and Tool Company Ltd. After three years, I took over the Rose and Crown pub in Upper Farringdon, Hampshire. Later on, I ran a sports shop in Cranleigh, near Guildford, and then I took over a newsagents in the village of Ewell in Surrey.

"That was seriously hard work," laughs Joe, "since I had to get up at 4.00am every morning and sort out the deliveries for the paper boys."

Joe reflects on his career by saying: "George Best was the greatest player I ever played against and his Irish team-mate, Derek Dougan, had the most to say for himself. I never got involved in verbals on the pitch but Dougan really used to wind me up. Also, I never liked playing against Don Revie's Leeds United – they were an unpleasant bunch."

Joe was never sent off in his career and was booked only once. It's an amazing statistic for a defender who played in almost 500 League and Cup matches and it is a testament to his cultured style of play.

There is an amusing sequel to West Ham's greatest night. The 1965 ECWC final was covered by the BBC and the commentator was Kenneth Wolstenholme who gained immortality the following year with the words "They think it's all over . . . it is now", as Geoff Hurst scored England's fourth goal to clinch victory in the World Cup final.

However, Wolstenholme did not always get things right and throughout his commentary during the West Ham v TSV Munich game, he persisted in pronouncing Joe's surname as "Keirkup".

Joe, who returned to London in May 2005 to attend the reunion dinner organised by *EX*, says: "Whenever I saw a recording of the game, and I now have the DVD, it used to drive me mad when Wolstenholme kept getting my name wrong. Years later, when I owned the newsagents in Ewell, I discovered that he was one of my customers and that we delivered newspapers to his house. It was an incredible coincidence and when Ken came in to pay his papers for the first time, I told him who I was and gave him some good natured flack for his error. I was pleased to put the record straight!"

These days Joe and Jill live in the medieval village of Mane (pronounced Man) which nestles amongst the picturesque hills in the Provence region of southern

France. It is the epitome of peace and tranquillity. There are only six shops in the village which has a population of less than one thousand people. The pace of life in Mane is gentle, to say the least.

Joe says: "We came out here six years ago and we love the relaxed lifestyle. At first, we lived near St. Etienne, but soon afterwards, we bought some land in Mane and we had a house and swimming pool built to our own specifications. I suppose it is our dream home."

Joe pictured at the Cup winners' reunion in 2005.

Joe has worked hard at turning the rest of the land into an imposing garden. He says: "It is approximately the size of a football pitch, although not the same shape! It takes me between two and three hours every week to cut the lawns and, afterwards, the swimming pool comes in very handy.

"The weather here is marvellous and we have our meals out on the terrace most days. Sometimes we eat in the village or we go up to the golf club. I play occasionally, but not as much as I would like. I hardly ever buy a newspaper, but I keep up to date with all the news on Sky TV. I watch plenty of football and I always look out for West Ham's result. We know enough of the language to get by but sometimes I have to ask the locals to slow down a bit when they are talking, so that I can understand them. We seem to get on well with everyone, though."

However, Joe admits that the peacefulness that usually exists in Mane was shattered one Saturday afternoon in July 2008, when the riders in the Tour de France sped through the village on stage 14 of the race – a 194.5km leg from Nimes to Digne-les-Bains. He says: "It was the first time it has happened and the whole village turned out to watch them. It was a fantastic spectacle.

"The only drawback to living here is that, obviously, we miss our family, but they come out for holidays and we go back to England at least a couple of times each year."

When Joe and Jill want to enjoy an occasional day away from their tranquil life in the village, there are plenty of attractions available to them. The glittering resorts along the Cote d'Azur such as St. Tropez, Cannes and Nice are less than two hours drive away, whilst the beautiful port of Marseilles with its spectacular restaurants and bars is even closer.

The final word rests with Joe when he says: "We know that we made the right decision about coming out here to live when we turn on the TV and see all the traffic jams on the M25."

Chapter 5

JACK**BURKETT**

"I'd say that Noel was among the top five left-backs of all time. I modelled my running style on his. He gave me probably the best advice anyone could have given. He explained that the reason he ran with his arms up and elbows sticking out was to stop opponents getting near him"

JACK Burkett once came perilously close to making football history, for all the wrong reasons, by almost becoming the first player ever to be sent off in a FA Cup final at Wembley. More than 44 years later, Jack still shudders at the thought of what might have been.

Jack was West Ham's stylish left-back in the 1964 FA Cup final against Preston North End. He recalls: "Preston settled more quickly than us and I was marking Davie Wilson, a tricky right-winger. In the opening minutes, I was very nervous and as Davie went past me for the first time, I mistimed a sliding tackle and brought him down.

"It looked bad. Five minutes later he turned quickly and ran straight into me and this time I obstructed him. A few minutes later, I brought him down again.

"At that point, the referee, Arthur Holland, ran across and told me in no uncertain terms that I was close to being sent off. There were no yellow or red cards in those days and I was very lucky to get away with it. I would definitely have been sent off in the modern game.

"I managed to settle down after that and we went on to win 3-2. Preston were better than us on the day, but it was still a great feeling to gain a FA Cup winners' medal so early in my career."

Clearly, the good people of Preston have long memories and at a players' reunion dinner in 2004, former right-back George Ross made an amusing after-dinner speech during which he jokingly said: "Can I please ask Jack Burkett to return Davie Wilson's kneecaps!'

Also, during a subsequent visit to the Lancashire town, Jack learnt that he is still known as 'The Cruncher.'

In truth, such a reputation is harsh and unfair because Jack was a class act and a typical West Ham player of that period – athletic, stylish and comfortable on the ball. He made a total of 185 league and cup appearances during his 10 years at Upton Park and was never booked or sent off in his career, despite his close call in the '64 final.

Jack, now 66, is a true football man and spent a total of 47 years in the professional

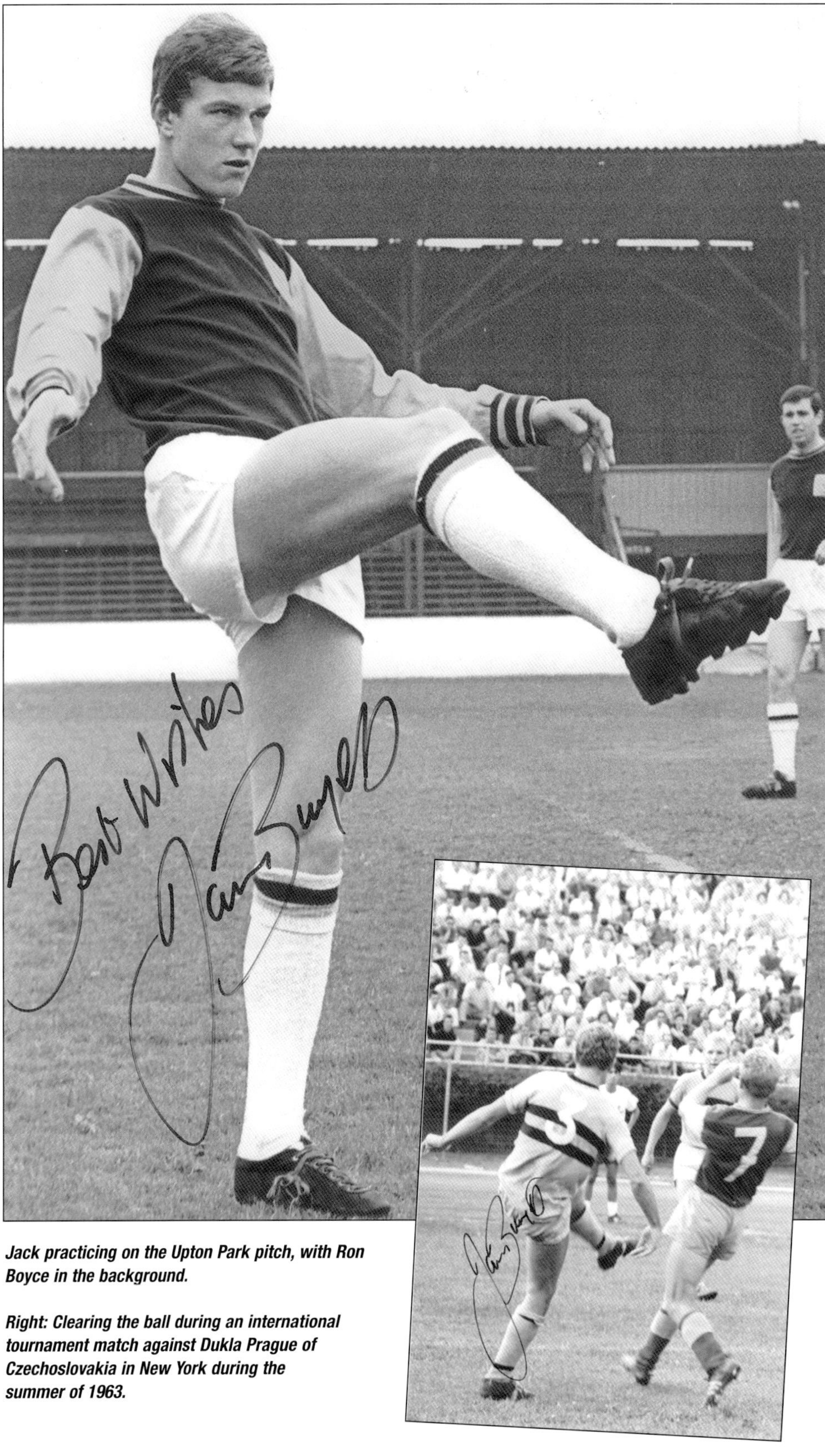

Jack practicing on the Upton Park pitch, with Ron Boyce in the background.

Right: Clearing the ball during an international tournament match against Dukla Prague of Czechoslovakia in New York during the summer of 1963.

Young Jack, 16, playing against Bristol City Reserves at Upton Park in 1958-59.

game until his retirement in September 2005. During that time, he was a player, coach, trainer, scout, manager and an employee of the PFA. He worked in various countries, including such football outposts as Norway and oil-rich Saudi Arabia.

"I would like to write my autobiography one day, if only to document my travels and experiences for my children and grandchildren," says Jack. It is indeed a compelling story which includes witnessing a gruesome execution in Saudi Arabia and his own personal battle against cancer.

Jack's ancestors originated from Germany and Ireland, ironically where he would also later work, but Jack himself is a true Cockney having been born within the sound of Bow Bells on August 21, 1942. Jack's parents, James and Lillian, had three other children, Ron, Doreen and Pat, and soon after Jack was born the family moved to Islington in north London and then on to Tottenham.

"I spent my formative years growing up near Tottenham's ground. Also, one of my uncles played football for Fulham during the war years, so I suppose football was in my blood," says Jack.

"I used to watch Spurs and Arsenal on alternate Saturdays. I remember seeing Ted Ditchburn and Alf Ramsey play for Spurs and Jack Kelsey and Wally Barnes for Arsenal. However, my first real hero was Nilton Santos, a World Cup winner with Brazil in 1958."

It comes as no surprise that Santos played at left-back, a position that Jack would later fill with such distinction at Upton Park. Jack's admiration for the Brazilian legend continues to this day – one of Jack's dogs is named . . . Santos!

He says: "I was a bit of a rebel at school but I was good at sport. I captained the school rugby team and I played for Middlesex at scrum-half. Also, I played football for Tottenham, Middlesex and London schools and my progress alerted the local scouts. I began training with Spurs a couple of evenings a week but there was just a great emphasis on running and I was a bit disillusioned.

"I was then approached by West Ham's chief scout Wally St. Pier and after getting permission from Spurs, I started training at Upton Park on Tuesday and Thursday evenings. It was great. We trained on the pitch and first teamers Malcolm Allison, Noel Cantwell and John Bond took the sessions. It was all ball work. I was hooked.

"I was about to leave school and West Ham's manager Ted Fenton came to the house and told my parents that he wanted me to join the ground staff. It was a great thrill, although I thought my chance had gone when my brother spilt a cup of tea over Ted's smart trousers!

"My first day with West Ham was on July 1, 1958 and I had to report to Upton Park together with the other new ground staff boys – all 15 of us. We were each given a garden fork and our first job was to dig up the pitch. Some of the jobs we had to do as ground staff boys would be illegal in the present day. I remember once having to climb up the floodlight pylon and collect footballs that had lodged on the roof of the stand. Health and Safety issues were non-existent in those days."

Despite such hair-raising tasks, Jack was making progress on the field and was a member of West Ham's successful youth team that reached the final of the FA Youth Cup against Blackburn Rovers in his first season with the club. Jack recalls: "We lost 1-2 on aggregate and our captain was a young, fair haired lad called Bobby Moore."

Jack's progress continued when he gained an England youth cap and he signed full professional forms in October 1959. West Ham's club captain Noel Cantwell was a huge influence on Jack's career. "I would say that Noel was amongst the top five left-backs of all time. I modelled my running style on Noel's. He gave me probably the best advice anyone could have given. He explained that the reason he ran with his arms up and elbows sticking out was to stop opponents getting near him."

After a series of poor results in the league and FA Cup, Ted Fenton left West Ham in March 1961 and Ron Greenwood took over as manager. Jack recalls: "We were all immediately impressed by Ron. He may not have been the greatest man-manager, but he was the best coach of all time."

Greenwood began to exert his considerable influence over a squad of highly talented young players and a new generation of Hammers, such as Bobby Moore, Joe Kirkup, Ron Boyce, Eddie Bovington, Martin Peters and Geoff Hurst, were rapidly emerging. It was against this background that Jack's path to the first team virtually opened up before him as Noel Cantwell was transferred to Manchester United and then tenacious John Lyall, once regarded as Cantwell's natural successor, sustained a series of knee injuries that would prematurely end his playing career.

As a result, Jack was given his league debut in the last match of the season, against Fulham at Upton Park on April 30, 1962. "It was a Monday night and we won 4-2. I wasn't nervous and I thought I played well," he says.

The following season, 1962-63, Jack firmly established himself with 45 league and cup appearances.

In the summer of '63, West Ham participated in an international tournament in the USA against some outstanding club sides such as Gornik of Poland and Dukla

Hammers line-up at Randalls Island, New York before beating Valenciennnes of France, 3-1, during the pioneering 1963 international tournament that taught the players so much and laid the foundations for the Cup successes that followed. Back row, left to right: Joe Kirkup, Martin Peters, Ken Brown, Alan Sealey, Jim Standen and Bobby Moore. Front: Ron Boyce, Johnny Byrne, Peter Brabrook, Geoff Hurst and Jack Burkett.

Prague of Czechoslovakia.

"That tournament was a great learning curve for us and it was the catalyst for the success that followed in the next couple of years," recalls Jack.

Indeed, within a year, West Ham had beaten Preston at Wembley to win the FA Cup for the first time in the club's history – but there was another memorable date for Jack in the summer of '64.

On June 20, Jack married Ann Rivers. He says: "I first saw Ann outside the Tottenham Royal dance hall at Christmas 1960 and then I met her shortly afterwards at a friend's party. When we got married, we bought a house at Chadwell Heath and we were close friends with Ron Boyce, Geoff Hurst, Martin Peters and their wives."

Newly-married and with a coveted FA Cup winners' medal to his name, Jack approached the 1964-65 season brimming with confidence. Clearly, Tottenham's legendary manager Bill Nicholson rated Jack highly and offered £40,000 to take him to White Hart Lane.

"It was a substantial transfer fee in those days," says Jack, "but West Ham turned it down. I was very happy at Upton Park, but a move to Tottenham would have been very tempting. Instead, Bill Nicholson signed Cyril Knowles from Middlesbrough and Cyril went on to have a good career at Tottenham."

Jack was in excellent form as the season progressed, but he sustained a serious back injury in a 1-2 defeat against Birmingham City at St. Andrew's on Boxing Day 1964. He explains: "I cracked a vertebrae and I was out for three months during which time I was encased in plaster. In fact, it was a potentially career-threatening injury." In the end, he just ignored the pain and got back into the side at the end of

March, in time for the semi-final of the European Cup Winners' Cup against Real Zaragoza of Spain which Hammers won 3-2 on aggregate.

He then played in the greatest match in West Ham's history, when we beat TSV Munich 1860 by 2-0 to win the European Cup Winners' Cup at Wembley on May 19, 1965."It was a fantastic achievement. Only seven of us played in the two successive Wembley finals against Preston and Munich. I am very proud to have been one of that unique group of West Ham players," says Jack. The others were Jim Standen, Ken Brown, Bobby Moore, Ron Boyce, Geoff Hurst and John Sissons.

Shortly afterwards, Jack's international aspirations came to an abrupt halt when he was selected for an end-of-season England under-23 tour. He recalls: "Unfortunately, West Ham were going back to the USA to take part in another tournament and I decided to go to the States with my club." Clearly, England manager Alf Ramsey did not take kindly to rejection and Jack was never called up for his country again.

While Jack may not have been top of Ramsey's popularity poll, there is no doubt that he was a huge favourite with West Ham's female fans of that era. Whenever Jack touched the ball at Upton Park, then Beatle type screams would ring out from the Upton Park terraces.

Jack says: "At first, I didn't understand what it was all about. I didn't feel embarrassed and it was quite amusing really. It certainly didn't bother Ann!"

Early in the 1965-66 season, Jack created a small piece of Upton Park history by becoming the first West Ham player ever to be substituted in a league match. It happened on August 28 when Jack was injured in a 2-1 home win against Leeds United and was substituted by Peter Bennett.

In March 1966, West Ham reached the two-legged Football League Cup final against West Bromwich Albion. Jack says: "I played in the first leg at Upton Park, which we won 2-1, but I was injured for the second leg when Albion took us apart at the Hawthorns and we lost 1-4. Only the players who played in the second leg got a medal, so I missed out."

Within four months, the West Ham trio of Bobby Moore, Geoff Hurst and Martin Peters won the World Cup with England. Unbeknown to Jack and his illustrious team mates, West Ham were about to drift into years of mediocrity. In the 1966-67 season, immediately after England's World Cup success, West Ham finished a miserable 16th place in the league and were humiliated 1-3 by Swindon Town in the third round of the FA Cup.

Towards the end of that season, Jack lost his place, albeit briefly, and played for West Ham's reserves in a 0-3 defeat to Southampton at Upton Park. Reserve team manager Ernie Gregory was so incensed by the team's performance that he reported the matter to Ron Greenwood and eight members of the team, including Jack, were each fined £5 for their poor display.

"It sounds ridiculous now," says Jack, "but it was still a fair bit of money in those days. It was the beginning of the end for me at Upton Park. My last appearance for West Ham came on December 16, 1967 against Sheffield Wednesday at Hillsborough. We lost 1-4 and the following week, I was left out again and Frank Lampard replaced me.

"I had lost form and in the summer of 1968 Wolves offered £25,000 for me, so I went up to the Midlands and met their manager Ronnie Allen. Wolves were still in the first division and I was all ready to sign when second division Charlton Athletic came in for me.

"I met their manager Eddie Firmani and decided to sign for Charlton because it meant I didn't have to move the family away from London. But it was the worst mistake I ever made. I just didn't get on with Eddie," he reveals.

"I never received a promised signing-on fee and I hated the training. It was virtually all running and nothing like the training that I had been used to at West Ham. In the end, I spent two years at Charlton and made only 15 appearances for them, although towards the end of my spell there I got involved with some coaching."

In July 1970, Jack went to Millwall on a free transfer and played around 20 games.

"I got on OK with manager Benny Fenton, brother of my previous West Ham manager Ted, and again I got involved with a bit of coaching, this time with the youth team.

"I had only been at Millwall for a year when I was offered the player-manager's job at St. Patrick's Athletic, who were based in Southern Ireland. I talked it over with Ann and decided that we would give it a go, so we moved out there with our two sons. In fact, we stayed in Ireland for four years and thoroughly enjoyed it. Our daughter was born while we were there and our sons ended up speaking Gaelic!

"The standard was the equivalent of the present day Rymans League and they were part-time players. St. Patrick's attracted crowds of around 500 for each home match. We lived just outside of Dublin and it was a brilliant four years. The people were fantastic and St. Patrick's became quite successful. We won their League Cup in my first season and we also reached the semi-final of their FAI Cup. In my third season, we got to the FAI Cup final, but lost to Finn Harps in front of 30,000 people at Dalymount Park.

"But in the summer of 1975, I felt the time was right to go back to England and I got a job as player-coach at Southend United. I played about six games for Southend but I didn't really get on with manager Arthur Rowley and I was only at Roots Hall for one year.

"In the summer of 1976, I was contacted by Jimmy Hill's World Sports Academy who were organising football in oil-rich Saudi Arabia. I was offered the job of managing Saudi's under-18 national side and I decided to take it,

April 1964 – Jack and John Bond watch as Jim Standen saves. The Bolton player is 17-year-old Francis Lee.

although I didn't take the family with me. I missed them dreadfully, but I usually got home for a few days at the end of each month.

"Nevertheless, it was a fantastic experience. We were always on tour and we went to France, Germany, Spain, Austria, Thailand, Iran, Malaysia and Iraq. The Prince of Saudi Arabia took a great interest in football and we used to fly everywhere in his own private jumbo jet."

Jack continues: "Law and order is enforced very strictly in Saudi. On one occasion, we were in Jeddah on a Friday, which is punishment day out there. Thousands of people attend and the sand around the punishment arena is stained dark from the blood of the victims. I saw one man, who was a thief, have his hand cut off.

"Another man was led in and as he knelt down, I realised that they were going to behead him. The executioner's sword glinted in the sunshine and as it flashed downwards, I looked away. There was a great roar from the crowd, reminiscent of football fans, and when I looked back again, the executioner was holding the severed head high into the air."

Despite witnessing such a horrifying spectacle, Jack says that he thoroughly enjoyed his time in Saudi.

"I had a three-year contract and I earned some good money.

"Towards the end of my time with the Saudi under-18 team, we went to Germany on another tour and I became friendly with the chairman of the second division club, Offenbach Kickers. Their manager was Siggi Held who had played against England in the 1966 World Cup final. After I left Saudi, I spent a few weeks with Offenbach Kickers doing some coaching, but I couldn't stay because I didn't have the German coaching badge.

"Later in 1979, I came home but I couldn't get a full time job, although I did a bit of scouting for Aston Villa. After that, I spent a few months working on my own running a sports shop in Southend."

In June 1980 Jack was off on his travels again when he was given the opportunity of being player-manager of Norwegian second division club Orsta, which is situated just north of Bergen. He says: "I had a reasonably good time there and the standard was OK – probably equal to the Conference League. However, although Orsta were only part-time players, we still had crowds of around 1000 for each home match. They had fantastic facilities and I had a good two-year contract, but it was very expensive living in Norway.

"I returned to England in 1982 and went back to Southend United as their youth team coach. Shortly afterwards, Bobby Moore took over as manager and it was good to work with Mooro again. But there were dreadful financial constraints on the club. Basically, we just didn't have any money. Even so, I stayed at Southend for four years.

"In 1986, Fulham manager Ray Harford asked me if I wanted to join Fulham on the coaching staff and I readily agreed. Unfortunately, they were in an even worse state than Southend. There was no money and we didn't even have a training ground. In fact, things were so bad that we had to take our own toilet paper into training with us!

"I remember that Liverpool came to Craven Cottage for a cup match and there was no heating in the dressing rooms and no soap either. I don't know what the likes of Kenny Dalglish and Ian Rush must have thought.

"Things gradually improved and when Ray Lewington took over as manager, I progressed to first team coach and then assistant manager. I was involved in so much at the club that I even turned out for the reserves against Watford at Vicarage Road when I was 46-years-old!

"We did turn things around and in 1989, we reached the play-offs, but lost to Bristol Rovers. There were huge pressures to keep things going at the club and I was working ridiculously long hours. Late one night, I was driving home from a scouting mission in the Midlands and I felt unwell while on the motorway. I pulled into a service station and completely blacked out. When I didn't arrive home, Ann got very worried and contacted the police. They eventually found me slumped in my car.

"I was literally worn out. I went to hospital and I was told by the doctor that if I didn't slow down, then I would be dead within a week. Clearly, it was time to look for an alternative role in football.

"In 1991, I took a job in charge of YTS boys in the south of England on behalf of the PFA. Basically, we helped young professionals with all aspects of their career and life including education, marketing and the football side of things. We even assisted one or two who were involved in unfortunate court cases. Also, there were dozens of boys who didn't make the grade in the professional game and we helped them start new careers. I dealt with young players from 32 professional clubs, it was extremely satisfying work and I stayed there for 14 years until I retired in 2005."

Unfortunately, none of Jack's experiences in his fascinating life could prepare him for the shattering news that he received in the spring of 2005. He explains: "It started off with nothing more than an irritation on my back which became quite sore. In the end, I went to the hospital for a check up and I will never forget the moment when the doctor told me that I had skin cancer, a full malignant melanoma. It was a huge shock. It put a completely different perspective on life and also meant a change of lifestyle. To say the least, the treatment was unpleasant and I am still having check-ups at the hospital."

Jack pictured at the Cup winners' reunion in 2005.

There is no doubt that Jack's family helped him through that very difficult period in his life. Jack and Ann have been happily married for 44 years and they are very proud of their three children, Darrell, who is a warehouse manager, Dean, who owns a french polishing business, and Elizabeth, who is employed by the NHS in property as a surveyor.

Jack and Ann are grandparents to Jacob, Owen, Isabella, Siena, Tobias and Isla. Jacob and Owen play football and Jack gets great enjoyment watching his grandsons play for their respective teams. Jack and Ann currently live near Southend, although they are contemplating a move to Hampshire at some point in the future.

He says: "I keep myself busy and I am currently researching my family ancestry. Also, I stay fit by playing golf, swimming and walking the dogs."

In fighting his illness, Jack has shown the same determination and fortitude that he displayed as a member of West Ham's defence in the glory days of the mid-60s. As one of the 'Magnificent Seven', Jack's career will always remain an integral part of Upton Park folklore. All West Ham fans, past and present, will wish him a long and contented retirement.

Chapter 6

PETER**BRABROOK**

"My calves were in knots and my socks were round my ankles – that was what the Wembley pitch did to you then. We were used to playing on mud-baths every week, but Wembley was so firm and the grass so lush, it just soaked the energy out of your legs"

PETER Brabrook eventually cost West Ham United the princely sum of £35,000 when they signed him from Chelsea in 1962 . . . yet they might have had him for nothing when he left school in the mid-50s.

Wally St. Pier, the famous Upton Park scout of that golden post-war era, didn't often miss out when it came to snapping up the finest local talent – but it's highly likely he would have been kicking himself at seeing the East Ham youngster and Hammers fan head west to Stamford Bridge and become a full England international.

Greenwich-born Peter had grown up just a stone's throw from the Boleyn Ground – the son of an East End docker – and when it came to his loyalties as a football-mad schoolboy, the blue of Chelsea was nowhere to be seen.

"As a young boy, I lived in Beconsfield Street in East Ham, down near the docks, and I followed both West Ham and Charlton Athletic," says Peter. "I used to go over on the Woolwich Ferry to watch games at The Valley, when they used to get amazing crowds. I remember going to watch them play Manchester City, when Bert Trautmann was in goal, and there were 70,000 people there – most of whom were packed onto that old terrace which almost seemed to reach the clouds.

"I also used to stand behind the goal at West Ham, though, in the early 50s when you had people like Harry Hooper and Dougie Wragg, who was my favourite player then. He used to be called 'Oily' – and what a player he was. He was a slight fellow but he was so good on the ball and had this trick where he dropped his shoulder and switched direction – it used to leave defenders on the floor!"

Despite his local background and familiarity with all things claret-and-blue, though, Peter didn't follow the usual route once his footballing abilities began to stand out in the East London area. In fact, with the Hammers unwilling to offer him anything other than part-time involvement, he faced an uncertain future. That was until a stunning performance in a prestigious representative match changed his life and resulted in the East End boy heading across the other side of the capital.

"In those days, the only organised football you played was through your school," recalls Peter. "I went to Napier Road School – which is now called Thomas Letherby

– on the Barking Road and was lucky enough to be picked to represent the district (East Ham Boys), the county (Essex) and eventually London, which was a real honour then.

"As a youngster, I was more of a central midfielder but I was strong and had a lot of pace, and I had trained with West Ham as a schoolboy. Wally St Pier, the famous old chief scout, had watched me on plenty of occasions but the club never really made it obvious that they wanted me.

"I was hoping to be taken on to the groundstaff once I left school – meaning that I would be at the club full-time – but West Ham said they couldn't offer me that and, instead, wanted me just to train with them twice a week in the evenings. That would have meant learning a trade and going out to work during the rest of the week – and I didn't want to do that! I just wanted to be a footballer, like all boys of my age then.

"Anyway, a few weeks before I was due to leave school, I played what would be my last game for London Schoolboys, against West Germany at Highbury. It was a big game, with a crowd of around 20,000 there, and I was picked to play from the start.

"We won 2-1 and I scored both of our goals – a diving header and a volley from 25 yards out! It was one of those days when everything went right for me and I could do no wrong. Afterwards, my uncle John – who used to drive me to all the matches – took me home and, when we got back in the early evening, I was met at my front gate by Jimmy Thompson, who was Chelsea's chief scout and recognised throughout the English game as probably the best around when it came to unearthing young talent.

"Jimmy, a real East End character, was just sitting there on the wall and said to me: 'Hello Pete, I've seen mum and dad and they said you'd be home soon – let's go in and have a cup of tea.'

"So we went inside the house and he told my mum to get the kettle on and get me a drink as well, then just sat us all down and said: 'We'd like Peter to join us on the groundstaff at Chelsea.'

"Of course, I was highly delighted and said 'yes,' then told him that I'd been training with West Ham. 'Don't worry about West Ham,' said Jimmy, 'we'll look after you. Come down to Stamford Bridge on Monday and you can meet Ted Drake, the manager.'

"My next question was: 'How do I get there?' To me, Chelsea was on the other side of the world – somewhere near Brazil! Jimmy told me that it was no problem – I could get a District Line train from East Ham all the way to Fulham Broadway and then walk down the road to the ground. I thought: 'Bloody hell, is he sure?' I was only 14 and I'd never travelled that far on my own, but I knew it was what I wanted to do and so I signed for Chelsea.

"A few weeks later, I actually received a letter from Wally St. Pier, wishing me and my mum and dad all the best and apologising for not being able to offer me anything at West Ham. That was a nice gesture and I've still got that letter to this day."

After finding his way to Stamford Bridge on that following Monday morning, Peter was taken aback to discover a groundstaff of around 30 youngsters (including eight or nine of the entire Welsh national schoolboys side!) – all vying for 11 places

Above: Peter (far left) training indoors with Ronnie Boyce, Johnny Byrne, Geoff Hurst and John Sissons.

Right: Following Don Howe and Bobby Charlton down the steps after returning home from the 1958 World Cup in Sweden.

Below: Swindon Town defender John Trollope tries to block Peter's shot during the 3-3 FA Cup third round tie in January 1967.

in the youth team.

However, undaunted by the prospect, young Brabrook set about establishing himself on the King's Road and enjoyed a dream start to his fledgling career.

"My early days at Chelsea were fantastic. We had a terrific youth team that was top of the South-East Counties League for three years and never lost a game. We played in the FA Youth Cup against Manchester United – the team that would become the Busby Babes.

"It was a two-legged match, there were 38,000 at Stamford Bridge for the first leg and we went 1-0 up. Duncan Edwards, who had been playing at centre-half, was then pushed up front and scored two goals to make it 2-1. In the second leg at Old Trafford, the crowd was nearer 50,000. Again, we went 1-0 up, and again Duncan was pushed forward and scored two goals! He was an amazing player even then, six foot tall and built like a tank, but he could play as well. They were a great side – but we weren't bad either.

"From my point of view, it was a wonderful start to my career. I was picked for England youth and seemed to be progressing in the right direction. Our youth team coach at Chelsea was Dickie Moss – a stern man who didn't hand out praise easily and would always rather talk to you about what you'd done wrong rather than right. But looking back now, his approach helped us to grow up and improve our game.

"I was quite a confident lad at that age, I had belief in my ability and was playing for the reserves at the age of 15. In those days they only did that if they thought a lot of you."

Boosted by the belief shown in him by his coaches at Chelsea, Peter continued to progress and, having matured physically in his teens, was handed his Blues debut in the momentous 1954-55 season, when they lifted the League championship for the first time.

His performances at Stamford Bridge didn't go unnoticed by the England selectors, either, and having made himself a regular fixture in Drake's young side, full international honours duly followed after he had once again produced a scintillating performance in a representative match.

"Unfortunately I didn't play enough games to earn a championship medal in 1955 but, at the time, I wasn't too disappointed because I was young and felt there would be more opportunities for me in the future. It was a great time to be at Chelsea and the following year I became a regular as an outside-right when Eric Parsons – who had previously played for West Ham – was injured. Ted asked me if I'd play out wide because I could run, and it all went from there.

"I was part of a forward line who were all under the age of 19 – there was me on the right, Jimmy Greaves inside, Les Allen as centre-forward, Tony Nicholas inside-left and Micky Harrison or Micky Block outside-left. We were known as 'Drake's Ducklings'.

"At the age of 18, I was playing regularly for England under-23s and, at the end of the 1957-58 season, I was selected to play in an England trial game between the 'probables' and the 'possibles' ahead of the World Cup finals in Sweden that summer.

"I was playing for the 'possibles' and was up against left-back Jim Langley, who wasn't the quickest, and I left poor, old Jim for dead that day. I had one of the best games of my life and it got me selected for the World Cup squad.

"In Sweden, I actually roomed with Bobby Charlton, who had flown for the first time since the Munich air disaster a few months earlier. I made my full international debut in the deciding game against Russia and had a great game but we lost 1-0. I hit the post twice and had a goal disallowed against the great Lev Yashin, and we were on our way home."

Having appeared in a World Cup finals tournament at the tender age of 20, the stage seemed set for Peter to go on and establish himself on the international scene and enjoy further domestic glory at Stamford Bridge. Unfortunately, things didn't work out that way. Chelsea failed to build on their title success and Peter won just two more England caps, against Spain and Northern Ireland in 1959.

As the Blues underwent a transitional period following the departure of star striker Jimmy Greaves to AC Milan at the beginning of the 60s, it soon became apparent that Peter would also be on his way when change occurred at the top – although it took some time and hassle before eventually got his wish of a dream switch to Upton Park.

"Ted Drake had been replaced by Tommy Docherty, who wasn't really my cup of tea," recalls Peter. "He used to do strange things. You'd be sitting at the table having breakfast and all of a sudden a bag of sugar would hit you on the back of the head – not really the kind of joke you expect from your manager.

"He didn't fancy me as a player, either, and put me on the transfer list soon after taking over. A few clubs showed an interest and I actually went up to Everton after they had a bid accepted. I'll never forget getting off the train up there – the station was absolutely heaving with Everton fans cheering me and asking me to sign.

"The manager, Harry Catterick, was a lovely man and, after meeting at Goodison Park, he showed me some beautiful houses in Southport. Deep down, though, I knew I wasn't going to sign. I had just got engaged to Doreen and it seemed too much of an ordeal to leave our roots and move all the way up to Liverpool.

"I told Harry I would think about it but I phoned him a couple of days later and told him that I wouldn't be coming, that I would prefer to hang on and wait for a London club.

"The trouble was, Tommy Docherty didn't want me signing for another London club, in case I did well and made him look silly. He cut my money in half after I turned down the move to Everton and a few others, but I stood my ground and just bided my time. Eventually, he realised I wasn't going to budge and they agreed to sell me to West Ham, who I knew were interested."

And so, more than 10 years after having him in the palm of their hand as a schoolboy, West Ham splashed out £35,000 – a record fee for a winger at the time – to finally bring Brabrook to Upton Park in October 1962.

New manager Ron Greenwood, who had been a Chelsea team-mate of Peter's in the mid-50s and coached him at England under-23 level, was building a new claret and blue empire that had seen Johnny Byrne arrive in another record fee just months earlier, and success was just around the corner.

For Peter, who had resisted the opportunity to live nearer Stamford Bridge and stayed loyal to his East End roots, it was the perfect move.

"Having been on half money for six months, I was just glad to get it all sorted out – I think Ron might even have offered me a little more than I'd been on at Chelsea. It wasn't about the finances, though. I just wanted to sign for West Ham and play football again – I'd been out for too long.

"I knew quite a few of the lads – Bobby from England duty of course and some of the others from schools football, plus it was closer to home and, as an East End boy, it wasn't too difficult for me to settle in. They were all nice people at West Ham and Ron was different class as a coach, so I knew I was doing the right thing."

An impressive Hammers debut followed, in which he set up a goal for Geoff Hurst after just 40 seconds against Burnley, and Peter went on to score seven times in 29 appearances in his first season as Greenwood's plans began to take shape.

The following year, he missed just four league games and, more significantly, played in every round of the FA Cup as Hammers reached Wembley and secured the first major cup triumph of their history thanks to a 3-2 victory over Preston North End – a performance he more than played his part in, setting up Ronnie Boyce's memorable late winner.

"Along with playing for England, winning the FA Cup was the pinnacle of my career," he declares. "We had shown great character to beat Manchester United in the semi-final at Hillsborough. They were an awesome side and big odds-on to beat us, but we unleashed a fantastic 3-1 win against them on a ground that was virtually unplayable because of the torrential rain.

"Everyone worked hard that day and the

Homecoming Hammers heroes. The players enjoying their triumphant bus journey through the streets of east London after winning the FA Cup for the first time, in 1964. Peter is the one facing the camera, with his legs dangling over the side!

*Above: Running round Wembley with the Cup . . .
Peter joins Jack Burkett, John Bond (his face hidden by the Cup) and Bobby Moore on a lap of honour after defeating Preston in 1964.*

Left: Practicing his ball skills at Chadwell Heath.

whole team was superb. Those who weren't usually great runners ran all day, those who couldn't pass very well were passing superbly, and it was just a fantastic performance, topped off by Mooro, who was simply immaculate. Despite the weather, I don't think he had a spot of mud on his boots, let alone his shorts!

"The final wasn't a classic match, Preston were the underdogs and played really well – at one point they were outplaying us. We kept battling away, though, and got our reward in the end.

"I can remember the winning goal well. Hursty popped the ball out to me and I just whipped it into the box. Boycey – someone who didn't get many goals usually – popped up in the right place with a superb header and that was it. I couldn't run to celebrate with him, though – my legs were completely gone!

"My calves were in knots and my socks were round my ankles – that was what the Wembley pitch did to you then. We were used to playing on mud-baths every week, but Wembley was so firm and the grass so lush, it just soaked the energy out of your legs.

"It was a great day, though, and brings back such wonderful memories. The celebrations afterwards, bringing the cup back on the bus the next day – I'll never forget it and I'm sure the supporters who were there won't either."

Of course, Hammers were back at Wembley just 12 months later to enjoy what many consider to be the greatest occasion in the club's long history, glory in the European Cup Winners' Cup final against TSV Munich. Sadly, Peter was one of three members of the FA Cup-winning side to miss out against the Germans through injury – his place taken by two-goal hero Alan Sealey.

"I missed out because of a calf injury that I had picked up in one of the earlier rounds," he recalls. "I remember running down the wing and it felt like I'd been shot in the back of the leg. It turned out I'd torn a muscle deep in the middle of my calf and Bill Jenkins, the physio, said it was quite an unusual injury and would take some time to recover from.

"Alan came in and took my place and, in the final, he was in the right place at the right time to become the hero. People have asked me in the past if I'd thought it might have been me but you can never think about what might have been. I was the first to congratulate Alan after the game and I was delighted for the team, because I was a part of it.

"It was a fantastic achievement for the club and most of us were supporters anyway, so it was extra special. They were magical times for West Ham and I was proud to be a part of it. People talk about the 1985-86 team but, in my opinion, the best-ever West Ham team was the '64 and '65 side. It was packed with international players – three of them went on to win the World Cup with England."

Peter returned to full fitness the following season and played his part as Hammers reached the semi-finals in their defence of the Cup Winners' Cup and lost out to West Brom in the League Cup final. But that was the last taste of success in the 60s as Greenwood's original dream team began to dismantle and a new batch of young talent broke through.

With a teenage Harry Redknapp starting to make an impact on the right-wing towards the end of the decade, Brabrook's opportunities were decreasing and, in

Re-United . . . Peter with Eddie Bovington and John Bond at the 1964 Cup final reunion hosted by Preston in 2004 and (right) before the EX magazine-organised dinner in London the following year.

1968, he joined Orient, then managed by ex-Hammer Jimmy Bloomfield.

A third division championship medal followed in 1970 at Brisbane Road, before Peter rounded off his career with a spell at Southern League side Romford, who regularly attracted big crowds during the early 70s.

After hanging up his boots for good, Peter built a successful business as a butcher – owning two shops in East Ham and Forest Gate – before the growth of large supermarkets forced him to sell up. However, he thankfully stayed in football as a coach on the non-league network, enjoying spells with the likes of Ford United, Tilbury, Billericay and Basildon – from where he recommended striker Steve Jones to Hammers' boss Billy Bonds in the early 90s.

When Harry Redknapp offered him the opportunity to return to Upton Park as a youth coach in 1995, Peter jumped at the chance and went on to spend six years in the role – overseeing the development of players such as Rio Ferdinand, Joe Cole, Michael Carrick and Jermain Defoe.

Now 70, Peter still works for the club in a part-time role as a scout and he enjoys spending his spare time with his family. Living in Laindon, Essex, with wife Doreen, they have two children, son Wayne – who has two young daughters, Daisy and Rosie – and daughter Donna, whose son PJ is a budding footballer himself who seems to have inherited grandad's skills.

Chapter 7

BOBBY FERGUSON

"I had a hard time from some of the press but Ron always left his door open to me if I wanted to talk things over with him. He was supportive. He was a brilliant talker, who could talk for five hours and never repeat himself"

WHEN most Hammers supporters think back to Bobby Ferguson's time as the West Ham goalkeeper, they tend to remember him most for his bravery and a couple of nasty moments that could have resulted in serious injury.

The most high profile incident saw him concussed after being kicked in the head during the 1972 League Cup semi-final marathon against Stoke City – a moment that passed into Irons folklore by virtue of the fact that his stand-in, Bobby Moore, saved a penalty while 'Fergie' was back in the dressing room receiving treatment.

Little more than a year later and Bobby was in the wars again, having to be replaced by another outfield player, Clyde Best, after damaging his neck in a fall during the home league game against Leeds United.

He once again left the field suffering concussion, although immediate fears that he had broken either his back or neck thankfully proved unfounded.

Bobby and his Australian wife Greer have lived in Adelaide, South Australia with their two children for the past 27 years. The last time he visited England was for a week in October 2004. He flew from the other side of the world to visit his seriously ill mother, who sadly passed away just hours before Bobby's flight touched down.

Bobby didn't manage to fit in a return visit to Upton Park, although he did contact former team-mates, Billy Bonds, Sir Trevor Brooking, Pat Holland and Jimmy Greaves by phone.

Fergie is still easy to recognise. His jet black hair has now turned grey, but he looks in good shape and confirms that he still weighs the same – 13 stones, 9lbs – as he did when he wore the number one jersey at Upton Park.

His battered, disfigured fingers, clasped around a cup of cappuccino as he chatted to *EX* in a Shenfield, Essex coffee bar, are testimony to the loyal service he gave and the knocks he took during 14 years with the club, in an era before padded gloves were invented.

Indeed, re-wind videos from the late 60s and 70s, and the chances are you will find plenty of footage of Bobby playing without any gloves at all.

Self-effacing with a dry wit, he knows that he wouldn't figure near the top of too many all-time greats lists at Upton Park. To be fair, though, he had a difficult act to follow in Jim Standen, a double cup-winner in the mid-60s, and the fact that he spent 14 years with the Hammers – he was still cover for Phil Parkes at the 1980 FA Cup final – says a lot about his strength of character and determination to keep bouncing back.

And let's not forget either that manager Ron Greenwood rated spring-heeled Fergie so highly that he paid Scottish club Kilmarnock £65,000 – a then British record fee for a keeper – in May 1967.

Bobby was so valuable to 'Killie' that Greenwood had to wait until they were eliminated from the European Inter-Cities Fairs Cup (forerunner to the UEFA Cup) after their semi-final defeat by Leeds United before he could land the man he chose to succeed Standen. The transfer was preceded by a specially arranged friendly between West Ham and Kilmarnock, held under lights at the Boleyn Ground in the February before Fergie moved south of the border.

Born in the small Ayrshire town of Ardrossan, some 400 miles north of East London, Bobby Ferguson played centre-half for the local Boys' Brigade team before their regular keeper suffered an injury and Fergie went between the sticks. He was the biggest lad in the team and was spotted by a Kilmarnock scout at the age of 14. He continued to progress for Kilmarnock Amateurs, a feeder club to Willie Waddell's Kilmarnock, who were main challengers to Glasgow Rangers in the pre-Jock Stein Celtic era.

He won a Scottish first division championship medal as a teenager in 1964-65, keeping a clean sheet in the decisive 2-0 victory at main title rivals Hearts on the final day of the season. It remains Killie's first, and only, senior league success in their history.

In November 1965, at the age of 20, Bobby's brilliant form for Kilmarnock earned him the first of seven senior Scottish international caps – as successor to Tottenham's Bill Brown. Bobby recalls facing England, skippered by Bobby Moore, in front of 134,000 at Hampden Park in April 1966, just weeks before Alf Ramsey and his team re-wrote football history. The Scots scored three times that day thanks to Denis Law and Jimmy Johnstone (twice) but a brace by Roger Hunt, and one each by Bobby Charlton and future club-mate Geoff Hurst, spoiled Fergie's biggest day on the international scene. A slick deliverer on witty one-liners, Bobby admits: "We lost 4-3 and I played like a prat, mate! Don't ask me why."

All seven of his full caps came within a calendar year and were gained before then Kilmarnock boss, Malcolm McDonald – a friend of Ron Greenwood's from their days together at Brentford – sold him to West Ham. By the time the Scots claimed their famous 3-2 victory over the world champions at Wembley in May 1967, Bobby had been replaced by Celtic's Ronnie Simpson.

He still, however, remains the fourth highest capped player in Kilmarnock's history and the second Scottish international keeper to join the Hammers following Lawrie Leslie in the early 60s. "I used to watch him play for Airdrie against Kilmarnock," recalls Bobby.

After making his West Ham bow in a pre-season friendly against HJK Helsinki in Finland, Bobby's league debut came at the Boleyn in a 3-2 home defeat by Sheffield Wednesday in August 1967, when fellow summer signings Billy Bonds and John Cushley also made their bow in a new-look back four.

Bobby on his Hammers' debut against Sheffield Wednesday, a 3-2 defeat on August 19, 1967, with fellow debutants John Cushley (5) and Billy Bonds also in the picture with Bobby Moore and Eddie Bovington.

But while Bonds quickly became a crowd favourite with typically surging runs from right-back, central defender 'Cush' – signed from Celtic to replace Ken Brown – and the new keeper found it much harder to settle in. Results told their own story as Hammers conceded 18 goals in the first six matches of 1967-68 in which the first 13 games produced just three wins.

Cushley was dropped and replaced by new signing, Alan Stephenson, from Crystal Palace some two-thirds of the way through the season but Greenwood kept faith with Fergie as West Ham recovered to finish 12th in the first division.

West Ham fans demanded to know why the West ham boss had chosen Ferguson instead of Gordon Banks, whose greatness had been there for all to see during England's glorious 1966 World Cup-winning campaign.

Greenwood revealed how he chose Ferguson instead of Banks in his autobiography, *Yours Sincerely*. He wrote: "Three members of the England team that beat the world in 1966 were West Ham men, and there was nearly a fourth. Bobby Moore, Martin Peters and Geoff Hurst could have been joined by Gordon Banks. Just think, the best goalkeeper in the world backing up the massive authority of Moore, the elegance and stealth of Peters and the goals of Hurst.

"I had the chance to sign Banks, he wanted to join us and I refused. Hindsight tells me that this was one of the biggest mistakes of my life – but the reason for my decision was at least honourable. To sign Banks I would have to break my word to an old friend and I could not do that.

"I enquired about Banks before the 1966 World Cup but Matt Gillies, his manager at Leicester, said he wasn't available. England's ultimate success changed things for a lot of people, though, and Banks decided soon afterwards that he wanted a move. He got his way and Matt, remembering my enquiry, rang me out of the blue to say, yes, Banks was now for sale. We could certainly have afforded him, and I was told that Banks was keen on joining us. The idea of linking up with Moore, Peters and

Above: Bobby made a specific request to Ron Greenwood to be able to practice at the empty Boleyn Ground.
Right: Harry Redknapp looks aghast as this shot creeps inside Fergie's near-post at Anfield.

Hurst must have been irresistible to him. It rather appealed to me as well!

"Alas, there was a mountain of an obstacle: my conscience. I had just made a huge and firm offer for Bobby Ferguson of Kilmarnock. The fee was £65,000, a record for a British goalkeeper, and I even agreed to hang on until the Scottish club was knocked out of the European Fairs Cup before completing the deal. I was prepared to wait to get my man. Kilmarnock's manager was Malcolm McDonald, a good pal from my playing days at Brentford, and we had shaken hands on the sale.

"Then Gillies made his telephone call. I had the chance to sign the best goalkeeper in the game, a man with every physical and mental quality a keeper needs. And he was a long-term buy as well; he had years left in him. But I had given my word to Kilmarnock. I told West Ham's directors about my dilemma, admitting that I would prefer Banks, but I insisted that we went through with the Ferguson deal.

"The story that Banks was for sale and that we were interested came out in the papers, and Malcolm McDonald phoned me to ask if I still intended to stick to our agreement. 'I've given my word: the deal is still on', I told him.

"Roland Brandon, one of our directors, told me it was one of the biggest mistakes West Ham ever made. He said we should have pulled out of the deal with Kilmarnock and gone for the best man. I know he was right in one sense. Professional football is a hard little world. Promises are broken daily. Expediency rules. Nice guys are supposed to finish last. But I did what I thought was right, and honesty should matter. Only if that is wrong was I wrong."

With typical honesty, Bobby told *EX*: "Banksy was a better goalkeeper than me and Ron had the chance to sign him, although I didn't know that until I read it in his autobiography. I don't know how much he really rated me compared to Gordon Banks but all I do know is that Ron had great integrity."

Goalkeepers made of less resilience would have crumbled under the London spotlight but Bobby was made of much sterner stuff. He says: "I never considered throwing in the towel and going back to Scotland. It was my job to see it through.

Take it, move on.

"I think the fans were fair to me – they pay their money, so they are entitled to say what they think."

But Bobby agrees that he suffered a bit at the hands of the press. "A few of them took liberties – absolutely. You accept their criticism of you as a player but I couldn't accept being misquoted and I had an issue with one guy who ran a piece with big headlines. I had him up against a wall asking for an explanation. I told John Lyall, after he'd taken over from Ron, that the guy had 'screwed me' and John said he believed me."

Bobby also appreciates the backing he received from Greenwood that helped him through the most difficult times.

"I had a hard time from some of the press but Ron always left his door open to me if I wanted to talk things over with him. He was supportive. He was a brilliant talker, who could talk for five hours and never repeat himself.

"In Scotland, the managers I played under all wanted me to call them 'boss'. With him, he just said: 'Call me Ron'.

"I went through a spell where I asked Ron if I could go back for more training in the afternoons, three days a week. But instead of doing the extra work at Chadwell Heath, I wanted to do it at the main ground, at Upton Park, so he arranged for a few apprentices to be there to help me by hitting shots and crosses in for me. The groundsman wasn't happy about us being on his beloved pitch but Ron told me to just go ahead and do it.

"He was an excellent coach, the technical knowledge he had was absolutely fabulous, although I probably only fully appreciated it as I got a bit older.

"Ron was more than helpful to me, he was 100 per cent."

Bobby also praised the help of Hammers' original specialist goalkeeping coach, Ernie Gregory. "We worked a lot on angles when I first came to the club. Ernie had a great saying: 'If you can bank five years' experience for five years' wages, take it'. That holds very true for a goalkeeper."

A dozen clean sheets – his highest-ever tally of shut-outs in an English league season – helped Hammers climb to eighth position at the end of 1968-69 but, in fairness to Ferguson, West Ham had never paid much attention to the art of defending. Neither Stephenson nor Tommy Taylor, the next centre-half to be tried alongside Bobby Moore in the early 70s, were top class.

But rather than criticise or question the quality of former team-mates, Bobby accepts that he joined a club where the emphasis was always on attack as opposed to defence.

"It was Ron's philosophy – just like the great Hungarians – that if we let in two goals, we'd score three. I didn't appreciate it much, though! It left us a bit short at the back at times but that's not a criticism of Ron as a manager, just an observation. It's the way we played at West Ham and it was good to watch."

Mind you, he did have England's greatest-ever defender conducting the orchestra in front of him!

Bobby acknowledges the presence and influence of the great man: "Mooro always did exactly what you asked him to do in terms of positioning himself, without question. He was a very good communicator, always available. And he could play a bit as well, which helps!"

Although Fergie was Greenwood's first choice in his first three seasons at Upton Park, he lost his place to Peter Grotier for four months at the start of 1970-71. But it had little effect on results as 'Grote' – himself not helped by the team's traditionally leaky defence – managed just one clean sheet in his 19 appearances and Hammers slumped even further, finishing just one place above the relegation zone.

Bobby says he gone on fine with all the challengers for the goalkeeper's shirt. He says of Grotier: "Peter 'Grote' was a top man – daft as a brush – but he was just a bit short of top level to be a great keeper, which I think he realised himself."

Fergie reclaimed the green jersey from the start of 1971-72 and only injuries denied him an ever-present record in a season memorable for a thrilling run to the League Cup semi-finals against Stoke City. After goals by Hurst (penalty) and a cracking half-volley by Clyde Best gave Hammers a 2-1 win in the first leg at the misty Victoria Ground, West Ham wasted the chance to reach the final when Gordon Banks saved Hurst's late, thunderbolt of a penalty in the return at Upton Park, where John Ritchie's goal was enough to force a replay.

And after a goalless draw at Hillsborough still failed to divide these two enterprising teams, a second replay was required at Old Trafford, where there were incidents and talking points galore. Not that Fergie remembers anything about the 3-2 defeat in the Manchester quagmire – apart from the bottle of brandy he helped down afterwards to drown his sorrows.

Ferguson and Moore were the central figures in an epic encounter that took the first of many twists in the 14th minute. The West Ham keeper was kicked in the head when he courageously dived at the feet of Terry Conroy and had to leave the field with concussion. During the next 20 minutes he spent trying to recover his senses in the dressing room, stand-in keeper Moore had to face a penalty. Remarkably, the England captain saved Mike Bernard's spot kick but could only parry the ball down in front of the Stoke player, who tucked away the rebound.

"I've got no recollection of that incident or the game itself. I went off the field and came back on again but I don't remember a thing about the game. I didn't 'wake up' until ten-past nine and, by then, there were only 10 minutes or so to play.

"I remember sitting in the hotel waiting to go to the game – I even remember what I was wearing – but nothing else stayed with me. I don't even recall the game starting.

"I think Bestie (Clyde Best) was meant to go in goal when I got injured, but he was too scared, so Bobby took over instead!"

Although midfielders Bonds and Brooking – two of Bobby's best friends at the club, along with Bryan 'Pop' Robson – gave Hammers a 2-1 lead, Stoke responded with further goals from Peter Dobing and Conroy that remain no more than a blur to Ferguson. *(For the full story of the epic League Cup semi-final, turn to p111)*

Fergie never played at Wembley and can now only wonder what might have been had Banks not pulled off that memorable save to deny Hurst's penalty in the second leg at Upton Park. He observes: "Hursty hit them in the same spot every time – he

Above: It's April 14, 1973 and Leeds United skipper Billy Bremner and West Ham players Kevin Lock, Clyde Best, John McDowell and Trevor Brooking join a concerned Ron Greenwood, his assistant John Lyall on the field as physio Rob Jenkins tends to the concussed Bobby Ferguson.
Right: Clyde Best deputised for the injured Scot and, despite close support from fellow defenders Kevin Lock, Bobby Moore and Frank Lampard, the big Bermudan manages to punch clear from underneath the crossbar at the South Bank end.
The game ended 1-1.

always blasted the ball high and to the keeper's right – so I think Pop should have taken it. It's easy to say that now, though, and it was a great save by Banksy, who took a chance and guessed right.'

Still the regular keeper in 1972-73, the season almost ended disaster for the former Scottish international after he was once again badly injured, this time in the home league match against Leeds United in April 1973.

Bobby recalls the incident that led to striker Clyde Best taking over the gloves and which has left a lasting legacy to this day: "It's not a problem but every 20 minutes, I have to 'click' my neck back into place," reveals Bobby. "I've had to do that ever since falling over the top of John McDowell in the Leeds game. It was all my fault, though – I should have called for the ball, but didn't, and I came down hard. I always used to tell my defenders, 'If I don't call for the ball, then you take it', but on that occasion I didn't call, so John was right to go for it. I just went over the top of him and landed on my neck.

"Now I've got the arthritic neck of a 75-year-old!"

Although Bobby began 1973-74 as No.1, Greenwood soon introduced what

Fergie with Bobby Gould and Trevor Brooking about to board the plane to the old USSR to play Ararat Erevan during Hammers' 1975-76 European Cup Winners' Cup campaign.

appeared to be his long-term successor in the precocious Mervyn Day. In fact, as Fergie stayed sharp with a five-game spell on loan to Sheffield Wednesday, the West Ham boss went out on a limb and declared that Day would keep goal for the Hammers "for the next 10 years".

His faith was to prove ultimately misplaced. After a very promising start and almost five years as the regular, Day lost his way and his early potential was unfulfilled.

Bobby can't pinpoint why Day didn't go on to fulfil his manager's bold prophesy, but says: "Bringing in Mervyn was natural progression and I didn't have a problem with Ron giving him his chance. He had two brilliant seasons but then fell away. He conceded a couple of bad goals against Derby in the Charity Shield at Wembley in 1975 and slipped from the brilliant, high standards he had set himself. But I don't know why."

However, Ferguson's patience was rewarded when he was recalled by Greenwood's successor, John Lyall, to make 19 appearances in 1977-78. Then, after just 11 outings the following campaign, he finally lost his place to the legendary Phil Parkes in February 1979 when Lyall set a new world record fee for a keeper.

Apart from a three-match respite as cover for the injured Parkes in November 1979, there was no way back for Fergie at Upton Park after 276 first team appearances.

Not that Bobby was ever desperate to leave the Hammers. He explains: "I spoke to a few clubs, as well as an agent who thought he could get me a team in Holland, but no one else could afford to pay me what I was earning at West Ham, where I still had two years left on my contract and also a testimonial to come.

"They were a good bunch of guys at Sheffield Wednesday, and I would have been

Bobby pictured on his last visit to England, when EX interviewed him in October 2004.

interested in moving there, but they couldn't afford my wages either.

"I read 'Big' Jack Charlton's autobiography where he said that he never earned more than £170 per week as a player in the great Leeds side of that era. We played at the same time as him, and were earning more than that, so I have no complaints, financially, about West Ham.

"I wasn't a problem to either Ron or John when I was not their first choice. I trained hard and I didn't go screaming and shouting to them. If I wasn't in the side, I remained professional about it."

Rather than sulk in the reserves, Bobby even became an unexpected asset. He explains: "I won a cup for the reserves one year while we were on tour in Zaragoza. We had so many injuries and I was the only sub left. Then Billy Jennings also got injured and so I said to Greenwood: 'Put me on, I can be a nuisance up front'. I was only joking but I went on and scored the winner . . . before doing about 15 laps of honour! I think I scored seven goals in all for the reserves."

Bobby also showed his talent on the golf course, where his regular companions were team-mates Pop Robson and Trevor Brooking.

"As well as those two, I also used to play a bit of golf with Greavesie, who lived just round the corner from us in Upminster. In fact, Jimmy is godfather to our son, Glenn. Greavesie and me sank a few lagers in our time together at West Ham but I'm very pleased to see him looking so healthy now he's off the drink completely.

"Greavesie probably finished playing at least a year too early at West Ham, but Ron played him wide on the left and expected him to track back, which wasn't his game. Maybe if he'd been allowed to play up front and just sniff around the penalty box for a few more goals, he would have played on for another year.

"I remember playing West Brom at home when we were in danger of being relegated, and Greavesie deliberately nutmegged their keeper to score. It was very deliberate and not many people can do that.

"Pop was also top quality. I used to share a hotel room with him on the away trips. I'd wake up at seven o'clock in the morning to find him standing on his head! He said it was good to let the blood get to his brain!"

After a well-earned testimonial match against Southampton at Upton Park in April 1981, Bobby and his family emigrated to Australia. He played for and coached Adelaide City FC for a couple of years before going into business – initially at a marina complex and then earning his living selling carpet and floor tiles. He then worked in property development with a friend.

When he is not busy working or taking an interest in his children, Kelly and Glenn, Bobby has kept in good shape as fitness trainer for a local rugby team. He also continues to enjoys his golf on the superb courses near his Leabrook home.

"I got my handicap down to four when I first went to Australia but it's up to nine now. Still, it's nice to be able to get around reasonably well in the sunshine – at least the weather doesn't bugger up my fingers any more!" he adds.

Even on the other side of the world, enjoying beautiful weather conditions unlike anything he could have experienced on a bleak winter afternoon at the Boleyn, Bobby Ferguson still cherishes the memories of his 14 years with West Ham United. "It was brilliant and so was the football we played. I loved the East End."

Chapter 8

ALAN STEPHENSON

"Billy's enthusiasm was just fantastic and he was such a superb all round player. I admired him totally, he had everything, and I can't believe that he didn't play for England"

WHEN Alan Stephenson looks back on his four years with West Ham, he reaches the conclusion that he was signed for a club record fee for one specific reason – to keep Hammers in the top flight.

Manager Ron Greenwood had given up on Scottish centre-half John Cushley when he renewed his interest in Londoner Stephenson and paid the £80,000 it took to bring him from Crystal Palace, where he had scored 13 goals in 170 senior appearances.

Before his arrival just before the transfer deadline in March 1968, West Ham's leaky defence had conceded 22 goals in its previous 10 league matches . . . and the team was fourth from bottom of the first division, just two places above the relegation zone.

But, despite stepping up a division in class, the then 23-year-old, six-foot Stephenson proved the saviour, slotting in comfortably alongside skipper Bobby Moore in the heart of defence. West Ham kept a clean sheet on his debut in a goalless draw at Southampton on March 18 – the first time in 12 games that the defence hadn't been breached – and conceded only 12 goals in its last 13 matches. A final league position of 12th, a leap of seven places in less than two months, confirms that 'Stevo' did exactly what was asked of him by Greenwood.

"I had a good debut and the clean sheet was just what I needed," he says.

Stephenson, now 64 and living comfortably at Wivenhoe, Essex, was aware that West Ham had shown interest in him almost a year before they completed the deal. Apparently, Manchester United and Wolves had also watched the tall, gangly stopper with interest, although he didn't need long to think about accepting Greenwood's offer to play alongside the England captain.

Alan told *EX*: "It had been rumoured a year earlier that West Ham were showing interest in me but nothing materialised until Palace had just been knocked out of the FA Cup at Walsall. Bert Head told me that he'd had a call from Ron Greenwood and that they were happy for me to talk to him. I'd been at Palace for about seven years then and I felt it was the right time to move and take the opportunity to play in the top flight with a fantastic club and their World Cup trio.

Not that joining the Hammers brought about a significant change of lifestyle. Alan went from earning £60-per-week in the second division at Selhurst Park to a basic of £80 per week at Upton Park. Add on first team appearance money and he was netting around £100 a week after collecting five percent – £4,000 – of his transfer fee – "which was a lot of money then, spread over the contract at £1,000 a year," he admits.

"Even though I had recently signed a new three-year contract at Palace, I think they had it mind to sell me sooner or later. They had brought in a couple of Scottish signings and with the money they got from selling me, they signed five or six more players.They did well by me!

"The strange thing was, I got married in June of '68 and we were in the process of moving into a newly-built house at Addington, Surrey when my move to West Ham came about. It meant that after having made the daily journey from where we used to live in Walthamstow through the Blackwall Tunnel to Crystal Palace's training ground every day, I was then doing the same journey in reverse! After a while, we sold the house at Addington and bought a place in Woodford Green, which was much nearer West Ham's Chadwell Heath training ground and not far from my roots.

Although born in Chesham, where his mother went to give birth just before the end of the war, the Stephenson family – who originate from the Islington area – returned to Barclay Road, Walthamstow, where he grew up in north-east London. Alan acknowledges the encouraging role Mr James and the head, Mr Maxwell, played in his development as a strong, all round sportsman and the excellent facilities at the secondary modern Warwick school. "They developed me, big-time," he says. "We played at Salisbury Hall, down by the Crooked Billet. I was always tall and there wasn't an ounce of fat on me."

With an amazing twist of irony, Alan revealed that his elder brother, Norman, played for Walthamstow Avenue, a successful non-league team of that era, who were then managed by . . . Ron Greenwood.

Alan and his father, Bill, used to stand on the terraces behind the goal at Leyton Orient in the late 50s, when he admired the centre-half efforts of O's legend Sid Bishop. But after 15-year-old Alan failed to catch the eye in a 45-minute trial for his local league club, it was Palace manager Arthur Rowe – the architect of Tottenham's glorious push-and-run side of the early 50s – who spotted him playing impressively for London Schoolboys against Glasgow at Stamford Bridge.

"That's when my career took off and I joined Palace's youth team at the age of 16. A couple of times I played a South-East Counties League game in the morning, went down the local café with the other lads for sausage, egg and chips and then, if the reserves were short, I was asked to play for them in the afternoon!

"Ron Greenwood didn't really have to sell West Ham to me. I only had to look around the place to see the quality. They had a reputation for playing good football but they were leaking goals at that particular time. I was confident that I could go there and do a decent job."

Alan knew a number of players who had represented both West ham and Palace who reassured him he was making a good career move, including Johnny Byrne, Trevor Dawkins, Dave Bickles and Eddie Presland.

"I was fortunate enough to play with Johnny in my last season at Palace. Budgie was Budgie – yes, he'd put on a bit of weight but he still had a tremendous touch, he was the life and soul of the team and a great ambassador for the club.

"Soon after I joined Palace as an apprentice, and before Johnny left Selhurst Park to join West Ham in 1962, he wrote a regular column in the Croydon Advertiser in which he gave me some rave notices, which was nice of him.

"I also knew Geoff Hurst from playing cricket together for Essex seconds."

When Alan arrived at Upton Park, he found himself among three World Cup-winning heroes, an emerging Trevor Brooking and two players who had signed the previous year, Billy Bonds and Bobby Ferguson.

"Bobby was my room-mate on away trips," says Alan. "Apart from having to get used to his Scottish accent, he was a good pro and, although he took some stick from the crowd, he just got on with it. He worked hard at his game and, as centre-back and goalkeeper, we struck up a good relationship. People said Bobby was a bit short for a keeper but I never had any problems with him. He'd come for crosses and he was brave."

Alan signing for West Ham for a club record £80,000 in March 1968, watched by Ron Greenwood.

Alan admits that it's only when he looks back on his career that he fully appreciates the privilege he had in playing alongside Moore.

"At the time, I didn't really think about the fact that it was Bobby who was always playing next to me, or that there were two other World Cup winners in the team. That was obviously a fantastic experience and thrill for me but it's only after I'd retired that I realised how lucky I was. I obviously wasn't on the same level as them but I was a professional footballer, West Ham had paid a record fee for me and I was paid to do a job."

Alan is the latest former team-mate of Mooro's to confirm the obvious – that Bobby always led by example and wasn't a skipper who gave specific advice to colleagues or issued them with verbal rockets.

"Bobby would gee you up a bit if he thought you needed it, or if you weren't in the position where you were supposed to be, but he never talked to me on a one-to-one basis or gave me advice about improving my game. He never said a lot, to be honest."

Apart from Moore, Alan describes Billy Bonds as "the best player I ever played

Leading the way in training, Alan (right) is followed by Frank Lampard and Billy Bonds. Geoff Hurst and Bryan Robson are at the front of the row of joggers on the left.

with." He went on to say: "Billy's enthusiasm was just fantastic and he was such a superb all round player. I admired him totally, he had everything, and I can't believe that he didn't play for England. But Bill was never one to force himself into the spotlight.

"We had great characters too, like 'Stag' and 'Charlo'," he added with a smile.

Alan was interested to read, in Moore's 1976 authorised biography by Jeff Powell, that Bobby believed Ron Greenwood's footballing principles had "ruined" both Stephenson and his predecessor, John Cushley. Moore claimed that Scottish centre-back Cushley "never made another tackle for West Ham" after Greenwood had expressed his dismay at what he considered to be some over-zealous challenges by 'Cush'. Bobby also suggested in print that the manager's purist beliefs had the same adverse effect on Stephenson and the way he played.

But Alan admits: "I was surprised to read that in Bobby's book, because Ron certainly never said anything to me about not wanting me to be aggressive or to adapt my style for West Ham in any way. I played the way I always had done. Maybe Ron might have said something about it to Bobby but I never heard him say anything about me in that respect

"To be honest, when he first signed me, he didn't go into detail about what he expected from me. But having watched me a number of times for Palace, he knew what he was buying and, at 23 or 24-years-of-age, it would have been silly to have tried to change my game.

"Ron never criticised me at all, although, having said that, he hardly said anything to me. Ron went about his business quietly."

Alan was under no illusions, though, about his role in the team. First and foremost, he was brought in to tighten up and add steel to a porous defence that let in too many goals. He knew he was not the next Franz Beckenbaur.

"I'd always been an aggressive defender – there were no thrills to my game – and what you saw was what you got. I was a natural ball-winner and a good marker, having been brought up in a very disciplined Crystal Palace side. We'd play people out of the game by tight marking and aggressive defending, although the way the game is played today, it's questionable whether I'd stay on the pitch! You used to go through the ball and the player in those days," he smiles.

"I always preferred being up against the bigger centre-forwards – I had some great battles with the Southampton and Wales forward, Ron Davies, and always managed to handle him OK. Tony Hateley and John Radford were others I relished playing against us, whereas the smaller forwards were more difficult for me to handle.

"I suppose I could have passed the ball better, especially on my weaker left foot, although I didn't think I was that bad a passer anyway. Ron did get me back in for extra training on some afternoons, though, to work on improving my left foot. He spent a few sessions working with me, getting me to clear the ball with my left foot, but other than that we didn't work much, collectively, on our defensive game.

"Most emphasis was on getting the ball wide – to our wingers, John Sissons and Harry Redknapp – and for them to then get crosses into the box for people like Geoff and Martin to score goals. It was very effective."

In his first full season at the Boleyn – 1968-69 – Alan enjoyed being an ever-present as Hammers rose to eighth place in the first division – their highest for seven years. His defensive qualities perhaps went unnoticed by many fans who revelled in the enterprising, attacking football that became the norm and brought thrilling home victories against Burnley (5-0), West Bromwich Albion (4-0), Sunderland (8-0 – Hurst scored six), QPR (4-3), Leicester City (4-0), Coventry City (5-2) and Bolton Wanderers (7-2, in the League Cup). Naturally, there was the obligatory, embarrassing defeat to a lower league side (3-0 at Mansfield Town) in the FA Cup but only a poor end-of-season run that yielded no wins from the last nine league games cost Greenwood and his men a top six place and possibly the club's highest-ever finish to date.

That season saw Hammers hold champions Leeds United and runners-up Liverpool to draws in E13, while Hammers were also unbeaten at Manchester United, Chelsea and Arsenal. "After we drew 1-1 at Old Trafford, I was pleased to get back to London that night and see that the Evening Standard classified edition made me man-of-the-match playing against Denis Law,"recalls Alan.

In the return clash, Reds' Irish full-back Tony Dunne could confirm the added physical presence that Stephenson brought to the West Ham back four after suffering a broken jaw in an accidental collision with Hammers' No.5.

As someone who was very fortunate enough to start attending home games as an eight-year-old that season, many of the performances were captivating and provided the very reason why we've continued supporting the club ever since. What many, like me, have struggled to comprehend, though, is why a team brimming with gifted individuals not only failed to build on the promise of that 1968-69 season, but spent the next few years flirting dangerously with relegation and achieving nothing in the cups either.

After slumping to 15th place in 1969-70, when a frustrated Martin Peters left in search of trophies at Tottenham after Stephenson had scored his only goal for the club in an FA Cup defeat at Middlesbrough, Greenwood's team plunged as low as 20th – one place off the drop zone – the following season.

Alan Stephenson provides an interesting perspective from someone who shared the fans' frustrations and he offers a very plausible explanation for the problem. Discipline, or rather a lack of it, was at the root of this woeful period of under-achievement and decline.

Stephenson agrees with Bobby Moore's view that Greenwood, brilliant and inventive coach though he undoubtedly was, might have coaxed a better response – and therefore results – from his players if he had got tough with them whenever playing standards or attitudes fell unacceptably short. After the team had been hammered on the field, Moore said he wanted the manager to show his disgust in the dressing room there and then, rather than delay his response until expressing a more considered analysis on the following Monday morning.

"I thought there was something lacking, discipline wise, in the club," says Stephenson.

"Players were taking training too light-heartedly, whereas the emphasis I'd been used to at Palace had been a disciplined approach and hard work. Manager Dick Graham had been a strict disciplinarian and while Bert Head was a bit laid-back, coach George Petchey was another firm man. George had played for West Ham and I think he would have done a good job there as coach or manager too.

"I don't think the West Ham players hurt enough after a defeat – there was never any shouting in the dressing room," admits Stephenson, who subscribes to Harry Redknapp's view that a 'win-or-lose, on the booze' culture did exist.

"I was a little bit surprised to find when I came to West Ham that there were a lot of players who were disillusioned with the club, which may have influenced the behaviour of certain people.

"We weren't going to challenge for the league title because the discipline wasn't there among the players. The general attitude wasn't right, there were a few cliques and the club wasn't bonded. Given the amount of talent around, we under-achieved. You looked around at the Liverpools and Manchester Uniteds and they had more steel about them. If anything, West Ham was too friendly as a club.

"I didn't think the players were reminded often enough how important it was to win – or, to put it another way, not lose. Defeats were just accepted . . . a case of go home, have a few beers, turn up for training on Monday and just go on like that from one game to the next.

"Not that I was a drinker. I had a young family at the time and although I'd go to social events if asked, I tended to focus on family life and would usually only see the players who lived nearby, in Woodford Green, on a social basis. Peter Eustace and Pop Robson, who later bought Peter's house, were the two I saw most away from football.

"I took defeat badly and knew it was important to win. I'd been brought up at Palace surrounded by good, disciplined pro's, where the team was promoted in my first season and there was a winning mentality around the club."

In August 1971, Greenwood appointed John Lyall as his assistant but injury was about to put Stephenson out of the first team reckoning. With the benefit of hindsight, Alan now wonders if the appointment of Lyall could have been made earlier in the interests of the team and Ron himself.

Like most ex-players who were coached by the man who brought European glory

West Ham United 1970-71: Back row, left to right: John McDowell, Paul Heffer, Bobby Ferguson, Peter Grotier, Trevor Brooking, Frank Lampard. Middle row: Billy Bonds, David Llewellyn, Tommy Taylor, Alan Stephenson, Bobby Moore, Peter Eustace. Front row: John Ayris, Harry Redknapp, Ron Boyce, Geoff Hurst, Bryan Robson, Bobby Howe.

and a fine reputation to West Ham, Stephenson acknowledges that Greenwood was a brilliant coach. But, on the other hand, Alan also shares the view of many fellow former Hammers when he says: "Ron didn't have a clue when it came to man-management or communicating with his players.

"I think he needed someone like John Lyall, who was coaching the youth team when I first went there, to work alongside him as his assistant, to provide a link between the manager and the players.

"Ron would have benefited as a manager from the way things are run today, where managers are supported very closely by a No.2, the person who can get close to the players and build bridges. Perhaps Ron needed more help at that stage than he realised.

"I think that was the reason for the demise of West Ham at that particular time. The talent was there, we had great technicians footballing wise, but it just needed to be co-ordinated better. We had three World Cup winners but those players needed help as well. At the end of the day, it's a team game

"I don't want to criticise Ron, God rest his soul, because he was a good man and he signed me. But, as so many others have said before me, he was lacking on the man-management side."

The turning point in Stephenson's Hammers career came in October 1970. A gradual knee problem forced Alan to undergo surgery to remove a damaged cartilage and in his place Greenwood splashed out £78,000 to bring Tommy Taylor from east London neighbours Leyton Orient. Alan doesn't believe that the signing of Taylor was as a result of his injury and he says that Greenwood would have lined

Training at Upton Park with John Sissons and Bobby Moore.

up the deal to bring in the player some weeks earlier.

It was another six months before Stephenson returned to the side, featuring in five of the last six games as the Irons just about clung on to their first division status.

"I'd had a bit of a knee problem a year or two before coming to West Ham. At Palace we used to work on our legs a lot, using weights, but West Ham didn't use any weights on the players' legs. As a result, I think my quad muscles got a bit weaker and I developed a problem with my cartilage. I had to go into hospital for an operation to have it removed and I went in at the same time Ronnie Boyce was there to have his knee operated on.

"When I got fit again, I just accepted the situation that I had to play well enough to get back in the side. I didn't feel that the injury affected me in any way, I didn't lose any pace or struggle because of it.

"I had no problem with Tommy either – he was fine. But I wasn't one to go knocking on the manager's door, asking or demanding to be in the team. I was just pleased to still be part of the club and didn't feel isolated until the following year, when me and Peter Eustace were bombed out, ignored and left to train with the reserves. I felt I could still have been a squad player, working with 15 or 16 first team players, and I was disappointed to be discarded like that."

Alan thought he had found the answer to the problem on the opposite side of London.

He explains: "I had 10 matches on loan to Fulham in Division Two and enjoyed my time there. The manager, Bill Dodgin jnr, wanted to buy me for the 40-odd thousand pounds Ron Greenwood wanted but Fulham wouldn't let him pay it. The fact that he was sacked shortly after my loan spell ended and I had returned to West Ham explained why, but I would love to have stayed at Fulham on a permanent basis."

At the start of 1971-72, Stephenson reclaimed the claret-and-blue No.5 shirt as

Greenwood tried to accommodate both him and Taylor, who switched to No.10 and started the first two matches in midfield. But the experiment lasted only two games – defeats against West Bromwich Albion (home) and Derby County (away) – before 'Stevo' was dropped and Taylor reverted to centre-half alongside Moore.

"Ron tried to find room for both Tommy and me but it didn't work. They clearly hadn't paid all that money for Tommy to play in midfield, so Ron put him back in defence for the third game – and that was really it for me at West Ham from then."

Apart from a sub appearance in a 1-0 defeat at Wolves in February, Alan's only other first team outing for the club before he left was in a meaningless final game, at home against Southampton on May 1, 1972.

"It's funny, my first and last senior games for West Ham were both against Southampton – and Ron Davies," Alan points out. "But Ron Greenwood explained to me beforehand that the only reason he put me in the side that night was to sell me – Portsmouth had shown interest and were about to make a bid."

Pompey manager, the ex-West Ham defender Ron Tindall, must have liked what he saw of Stephenson in the 1-0 victory over Saints, because he signed him for a fee of £33,000 in the summer of '72.

"I'd spent a year out of the side, Tommy Taylor was well established and playing well, so I decided I'd sooner play first team football somewhere else rather than stay and continue in the reserves at Upton Park.

"Ron Tindall was a good communicator and I enjoyed playing for him, but he didn't last long and moved 'upstairs' to become Director of Football after they brought in ex-Chelsea player John Mortimer as manager."

Alan spent two years and played 98 matches for Pompey before moving to South Africa and a fresh start with Durban United – where ex-Hammer Trevor Dawkins was captain – in 1975. "It was part-time football, so I also worked for Leyland South Africa in their parts department for trucks and buses, which wasn't what I wanted to do.

"We had a very good side, including Barry Bridges, and won the Embassy Cup, their equivalent to the FA Cup. But then, as I was running back towards my own goal, someone clipped my heel, I fell and I couldn't straighten or bend my knee. I had to have another operation on it and the specialist advised me never to play again. The bone had been flaking over a period of time and had become brittle. When the guy clipped my heel, a piece of bone had got locked in between the joint, so I had to have that cleaned out. It was the same knee I'd had trouble with at West Ham."

When he returned to England in 1977, Alan got back into football thanks to his old Palace coach George Petchey, who was managing Orient by then. Alan trained with the O's and was then grateful for the chance to become Youth Development officer. When Jimmy Bloomfield – another ex-Hammer – succeeded Petchey, Alan was promoted to reserve team coach but, after four years, he couldn't see a future at Brisbane Road and decided to quit football and go into business.

He bought the Queens Head freehouse pub at Wormingford, which is no longer there and which he had to sell after six years as part of his first divorce settlement.

His next job, which lasted 11 years, was for Essex County Council's education and welfare department, specifically working to reduce truancy in schools. This, in turn, led to his current job, working at Sir Charles Lucas Arts College in Colchester, where he takes satisfaction from helping vulnerable kids, some of whom come from disadvantaged backgrounds. "I've done it full-time for eight years now, working on kids' problems and their attendance, which can be very rewarding when you can turn around a lad who's been on a route to nowhere," says Alan. "I have to liaise with and visit parents, write letters and generally monitor the kids' school attendance, which also involves me working in association with other agencies like Social Services, the police and the local health authority."

Alan has two children from his first marriage – son, Craig and daughter Vicky, who both live at Loughton, as well as one grandson, Tom.

The school summer holiday has given Alan the chance to reflect more thoroughly on his four years and 108 matches for West Ham. "I suppose my time at West Ham was a bit like a school report for me – 'could have done better.' I was a bit disappointed that I was only there a short time, and at not having played in a successful side that won something. My only claim to fame is that I helped to keep them up in my first season.

"It's not sour grapes from me but I'm convinced that I was signed simply to keep the club in the top flight at the end of the 1967-68 season in which I joined them. I was brought in to do a job, to keep them up.

"But I enjoyed my time at West Ham, it was a wonderful experience I would have hated to have missed. I would thank Ron for not only giving me the chance to play in the top flight of English football but also in tour matches against the likes of Pele, in New York, and against Bayern Munich's Franz Beckenbaur and Gerd Müller, in Germany.

I played with and against some of the world's best players and I appreciate the chance I was given," Alan added.

Alan pictured when EX interviewed him at his Essex home in the summer of 2006.

Chapter 9

PAT HOLLAND

"I called the club a 'grammar school' because it was like receiving an education in football. It sounds a bit snotty to people in football, but it was a coaching club and people like Ron and John were fantastic to learn from"

HAD it not been for the imposing figure of legendary West Ham United scout Wally St Pier, 70s hero Pat Holland might have ended up wearing the white and navy of arch-rivals Tottenham Hotspur rather than the claret and blue of his local side.

As a schoolboy starlet growing up in East London, the curly haired youngster had none other than Spurs' Double-winning manager Bill Nicholson chasing his signature after an exciting display for his district side in the mid-60s.

However, when Upton Park's most famous talent spotter got wind of the possibility that the Lilywhites were about to pounce on his catchment area, he wasted no time in offering Holland the chance to remain firmly settled in the East End – and the nervous and bashful 15-year-old certainly wasn't going to turn down the opportunity.

Turning the clock back 40 years to reflect on where it all began for the future FA Cup final hero and Boleyn Ground favourite, Pat can't resist a smile when reflecting on the tussle for this signature.

"I was playing over at Poplar, on a pitch near where I lived, and had just been selected for the East London Boys' side at under-15 level," he recalls.

"I had played for the side at 13 but was bombed out at 14 and had just got back into it again and started showing more promise.

"An old boy called Arthur Lamb, who did a lot of scouting for West Ham, recommended me to Wally St Pier. I'd been wearing the number 10 shirt, so Arthur told Wally to look out for that number.

"I played in a game over at Enfield, and Bill Nicholson also happened to be watching. Amazing, really the manager of Tottenham Hotspur's Double-winning team watching a kids' district team match.

"Anyway, it so happened that me and Billy Gardner – a friend of mine who I went to school with – had put the wrong shirt on. He had my number 10 and I had the eight dog.

"The story goes that Wally told Arthur that he didn't go much on the number 10, but he liked the number eight. As did Bill Nicholson – and Wally used to tell my dad how he had to get in quick before Spurs made a move!

So much for modern training methods, use of computerised technology and a staple diet of pasta and salad . . . in the 70s they had the players running round a plastic rubbish bin up on the East Stand concourse!

Above: Pat leading the way from Alvin Martin, Billy Bonds, John McDowell and Bertie Lutton (can anyone recognise the back-marker?).

Right: McDowell watches Pat going through his paces on makeshift benches in the dressing room at Upton Park.

Pat turns away to celebrate his goal at Newcastle in January 1974, leaving Magpies' keeper Iam McFaul helpessly on his knees.

"When I first met Wally, though, he frightened the life out of me. He was a giant of a man, with great big hands and when he said: 'Would you like to come to West Ham, son? 'I was so scared I just said: 'Erm...Yeah'.

"So I went over to Upton Park and, on my first night, John Lyall was taking the training. I had a wonderful start because he was superb with youngsters, and it was no surprise to me that he went on to become a great manager.

"That was in 1965, when West Ham had just won the European Cup Winner's Cup...and were about to win the World Cup! It was a magnificent honour to be signed by the club because in those days, it was quite a shock for someone like West Ham to come to you.

"I went to a Grammar School and, to be honest, it was frowned upon really. There had been a lad called Ray Whittaker who went to Arsenal and was an England youth international, but didn't make it so they saw it as a waste of education.

"The headmaster was okay but I remember getting an awful rollicking off the deputy head, accusing me of wasting the school's time. I stayed on and did my 'O' levels but they still didn't look kindly on me attempting to become a footballer.

"It was ironic, though, because when I later played in the FA Cup final, they wrote to me asking if I would do a presentation for them!"

As a young teenager lacking somewhat in self-belief and confidence, Pat beat the odds to progress through the youth ranks and prove he had the attributes to forge a professional career at Upton Park. He admits that the education he received at the club played a huge part in ensuring he came out of his shell.

"It was my local club, I could get the number 15 bus straight to the ground in 20 minutes and I enjoyed every minute of it," he says.

"In 1967 I was offered a two-year apprenticeship – it was normally three years in those days – and, funnily enough, Billy Bonds had just signed from Charlton, we both started work at the club on the same day.

"It was a terrific time for West Ham. They had three players who had just played a vital part in the World Cup triumph, including the captain of course, and it was just great to be part of that atmosphere as a young lad.

"I was quite a nervous kid, never very confident, but being at West Ham was a great learning curve for me. I called the club a 'grammar school' because it was like receiving an education in football. It sounds a bit snotty to people in football, but it was a coaching club and people like Ron and John were fantastic to learn from.

"John was 10 years older than me, so he was 25 when he was coaching the youth team, and he was exceptional. He had a lovely way about him and I think he was instrumental in the way I coach now. I took a lot from him – his mannerisms and the way he spoke to people – and tended to pick up things without realising it.

"He had that talent of being able to make players think for themselves and the way he spoke made you respect him instantly. I read every issue of *EX* and no-one ever has a bad word to say about him – he was that kind of fella."

After serving his apprenticeship and progressing to the third team and reserve side. Pat made his first team debut against Arsenal – the side he had supported as a youngster – as a raw 18-year-old on Monday, April 21, 1969...just hours after signing professional forms. Understandably, his recollections of the day are as clear as water.

"I remember it as if it was yesterday. I'd played for the 'A' team against Cray Wanderers in the Metropolitan League on the Saturday and I had a bit of an indifferent game.

"On the Monday, I was told to go up to see Ron Greenwood and I was shaking like a leaf as I went in to talk to him. I was aware they were going to sign me as a pro but all sorts of things were going through my mind as I walked through the door.

"Anyway, he told me that the club would be offering me professional terms, which settled me down a bit, and then he said: 'Oh, by the way, would you like to play against the Arsenal?'

"I was so stunned that I just said 'yes' and sat there open-mouthed. So Ron said: 'We've got tickets for mum and dad, so get yourself home and I suggest you have a bit of a rest, I'll see you at 6pm'.

"I went home, of course mum and dad were delighted, and I just tried to calm my nerves for the game that night.

"It was a full house at Upton Park and I think I got two kicks all night – and one of those was from Bob McNab! The thing I remember most, though, is an incident before the game. Georgie Armstrong was playing outside-left and I'd seen him make his debut for Arsenal when I was a kid. He came over to me as we were about to kick-off, shook my hand and wished me all the best.

"It was a lovely gesture but, if I'm honest, the evening was a bit too much for me and I found it very difficult to handle the whole situation. It was a tremendous experience, though, and I've never forgotten it."

After that dream debut, it was back to reserve and A-team football for the young winger. A brief spell in Ron Greenwood's side followed the next season but, just months later, Pat encountered a knee injury – a phrase that would come back to haunt him throughout his career.

"My injury problems actually started at the age of 20, when I suffered a cartilage problem in my knee," he says. "I'd gone on loan to Bournemouth and when I came back I was included in the squad that went on tour to the USA in the summer of 1971.

"So I was creeping into the first team plans and mixing with all the senior boys like Mooro and Boycey. While were out in the States we played a game against the

Italian side Bologna and, as I ran up the steps to go out on to the pitch, my knee just locked. I literally couldn't move and they discovered it was the cartilage. In those days you never really knew what that meant, but I was out for nearly a year, which was a big blow for a young lad.

"I fought my way back, though, and finally had a really good run in 1972-73, playing at outside left, Ron changed the system, with three at the back and Bobby playing just in front of them, and it worked wonders.

"I think we ended up finishing sixth and I only missed 10 games all season. That was my best run in the team up to that point and things were going really well."

Sadly, his splendid run in the side didn't continue at the start of the 1973-74 campaign and Pat found himself on the verge of leaving the club after just one full season in the first team. However, if ever proof was needed that circumstances can change so quickly in football, Pat provided it.

"The following year, it went a bit sour again and I fell out of favour. The club had made up their mind that they wanted me to go and I was lined up to be part of the deal that brought Graham Paddon to West Ham from Norwich.

"I was supposed to go down to Carrow Road one day but I phoned Ron Saunders, the Norwich manager, and told him that I didn't want to go. He was fine and wished me all the best, not seeming at all that bothered. Two days later he became Manchester City manager!

"John Bond took them over at Norwich but I just didn't want to leave London. It was a bit of a sad thing really. I had a call from a guy called Len Whaley, who was

Pats gets his hands on the FA Cup after victory over Bobby Moore's Fulham in 1975.

a reporter on the local East London Advertiser, and just did a bit with him about being disappointed at not playing and that kind of thing.

"Then the story got in the national papers and I got a phone-call on the Monday saying that the manager wanted to see me the next day. Of course, Ron wasn't happy and wanted to use that to get me out. It was a shock, but I had just started courting and I thought: 'No, I'm gonna stay where I am.'

I was really out of favour but then came the FA Cup third round tie against Hereford in January 1974. The only reason I got on the bench that day was because there were so many injuries – the team was decimated. And if I remember rightly Mooro was carried off about 30 minutes in what turned out to be his final team match for West Ham.

"I came on, and I actually scored a header that was disallowed because Clyde Best was offside, but then I scored that late goal to equalise. I beat three or four players – although the number gets bigger every year! – before cutting it in. I suppose that changed everything for me, because I had done something to help the club out.

"In the summer of '74, John took over team affairs, with Ron moving upstairs and of course the following season turned out to be the FA Cup year.

"John knew me, he knew my strengths and weaknesses, and I was more of a squad player that year. That was in the days when you only had one sub and I was on the bench so many times that I had splinters in my arse!

"You had the midfield three of Paddon, Brooking and Bonds, and then it was Alan Taylor, Billy Jennings, Keith Robson, Bobby Gould and me competing for the places up front and out wide. I could play in a number of positions, so I suppose John saw me as the ideal player to bring on.

"Near the end of the season, Keith Robson got a knock and I came in for the last few games. The cup final was approaching and John made a big decision by leaving bobby Gould out in favour of me. Gouldy never lets me forget that. To this day, whenever he sees me he says: 'Where's my number 11 shirt!'

"Anyway, I can always remember, we played the Arsenal on the Monday night beforehand and, as I was walking past John's little office next to the dressing-rooms, he called me in. I thought: 'Here we go', but he said to me: 'I'm gonna play you on Saturday against Fulham. Now you get out there and do it for me tonight because I've put my neck on the line for you a bit'.

"So I went out against the Arsenal and had it right off. I think I kicked Peter Storey and Alan Ball up in the air and it was just one of those nights where everything went right for me. Later in the week, Bally said to the press that I would be one to watch in the Cup final, because I had played exceptionally well.

"Sadly, on the Saturday, it wasn't so exceptional. It was a lovely day, but I think I got caught up in it a little bit. I remember lining up to go out and I was standing next to Mooro, who was of course playing for Fulham. He turned to me and said: 'You all right Patsy, boy?' – that what was he always called me. I said: 'I'm so nervous Bob,' and he just smiled: 'Nah, you'll be all right, son,' and out we went.

"It was a fantastic experience, just to get that medal and be part of the winning side. I didn't have a great game but just to be playing in the FA Cup final – the game you dream about as a boy – was magnificent.

"I was also involved in both the goals and people make a big thing about that. When I say I didn't play all that well, they say: 'Yeah, but you made both the goals.' So if they want to say that, it's fine by me!"

Having gone from being a virtual Upton Park outcast to FA Cup final hero in the space of just over a year, a confident and happy Pat Holland kicked-off the 1975-76 campaign as Hammers came within touching distance of glory on the continent. Looking back, he admits the year signalled the peak of his playing days.

"I really felt a part of it in 1975-76 and I was on top of my game. I was high in confidence and everything was great. It was a shame that we didn't finish much higher in the league because, before Christmas, we were playing so well.

"Suddenly, it just dropped off. I think we only won one league game after Christmas, which was unbelievable really yet, when it came to the European nights under the floodlights, we were superb.

"For me, the tie that really sticks out is the semi-final against Eintracht Frankfurt. We lost the first leg 2-1 in Germany and the one thing I remember is being in the hotel room with Johnny Ayris, my room-mate for the trip. He was sitting on the bed thumbing through a telephone directory one evening, so I said to him: 'What are you reading that for?' Typical Johnny, he said: 'I', looking up Hitler!'

"We were both laughing about it, so I said to him that, if we scored, I was going to do the Ken Dodd impression of him. I'll always remember running to the touchline and doing it in front of the crowd when Graham Paddon scored, but on TV they only showed the goal going in!

"I think the second leg at Upton Park would have to be my all-time favourite game. The rain was absolutely lashing down and, as the two teams walked out together, even I felt the hairs on the back of my neck stand up.

"I'd never heard noise like it, it was better than Wembley, a fantastic atmosphere. The Frankfurt player next to me looked at me and pulled a face – you could see the fear in his eyes – and I just laughed!

"The team played well that night and Trevor Brooking was head and shoulders above everyone. It was one of those nights when he had no mud on his shoes and he was just in a different class to everyone else.

"We went to Heysel for the final and there was tremendous support out there, it was just a shame the way things turned out. I scored first but then we gave away that goal where Frank Lampard got his stomach injury and it couldn't have gone to a worse opponent, because Rensenbrink was absolutely top notch.

"I gave away the penalty for their third goal late on. I've looked at it since on the video and I think the key is that he gets up and tries to run on. I got a toe-end on it but the referee gave the spot-kick and that was it. It was a shame because we had gone so close and it would have been nice to repeat the feat of the team 11 years before."

Having reached such a memorable high, it was perhaps typical of Pat's career that a depressing low was just around the corner, and it arrived in the shape of another serious injury that signalled another lengthy spell on the sidelines.

"The following season it all went wrong," he says. "I broke my leg just six games

adidas

in, at Bristol City. It was a bad tackle by the fella, Jimmy Mann, as I touched the ball past him. The amazing thing was that, when we played at Bristol City exactly a year later, he tried to do me again. This time the tackle split my boot in half and they reckon that John almost jumped out of the director's box because he was so angry.

"The broken leg really put me back, though, because my knee on that leg was already weak and it took a long time to get over. I wasn't a good healer and that's when I first started limping a bit. I also think I lost a bit of pace. I didn't notice it at the time but later on a few journalists told me that they thought I'd lost half a yard after breaking my leg.

"The following summer I went out to America to play for Team Hawaii in the NASL and that was an interesting experience. Mooro, Georgie Best and Eusebio were out there and I'd missed playing against Pele and the New York Cosmos by a few days. The trouble was, we were playing on an Astroturf pitch and that caused problems with my knee again, so I had to come back after two months.

"The club's surgeon, Brian Roper, a nice man who sadly died a few years ago, said there was an operation he could do, but it would put me out for a year. I'd already missed a year so I didn't fancy that again and I decided just to build it up by running and, thankfully, it worked.

"I came back in 1977-78, but we were relegated at the end of the season. It was a transitional period for the club, certain players left and a new breed of players arrived. Bill was pushed back to centre-half and the likes of Phil Parkes, Ray Stewart and David Cross were fantastic signings. The likes of Alvin Martin and Paul Allen also came in and they developed into the 1980-81 side that I thought was the best team in all the time I was at the club."

Having yet again showed outstanding determination and willpower to battle back from what was, in those days, a career-threatening injury, Pat had won back his place in the late 70s as John Lyall rebuilt his team in the second division.

Minor injuries in the 1979-80 campaign restricted him to 26 league appearances but, having returned to action later in the season, Pat was dreaming of another glorious Wembley appearance as Hammers again reached the FA Cup final. Sadly, this time it was Pat's turn to face the Bobby Gould treatment and endure personal heartbreak in the days leading up to the big event.

"I was a bit unlucky that year. I'd started the season in the team but I had a few niggly injuries and missed quite a few games," he recalls. "Then, out of the blue, John brought me back in the FA Cup semi-final against Everton. I think he had a lot of faith in me to do a job down that right-hand side and I was delighted to get back in.

"We were drawing 1-1 and it was heading for the replay, when Andy King did me with 10 minutes to go. He came down straight on my ankle as I turned away from him but, because Stuart Pearson had already gone off injured, I had to hobble on for the last few minutes.

"I was in agony and on crutches for a good few weeks afterwards. I got myself fit but it was too late and young Paul Allen got his chance. Just like Gouldy does to me, I always remind Andy King that he cost me a Cup final place, against the team I had supported as a boy. It was a tough day at Wembley because, although I was in the

adidas

squad, I didn't feel a part of it and it was hard to see the boys enjoying themselves so much afterwards.

"Bonzo knew I was upset and, when we were back at the hotel getting ready for the reception dinner, he came up to my room for a chat and said: 'Fancy a drink, Dutch?' as he always called me. My missus was in the bathroom getting ready and, before we knew it, an hour had passed and we were late for the reception! As I walked in, though, all the lads started clapping, which was really nice of them."

Pat can't speak highly enough of Billy Bonds. He says: "I've always had the utmost respect for him and we've always got on well. I remember John used to do this training routine called 'man-for-man', where you were paired up with an opponent during a practice match and only allowed to mark that person, and vice-versa. I got paired with Bonzo once and John said it was fantastic to watch the two of us going at it together and giving it everything. There was only going to be one winner, though – and it wasn't me!

"Bonzo was good for me, though, he was always on my side. Someone once asked me who had been the best captain I ever played for, and I said Bill. Mooro was something special but, for some reason, I always felt in awe of him and so far below him in terms of ability. He was like a film star while Bonzo was more of a street fighter and it was easier to feel as though you were on his level.

"It's funny, I came from a boxing family – my dad and my uncles all boxed – but I would run away from a fight, so I never considered myself to be a brave person in any way. I remember sitting at home one day, though, and saying to my dad: 'Do you sometimes think I'm not a real Holland because I don't like a fight?"

"Don't get me wrong, Dad was a lovely man, but he said: 'Son, when I watch you on the pitch I can see you're a fighter'."

In 1980-81, Pat once again defy the odds and play an influential part early on as Hammers romped to the second division title in tremendous style. However, while in the act of scoring a typically brave goal at Notts County in January, he sustained a blow to the knee that would finally signify the end of the road.

"We had a very good side that season and we blazed it really. Things were going really well and I was in the team every week, then Holland's luck struck again. We were playing at Notts County and I got injured scoring our goal. Trev played the ball through and I dinked it over the keeper but he came out with his studs showing and caught me on the knee.

"I hobbled on, trying to run it off just before half-time, but we went out for the second half and, after 10 minutes, the whole knee just went completely. There was no-one around and I just sat on the ground. Rob Jenkins came on and they took me straight off.

"I was in plaster for a week and we were due to be playing Coventry City in the League Cup semi-final a few days later. Mr Roper said: 'That'll be fine, we'll take the plaster off and you can go and train on your own'.

"As soon as I moved it, though, I was in agony and it turned out there was a chip of bone floating around in the knee. I was rushed to Harley Street and they opened me up, but it took ages to find the thing and the operation had done so much damage. The knee was too weak to take it and I remember telling my dad that I

Pat with Sir Trevor Brooking at the unveiling of the Sports Heritage blue plaque in honour of their former manager John Lyall at the Boleyn Ground in January 2008.

thought I was finished. I was right."

After finally being forced to call it a day, Patsy continued a natural progression into coaching, having originally been introduced to the field by Lyall as a shy 18-year-old low on self-confidence. He helped out with the youngsters at Upton Park before finally cutting his claret-and-blue ties in 1984, after 19 years at the club, to take up a player-coach role at Leyton Orient.

From there he embarked on a coaching tour of the capital that saw him head to QPR, back to Orient and then on to Tottenham, before moving into the hotseat at Brisbane Road under chairman Barry Hearn in April 1995.

After leaving the O's 18 months later, he returned to White Hart Lane as a member of the Youth Academy coaching staff. But, Spurs being Spurs, they had another of their seemingly annual management and backroom staff upheavals and Pat was released in the summer of 2006.

Millwall manager Nigel Spackman then appointed Pat as his as chief scout, a position he held for 18 months until Kenny Jackett decided to bring in his own staff, so Pat again found himself temporarily unemployed. Luton Town's cash-strapped boss Mick Hartford turned to Pat when he needed a part-time scout, and that's the role the popular former West Ham winger has also fulfilled most recently for Roberto Di Matteo at MK Dons.

Pat's full-time job from early in 2008, though, was as head of the sports academy at Queens School in Bushey, Hertfordshire. Now 58, he lives at Upminster, Essex with his wife Jeanette and their two children, Sara and Mathew.

Remember the days when young lads played street football? Johnny Ayris did in East London.

Chapter 10

JOHN AYRIS

"I wore the claret-and-blue of West Ham United and I am very proud to have done so. I would be happy if that was inscribed on my tombstone"

IN 1971 the Upton Park faithful witnessed an horrific incident that left West Ham's diminutive 18-year-old right-winger John Ayris in hospital with a potentially life threatening condition.

The perpetrator was Chelsea's notorious defender, Ron 'Chopper' Harris.

Many West Ham fans who were present that day felt that despite making a complete recovery, John's confidence was severely affected and he was never quite the same player again, although he went on to make a total of 65 league and cup appearances for the Hammers during his eight years at Upton Park.

These days, John – now 55 – remains remarkably stoical about the incident and bears no malice towards the Chelsea hard man.

Recalling the incident on September 11, John told *EX*: "I had made my league debut a year earlier and I felt that I was beginning to establish myself. We had started the season well and fancied our chances against Chelsea. Ron Harris had a formidable reputation, but I was having a good game against him.

"I sensed that he was rattled and the West Ham crowd were really getting after him. Unlike some opponents, Ron never said anything during a game. No verbals – nothing. He didn't even look at you. His concentration was total.

"Clyde Best had given us the lead after 60 minutes but John Hollins equalised for Chelsea 10 minutes later. Even so, we were well on top and really pressing for the winner. The ball was in the air and I remember running forward and then leaping to get in a header, but Ron was ready for me. He anticipated my move and instead of jumping with me, he checked and held his ground.

"He seemed to flip me up and over his shoulder and my momentum caused me to come crashing down behind him, with my chest taking the full impact of the fall.

"I knew it was bad, but I got up and after a few minutes treatment, I tried to carry on. However, it was impossible. I was struggling to breath and badly shaken. I went off and Bobby Howe came on as substitute for me after 80 minutes. I sat in the dressing room listening to the roar of the crowd as Clyde Best scored the winner for us with five minutes to go."

Incredibly, West Ham allowed John to go home after the game but he admits that he was still having severe breathing difficulties throughout the night. The following morning, John returned to Upton Park – a strict rule for all players injured on a

Saturday – and was promptly despatched to The London Hospital in Mile End Road.

John continues: "They conducted a lot of tests and the diagnosis was that I had an air embolism in my lung. It was like a blood clot except that it was filled with air and I later discovered that it was potentially life-threatening. It was a very frightening experience and I was in hospital for two weeks.

"Looking back, I have to say that it did affect my confidence as a player," he admits. "I am sure Ron didn't intend to put me in hospital with an injury which ultimately affected my whole career, but I think he knew what he was doing and really wanted to teach me a lesson for giving him a bit of a run around."

Ironically, Harris was not cautioned for the incident, but it is safe to assume that West Ham were not exactly best pleased at the perceived physical assault on their young winger. The club remained ominously tight lipped about the affair and even the programme notes for the following home match were equally non-committal.

In the biggest understatement of all time, the programme merely reported: "Our only major regret was that following a collision with a Chelsea defender, John Ayris had to spend a few days in London Hospital. A bruised chest had a side-effect on his lung and it was necessary for them to keep him under observation. He therefore missed last Saturday's game, but we hope to have him back soon."

John says: "The game was tough in those days. There were a lot of hatchet men and unlike today, referees offered little or no protection. Defenders could kick your legs away from behind to get the ball and still not be penalised, let alone booked. I remember Geoff Hurst used to come into the dressing room after a game and the backs of his legs were black and blue.

"The likes of Ron Harris wouldn't last five minutes in the modern game."

There was no danger that John Ayris could ever be described as a hatchet man. Standing only 5ft 5ins tall and weighing just nine stone, John relied purely on his considerable skill and trickery, which had been perfected as a young boy by spending hours kicking a tennis ball against a wall near his home at Wapping in east London.

Wapping was John's birthplace on January 8, 1953, and where he lived with his parents and sister. He says: "I was football-mad as a kid and I supported Manchester United, mainly because of the legend of the Busby Babes and the Munich air crash, plus the magic of George Best.

"I used to have a long journey to school across London each day on the tube. I attended a Catholic grammar school in South Kensington. My P.E. teacher had some connection with Fulham and I had a trial there, but nothing materialised."

John recalls: "I was always a winger and I was playing for a boys' team called St. Patrick's in Wapping, where I was spotted by West Ham scout Wally Wood. I had a six-week trial and then started training with some of the other young players on Tuesday and Thursday nights at Upton Park. I was offered terms and signed as an apprentice professional at the age of 16 on August 26, 1969."

John's first appearance as an apprentice professional came a few days later in a South-East Counties League match against Watford at West Ham's Chadwell Heath training ground. The young Hammers won 4-2 with John notching a rare goal.

Among his team-mates that day was Kevin Lock who would later enjoy a distinguished career at Upton Park.

John says: "They were great days. John Lyall was in charge of the youth team and some of my contemporaries were Joe Durrell and Ade Coker, who both went on to play for West Ham's first team in the early 70s."

"It was a bit awesome training with the likes of Bobby Moore, Geoff Hurst and Martin Peters, but I have to say that they were very welcoming to young players. In particular, Bobby went out of his way to speak to me. It was just typical of him. I still get a lump in my throat when I think about the great man."

John's progress was meteoric and within a few weeks of signing apprentice forms, he was playing in the reserves – ironically, alongside Martin Peters on one occasion. "I think Martin was coming back from injury," says John, "and it was the only time I ever played with him in a competitive game for West Ham. By the time I made my league debut the following year, Martin had been transferred to Spurs."

Incredibly, John's league debut came while he was still an apprentice professional. He was just 17 years and nine-months-old. West Ham were playing Burnley at Upton Park on October 3, 1970 and John had been told to report to the ground around mid-day.

He recalls: "I just assumed I would be playing in the reserves against Chelsea and that I would be on the coach for the journey across London to Stamford Bridge. But Ron Greenwood took me to one side and said that I was playing in the first team. I didn't have time to be nervous and, looking back, my league debut was a bit of a blur. It sort of passed me by."

John is typically modest about his league debut. In fact he made a highly impressive contribution to West Ham's 3-1 win. Geoff Hurst scored a hat-trick, with John having a hand in two of the goals.

John's skill and trickery gave Burnley's experienced left-back Dave Merrington an uncomfortable afternoon and, post-match, Ron Greenwood – who was not known for lavishing fulsome praise on his men – was highly complimentary about the young winger's performance.

The following week, John signed full professional forms to complete a remarkable seven days. However, despite such an impressive debut, Greenwood had no intention of rushing his protégé and John played in just nine league and cup games throughout the 1970-71 season.

One of those games was the infamous FA Cup third round tie against Blackpool at Bloomfield Road on January 2, 1971. It was one of thc blackest days in West Ham's history as Blackpool annihilated the Hammers, 4-0, on an ice-bound pitch.

However, it was the events after the game that caused front page headlines. Ron Greenwood discovered that four players – Bobby Moore, Jimmy Greaves, Clyde Best and Brian Dear, together with physiotherapist Rob Jenkins – had been out drinking in ex-boxer Brian London's 007 night club in Blackpool's town centre until the early hours of the Saturday morning.

The guilty players were dropped, fined and suspended and the ensuing fall out was spectacular. The incident caused a major rift between Moore and Greenwood which never healed. Dear never played for the club again and the incident hastened

Greaves' retirement from the game. A sad end to a glittering career.

Only Best and Jenkins survived relatively unscathed, but even that was a close call.

John says: "It was a shocking display by the team. There had been rumours the previous evening when we arrived in Blackpool that the game would be called off, but the referee gave it the go ahead. We were slipping and sliding all over the place and they had a midfield player called Tony Green who was just sensational."

Despite the Blackpool fiasco, John's progress brought international recognition and he won seven England youth caps, including being a member of the victorious England team that won the European Championship in Czechoslovakia in the summer of 1971.

John recalls: "We were a good side and beat Portugal 3-0 in the final – I scored a goal. Among my team-mates was Steve Daley, who went on to play for Wolves and Manchester City, and also Trevor Francis, who had such a great career with Birmingham City, Nottingham Forest and England. Trevor was the star of our team – what a player!"

Two other highlights of John's early career were playing in the testimonial matches in honour of Bobby Moore and Geoff Hurst. He says: "Bobby's testimonial was against Celtic at Upton Park just a few weeks after I had made my league debut. Celtic made a real game of it. We drew 3-3 and I scored one of the goals. It was real end-to-end stuff, but I will always remember that game because of an incident with Celtic's Scottish international defender Tommy Gemmell.

"There was a hold up in play and Tommy started chatting to me. He was most engaging, but suddenly there was an excruciating pain in my foot. When I looked down, I realised that Tommy was treading on my boot, grinding his studs into my foot. When play restarted, he just ran off. I learnt a lot that night.

"The following year, I played in Geoff Hurst's testimonial against a European all-star team at Upton Park. We drew 4-4 against a side including such legends as Eusebio, Uwe Seeler, Rodney Marsh, Jimmy Johnstone, Dave MacKay and my old friend Tommy Gemmell! I felt a bit overawed being in such company, but it was an unforgettable experience."

John talks movingly about Bobby Moore who he admits made the biggest impression on him over the years, together with that other Upton Park legend Billy Bonds.

He says: "There will never be the like of either of them again at West Ham. People thought that Bobby was arrogant because he had such an aura about him. They hated him up north and also in Scotland, but he was such a nice man and so approachable.

"Early in my career, I vividly remember coming back from a game against Wolves at Molineux. I was sitting next to Joe Durrell on the train and we agreed that when we got back to London, we would go for a drink at the Globe pub in Stepney. At that point, Bobby came over and sat at our table and started chatting to us. He asked what we were doing when we got back to London and we told him of our plans about going to the Globe. Bobby said he thought it was a great idea and asked if he could come along. Can you believe it?

"When we got back to London, Joe and myself got into Bobby's red Jaguar – with

John receives the appreciation of Geoff Hurst, who scored a hat-trick largely courtesy of the little right-winger's dazzling debut display in our 3-1 win against Burnley at Upton Park on October 3, 1970.

John with daughter Vicky and a friend at Cardiff before the 2004 Play-off final.

leather seats and all – and off we went to The Globe pub. We never had to pay for a drink all night. Bobby was real class and had time for people. It was a great honour to have played alongside him and to have known him."

Around this time, the injury following the Ron Harris challenge had begun to take its toll on John's career. In the 1971-72 season, he made a total of 13 league and cup appearances and this was followed by just 30 appearances over the next three seasons. His career had hit the proverbial buffers and he was an unused substitute in numerous matches.

One such occasion was the FA Cup third round tie against Southampton at The Dell on January 4, 1975. West Ham won 2-1 and after the game, John and his team-mates duly obliged the numerous autograph hunters on the train journey back to London.

There was one female autograph hunter to whom John was particularly attracted and he discovered that her name was Lyndsey – whose entire family were fervent West Ham fans.

"She looked fantastic," says John, "and I asked Lyndsey out the following weekend. It was the best decision I ever made and we ended up getting married."

The FA Cup win at Southampton set West Ham on the road to Wembley and they went on to win the FA Cup that season, beating Fulham 2-0 in the final. Sadly, John was 6,000 miles away at the time.

He explains: "A few months earlier, I had been given the opportunity to spend three months playing for Cape Town City in South Africa. They were managed by Roy Bailey, the former Ipswich goalkeeper and whose son, Gary, later kept goal for Manchester United. I was clearly out of favour at West Ham and I obtained the club's permission to go out to South Africa for three months during the summer. I felt it was a good opportunity to see another country and also the money was good.

"Unfortunately, my stay in South Africa coincided with the 1975 FA Cup final and I listened to it on the radio in my hotel room in Cape Town. I seriously regretted missing the big day. I accept that I would not have been selected for the game, but I missed being a part of it – all the celebrations afterwards and the parade through the streets of east London the following day.

"I returned to West Ham in time for the start of the 1975-76 season and I managed 10 league and cup appearances during that campaign, plus an appearance in the Anglo-Italian Cup against Fiorentina. The lads were tremendous in the European Cup Winners' Cup and I was one of the substitutes in the final against Anderlecht in the Heysel stadium in 1976. I didn't get on during the game and we lost 4-2. I still have my runners-up medal and the tracksuit top as well!"

In 1976-77, John played just three games and his last appearance for West Ham came as a substitute in the 2-0 defeat against Ipswich Town at Upton Park on October 16, 1976. John acknowledges: "By the end of the season, things didn't look too good for me and I tried not to think about the possibility of leaving the club. However, I was called into Ron Greenwood's office and he told me that I was being released. He said I needed regular football and also a new challenge and while I knew he was right, it was still a huge blow.

"Within a few days, I signed on a free transfer for Wimbledon who had just been elected into the Football League from the old Southern League. Dave Bassett was one of the players there, but they were all still part-timers and only trained on Tuesday and Thursday evenings. Ron Noades was the chairman and after one week, I decided to call it a day. I went to see Ron and explained the situation. Wimbledon were very good about it and, looking back, it must have been one of the shortest stays by any player.

"I was very concerned about the future and I contacted John Lyall, who had always been there for me. I was only 24-years-old and I had no qualifications. John got in contact with Brentford's manager, Bill Dodgin, and I had a trial at Griffin Park.

"I did OK and Brentford offered terms, but I talked it over with Lyndsey and in the end, I turned it down. Quite simply, I knew that I would never find another club like West Ham and felt that perhaps it would be better to start another career with better long-term prospects. But, looking back, it was one hell of a gamble.

"It is strange how luck can sometimes turn in your favour. I had only been out of football for a few weeks, when the *Daily Express* wrote an article about me and in particular about the pitfalls of young footballers not making the grade and what happens to them after their career has come to an end. Incredibly, someone from Selfridges store in Oxford Street, in London's West End, read the article and made contact with me. I was offered a job in their sports department, which I readily accepted.

A recent picture of John working at the sports centre.

"After enjoying the life of a professional footballer, it was a bit of a culture shock at first, but I thoroughly enjoyed my time there.

"Lyndsey and I got married in 1981 and we moved out to South Woodham Ferrers in Essex. However, I have to say that travelling into the West End each day started to get me down and in 1982, I saw an advertisement for an assistant manager's job at the new South Woodham Ferrers sports centre. During my years at West Ham, I had got some coaching badges and I think this must have helped, because I was offered the job and I have been there ever since. I am now manager of the sports centre and it's great. I live close by and I can just walk to work."

John and Lyndsey have two children – Vicky and Christopher.

"I love football and I still play in the occasional veterans' match," says John. "However, I don't tend to go to many professional games these days, although I went to the 2004 play-off final between West Ham and Crystal Palace in Cardiff. Living in Essex, I sometimes come into contact with some of my old team-mates such as Geoff Pike, Paul Brush and Kevin Lock. Also, Pat Holland and Billy Bonds attended my 50th birthday party in 2003. It is always great to meet up with the lads again."

John reflects: "It is only now that I realise what being a West Ham fan really means. When I went to the play-off final at Cardiff, I thought the intensity of the fans was quite amazing. It transcends everything. I still have a great affection for the club."

In retrospect, it must be said that John Ayris was a good player. When skill was handed out, he was at the front of the queue. But, sadly, lady luck was not so kind to him. The spectre of that fateful challenge by Ron Harris cast a long shadow over the remainder of his career.

John adds: "I would have liked to have played more games for the Hammers, but I enjoyed my time there. I wore the claret-and-blue of West Ham United and I am very proud to have done so. I would be happy if that was inscribed on my tombstone."

What an epitaph. And what a pity that some of the football mercenaries who have recently plied their trade at Upton Park are unlikely to voice a similar opinion in the years to come.

Chapter 11

LEAGUE CUP EPIC

Looking back at West Ham's heroic performance in the 1971-72 League Cup semi-final against Stoke City – a marathon tie that went to four gruelling matches. Terry Roper re-lives the drama . . .

IT happened more than 36 years ago – a marathon encounter between West Ham and Stoke City in the semi-final of the Football League Cup. It was a titanic struggle, lasting a total of seven hours that, in the end, resembled two heavyweight prize fighters who had almost fought each other to a standstill. Sadly for the Hammers, it was Stoke who delivered the ultimate knockout blow.

In the early rounds of the 1971-72 competition, Stoke – who were in the old first division at the time – had beaten Southport, Oxford United, Manchester United and Bristol Rovers to reach the semi-final stage. West Ham had disposed of Cardiff City and Leeds United (away) after replays, while Bryan 'Pop' Robson was the hero of both the fourth round victory at home to Liverpool and the 5-0 fifth round thrashing of Sheffield United under the Upton Park lights. Pop's hat-trick to slice apart the Blades marked a brilliant performance by both himself and the team.

The Hammers were considered slight favourites to reach Wembley. In the other semi-final, Spurs met Chelsea in the all-London tie.

Each semi-final was a two-legged affair and West Ham travelled to Stoke on Wednesday, December 8 for the first meeting. Indeed, it was Hammers who gained the advantage with a 2-1 win.

Peter Dobing gave Stoke the lead after 14 minutes, but Geoff Hurst blasted home a penalty past England World Cup colleague Gordon Banks just before half time to level the scores. In the 63rd minute, following a fine move down the right, Bermudan striker Clyde Best volleyed home Harry Redknapp's pinpoint cross for the winner – West Ham had the Twin Towers firmly in their sights.

In the return leg at Upton Park on December 15, the gates were closed 30 minutes before the evening kick-off with 39,000 crammed inside the floodlit Boleyn Ground. When Tommy Taylor failed to clear, West Ham allowed Stoke's John Ritchie to fire home after 73 minutes to level the aggregate score at 2-2 and take the tie into extra-time.

In the dying minutes of the extra period, Upton Park witnessed one of the most dramatic moments in its long history. As West Ham surged forward for the winner, Redknapp raced into the Stoke penalty area and appeared to be wrestled to the

Gordon Banks saves Geoff Hurst's thunderbolt penalty under the Upton Park lights to send the tie into replays....

ground by Banks, who had fumbled a cross. The Boleyn Ground erupted as referee Keith Walker, from Maidstone, pointed to the spot. The Stoke players – including Banks – surrounded Walker with their protests, but the official remained unmoved.

West Ham were a penalty-kick away from reaching Wembley and the responsibility fell to Hurst – the game's most feared striker facing the world's greatest goalkeeper.

As Hurst placed the ball on the spot at the North Bank end, several West Ham players – including Billy Bonds, John McDowell and Tommy Taylor – looked away, such was the intensity of the moment. Hurst was the penalty king for West Ham and England at the time and always went for power. His cheeks would puff out at the moment of impact.

This occasion was no exception and as referee Walker signalled for the kick to be taken, Hurst ran forward and fired a venomous shot high towards Banks' right-hand side. It was a shot of such ferocity that it would have beaten any goalkeeper in the world, with one exception – Gordon Banks.

The Stoke goalkeeper dived to his right and, incredibly, deflected the ball over the bar. The game was over. Stoke had escaped and taken the tie to a replay at Hillsborough.

A crowd of 46,000 witnessed the replay on January 5 and again, it was a stalemate. There were no goals after 90 minutes and still none at the end of the lifeless extra-time period. West Ham and Stoke had now faced each other for five-and-a-half hours and Chelsea – who had overcome Tottenham in the other semi – still didn't know who they would be facing in the final at Wembley.

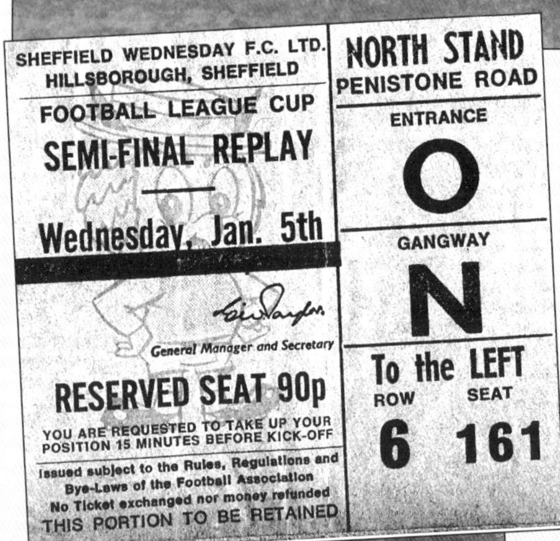

Gordon Banks at full stretch to deny Clyde Best in the goalless first replay at Hillsborough.

The second replay was held in torrential rain at windswept Old Trafford on January 26. This time, almost 50,000 were in attendance and the drama that unfolded exceeded anything that had been experienced in the three previous encounters.

After just 14 minutes, goalkeeper Bobby Ferguson dived at the feet of Stoke's Terry Conroy and received a sickening kick in the head. Ferguson was concussed and left the field accompanied by physiotherapist Rob Jenkins.

In those days, teams were allowed just one substitute – always an outfield player – and if their goalkeeper was injured, then one of the outfield players would take over in goal. Teams were always aware who their emergency goalkeeper would be in such circumstances and, on this night, Clyde Best should have taken over from Ferguson.

However, as skipper Bobby Moore handed the green jersey to Best, the giant Bermudan's nerve cracked and he turned away saying: "No, man – not me."

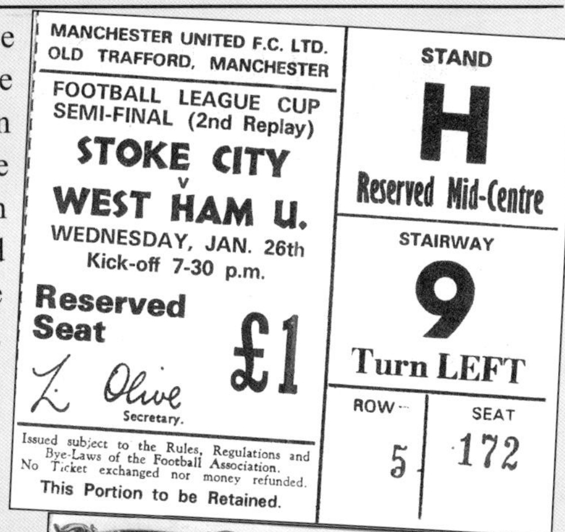

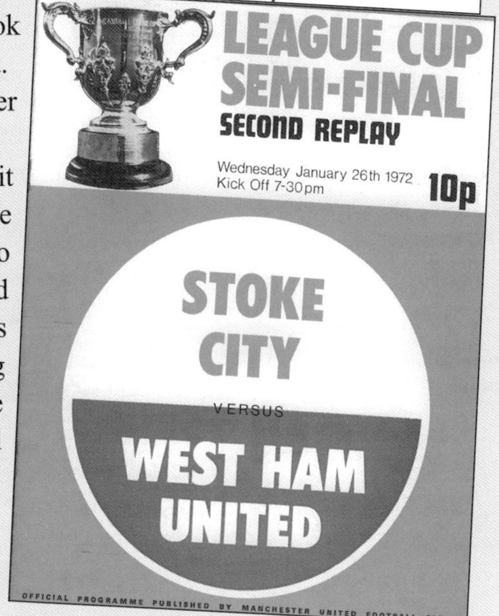

It may sound harsh, but why agree to be an emergency goalkeeper when you are not prepared to go in goal in an emergency – however important the occasion? It rather defies logic. But then this was an extraordinary occasion and the stakes were very high. The incomparable Moore looked around his team-mates and clearly, there were no other volunteers.

Moore, the captain, simply led by example and pulled on the green jersey – and also Ferguson's gloves – and took over in goal in front of the Stretford End.

Within a minute, the England skipper was facing a penalty kick!

John McDowell had dreadfully under hit a back-pass and committed a desperate foul in the penalty area as he tried to rectify his error. Stoke's Mike Bernard placed the ball on the spot, but was clearly inhibited at the thought of facing Bobby Moore in goal. Incredibly, Moore parried the spot-kick – but Bernard followed up to net the rebound.

Even so, Moore's confidence was unshakable and twice he held crosses despite being under pressure from Stoke's onrushing forwards. Inspired by their captain's heroics in goal, 10-man West Ham – who had chosen not to bring on substitute Peter Eustace at this stage – fought back and Billy Bonds equalised with a deflected shot past Banks.

Meanwhile, feverish work in the West Ham dressing room had resulted in Ferguson coming round despite the fact that he was still groggy. To test Fergie's reactions, Eustace had been firing shots at the stricken keeper in the players' tunnel.

The decision was made by manager Ron Greenwood and assistant John Lyall to send Ferguson back in goal, thus releasing Moore into his usual position at the heart of West Ham's defence.

After 39 minutes, their gamble appeared to be vindicated as West Ham went ahead when Trevor Brooking drove home from the edge of the penalty area after a typically rampaging run down the right flank by Bonds.

However, all was far from well with Ferguson, who merely watched a 20-yarder from Dobing flash past him, just before half-time, to level the scores.

Throughout much of the second half, West Ham, not surprisingly, appeared to be more intent on protecting their goalkeeper than pushing forward for the winner. In

the end, the burden was too great and inevitably, Stoke snatched the lead.

Ironically, the scorer was Terry Conroy who had been involved in the early collision with Ferguson – a fact not lost on Hammers' fans who mercilessly booed Conroy throughout the remainder of the game.

Greenwood subsequently criticised Stoke's treatment of Ferguson, but the keeper himself told the press that Conroy was blameless in their collision.

At the end, Stoke's players – and their fans – rejoiced in a manner befitting a team who had just reached their first-ever major cup final at Wembley. It was in total contrast to the emotions experienced by the men in claret-and-blue and also their watching

Bobby Ferguson, West Ham's goalkeeper, lies injured at Old Trafford last night after a headon clash.

League Cup Semi-Fi

BRAVE M

GOALKEE

STOKE G

By DON

Stoke City ......

STOKE CITY stagge
little luckily in
last night after re
eous West Ham fron
marathon that came
Old Trafford.

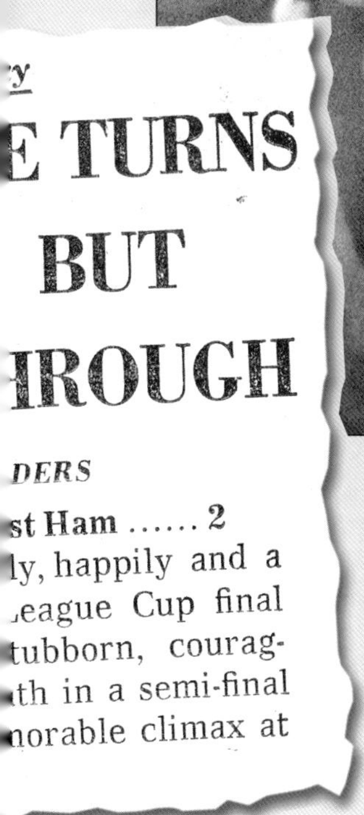

y

E TURNS

BUT

IROUGH

DERS

st Ham 2

ly, happily and a
League Cup final
tubborn, courag-
th in a semi-final
norable climax at

One of the key turning points in the marathon tie . . . the injury to keeper Bobby Ferguson that meant Bobby Moore had to take over in goal and then face a Stoke penalty. Above: A still dazed Fergie shaking hands with Gordon Banks at the end.

fans. Defeat on that rain-soaked night in Manchester was like a proverbial dagger in the heart.

A total of 171,000 spectators watched the four West Ham v. Stoke matches, which produced gate receipts of around £82,000 – a considerable amount in those days.

West Ham fielded an unchanged team for all four games: Bobby Ferguson, John McDowell, Frank Lampard, Billy Bonds, Tommy Taylor, Bobby Moore, Harry Redknapp, Clyde Best, Geoff Hurst, Trevor Brooking, Bryan 'Pop' Robson.

Only one substitute was used throughout – Peter Eustace, who replaced Harry Redknapp after 80 minutes in the second replay at Old Trafford.

Stoke went on to beat Chelsea, 2-1, in the League Cup final, while West Ham would have to wait another three years before they returned to Wembley again.

Chapter 12

DUDLEY**TYLER**

"He wanted the ball played purely on the ground, so we worked all the time on one-touch, two-touch, with the ball being pinged around. Even these days you don't see the levels of control in the Premier League that we had at West Ham back then"

IT happens, without fail, every year. FA Cup third round time comes around and we are treated to endless reruns of the 35-yard piledriver from Ronnie Radford that set Hereford United on the way to one of the most famous cup upsets of all time in 1972.

When the Southern League part-timers humbled mighty Newcastle United 2-1, to delight the hordes of parka-clad home fans who came, repeatedly, swarming on to the Edgar Street pitch, a depressed nation, which was in the midst of industrial unrest, three-day weeks and power cuts, rejoiced and the names of Radford and Ricky George, who scored the winner, became immortalised in the annals of FA Cup history.

For one member of the Bulls' victorious side, however, even greater things lay ahead. Dudley Tyler, Hereford's 27-year-old right-winger, had torn Newcastle's left flank to shreds that day with his pace and direct running, impressively enough to attract interest from league clubs up and down the country, including West Ham, who, by coincidence, had been drawn to play at Hereford in the fourth round.

As a 15-year-old living in Swindon, Tyler had undergone an operation to fix a hole in his heart and any hope of a career in professional football had seemingly long since passed him by. But Hammers boss Ron Greenwood knew a good player when he saw one and at the end of that season 'Deadly Dudley' got an unexpected tilt at the big time when West Ham paid £25,000 – a record for a non-league player at the time – to acquire his services as a replacement for the departing Harry Redknapp.

"I hadn't dreamed of going anywhere else," said Dudley, 64, who now lives in Hereford and works as a sales manager for Glazpart, an injection moulding company based in Banbury. "I lived in Swindon, had a job, played part-time for Hereford for a tenner a week and was happy. But then came that cup run and all of a sudden our confidence was sky high.

"At 23, I'd impressed in a trial game at Swindon but they said I was too old, so I thought that was that. But there had been some enquiries about me the previous season, by Fulham I think, and after the Newcastle game Colin Addison, our manager, told me West Ham were interested.

Dudley and wife Margaret on arrival at The Boleyn in 1972.

"They were heady days at Hereford and when West Ham, with Bobby Moore and Geoff Hurst, came to town it was big news. We actually thought it was going to be harder than the Newcastle game because of West Ham's tradition and the way they played, but we still felt we had a great chance.

"The first game ended 0-0, though, and I'll never forget the replay, played on a Monday. We were right in the middle of all the power cuts, so the game was due to kick off at 2.30, but because everybody was off work everyone wanted to see the game. Over 42,000 turned up at Upton Park that day and our bus couldn't get near the ground. At quarter-past-two we gave up and had to get off, with the skip containing our kit, and run to the ground. Class told in the end and we lost 3-1, with Geoff Hurst getting a hat-trick.

"Not long after, West Ham said they wanted a chat and at the end of the season I went down and played in a testimonial match for Harry Cripps at Millwall. Ron invited me to sign and I finally became a pro at the ripe old age of 27! Looking back

Dudley and Trevor Brooking watch as Clyde Best gets stuck into Manchester United keeper Alex Stepney and full-back Tony Dunne during the 2-2 draw on September 2, 1972.

now, I had a good job with a large engineering firm so in the cold light of day it was probably a dopey thing to do at that age, but it was a dream I'd had for a long time so I gave it a go."

And give it a go he did. From playing against Bobby Moore in a one-off cup tie, Dudley was now training alongside the England legend – "and out-sprinting him!", he laughs – and did enough to impress Greenwood on a pre-season tour of Sweden to earn a place in Hammers' starting line-up for the first match of the 1972-73 season, at West Bromwich Albion.

In typically relaxed fashion, Dudley took it all in his stride and was soon providing the kind of service our ace marksman, 'Pop' Robson, thrived upon.

Dudley adds: "It was a bit difficult to start with. I was a quick winger who could go past people but I remember my first training session, when the ball was just flying around, all one-touch stuff, and wondering how I could cope with it. But doing it everyday, eventually it happens for you.

"I felt a little bit on trial because I'd come from non-league and it was a big jump, but they were a good bunch at the club and I never had any problems settling in. It was funny in a way, though, because on the one hand you had a lot of young guys like Tommy Taylor, John McDowell and Kevin Lock, who probably saw me as not daft enough to be with, then you had established people like Trevor Brooking, Billy Bonds and Frank Lampard, who just liked to play cards, have a chat or have a beer. I was somewhere in the middle.

"I thought I had a chance of starting in the first team after Harry left for Bournemouth – why else would they have bought me? I made my debut at West Brom, it finished 0-0 and Ron said I'd done all right. So I stayed in and scored my first and only goal – a very rare header – against Leicester City in my third game.

Left: In a chase with Liverpool's Larry Lloyd at Anfield. Right: Ade Coker is about to join Dudley in celebration of his only Hammers goal – a header against Leicester City.

"It was a dream start and I played all the way through to November, but then I broke my collarbone in training and was out for three months. I came back in time for our trip to Manchester United, the most memorable game of my time at West Ham, when we drew 2-2 and I was up against the likes of Bobby Charlton and George Best.

"For someone who'd been playing non-league a few months earlier, you couldn't really believe someone was paying you to play football at such places and, in retrospect, it was a huge leap which I probably didn't appreciate at the time. You just went along with it; you trained, played and had a bit of fun with the lads."

Dudley played in half our league games that season as the Hammers scored 67 league goals, the third highest tally, to finish sixth in the old first division, a position that, in all likelihood, would nowadays be sufficient to bring European football to The Boleyn and spark wild celebrations down the Barking Road.

Back in 1973, however, there were no rewards for finishing sixth so the significance tended to pass people by. "It was superb really and nowadays they'd be partying," says Dudley. "But at the time there were no big money-spinning competitions like the Champions' League or extra UEFA Cup places up for grabs, so there was no great talk about it.

"But it was a good season and Pop ended up getting 28 goals in the league. He was one of the best strikers of a ball I've ever seen and could score goals from any angle with either foot. He was a good Geordie lad, too, with whom I played golf and got on with particularly well.

"That season, I did for West Ham exactly what I did for Pinehurst, my old youth team in Swindon. I was able to go at people, knock crosses in and I think the crowd appreciated that. It's the same now with people like (Paolo) Di Canio and (Joe) Cole, who run with the ball, and I never had any problem with the crowd, even from the Chicken Run. You got the odd comment about being a West Country boy but that was about it.

"Ron (Greenwood) was different and he had some ideas that were new to English football because a lot of his studies had been based on the continental game. He had

Dudley pictured when EX interviewed him back in 2003.

good views on how he wanted the game played; he wanted the ball played purely on the ground, so we worked all the time on one-touch, two-touch, with the ball being pinged around. Even these days you don't see the levels of control in the Premiership that we had back then."

Sadly, Dudley's sojourn at Upton Park ended as suddenly as it began. In contrast to his first season, the 1973-74 campaign had begun disastrously, with just one win from our opening 18 games fuelling dissension in the camp.

Goalkeeper Bobby Ferguson was moved to famously remark that there were "too many gutless, spineless men in the team" and Bonds later decided to do some sparring with Ted MacDougall, our hopelessly off-form striker, in the bath after a 4-1 defeat at Leeds.

Even Bobby Moore had seen enough and was soon off to Fulham, so it was almost a relief when, in November 1973, Dudley was invited to return to Hereford, who were by now a third division club. Of his departure, Dudley said: "The side had been chopped and changed a lot. I was in and out and didn't get a really good run, then Ron just said to me that Hereford were interested in taking me back.

"I didn't really know what to do, but with Hereford being in what is now the Championship, it wasn't as if I was dropping down too far and they still had a good crowd. It was a bit like going home, but it was disappointing that things hadn't gone better at West Ham at the time.

"The biggest irony, of course, is that I'd been back at Hereford just a few weeks when, who should turn up in the FA Cup third round? Yes, you've guessed it, and we beat West Ham 2-1 at Edgar Street after a 1-1 draw at Upton Park. No motivation was needed for those matches but it wasn't through revenge – I just needed the win bonus again!"

Dudley eventually retired from football in 1978 after an enjoyable, but totally unexpected, six-year professional career. He has been in sales ever since but still follows the Hammers, as does his son Nick, who was born during his father's time in London.

Now settled in Hereford with wife Margaret, Dudley says: "I thought my football career would end as a part-timer at Hereford, where playing football just meant a bit of extra money on top of working. But I had the opportunity of playing pro and I wouldn't change a thing."

Chapter 13

MERVYN**DAY**

"I honestly believe I should have been taken out of the side a little bit earlier, given a rest and then rebuilt my confidence that way. I needed more moral support and a little bit more backing in the press but that that's the way people managed in those days. John wasn't any different to anybody else"

WHEN Ron Greenwood died in February 2006, few of his former players was more saddened by his loss than Mervyn Day, who will never forget the help and attention he received from West Ham's celebrated ex-boss at a difficult time in his life.

"Nothing was too much trouble for Ron," Mervyn told *EX*. "He started to watch me play for my grammar school, King Edward VI in Chelmsford, and for one particular match for the school district team that was played at Chelmsford City's ground, he even stood on the terraces behind my goal. I still have a picture at home, showing a deserted Chelmsford City stadium with Ron on his own dressed in raincoat and trilby, watching the game.

"I had no idea he'd been stood there until somebody told me after the game. Can you imagine a Premiership or Championship manager bothering to go and watch an under-15s game now!

"I was made to feel part of the West Ham family very early on and I came here because of the type of people who were at the club – Ron, John Lyall, Ernie Gregory, Wally St Pier and Arthur Lamb, the scout Wally used to send to watch my school matches.

"The first football match I can really remember watching was the televised coverage of the 1964 FA Cup final, when Alan Kelly did his back and was a virtual passenger for Preston against West Ham," says Mervyn. "I had three teams – West Ham, Ipswich – the town my parents came from – and Chelsea. Peter Bonetti was my schoolboy idol and I had the green goalie gloves and all the sort of stuff he used to wear.

"Tottenham, Birmingham and one or two smaller clubs were interested in signing me as a kid, although I thought I was set for Ipswich, who were then managed by Bobby Robson. But I was brought to West Ham by the famous chief scout, Wally St Pier, and Ron Greenwood made such a fuss of us, really welcoming us to the club, that he made my mind up to come to Upton Park," said Day who played at right-half before going in goal for Chelmsford district schools at the age of 10 after the regular keeper failed to turn up.

Mervyn signed for Hammers as an apprentice in the summer of 1971 and within two years he had made his first team debut at the age of 18.

"To be honest, I didn't expect to be picked so soon," he says, although Greenwood clearly rated his young goalkeeping discovery very highly and their respect was mutually strong. Mervyn recalls a difficult time in his life which, despite his subsequent spells with Leyton Orient, Aston Villa, Leeds United, Carlisle United and Charlton Athletic, reinforced his affections for West Ham forever. His story also conflicts with many who have claimed that Greenwood possessed no man-management skills to complement his undoubted qualities as a coach.

"My father (Albert) died when I was 17. It was the February and, you know, one of those nervous times when a youngster is unsure whether he'll be offered a pro contract. No-one had said anything to me but within a week or two of my Dad passing on, Ron called me in and I signed pro there and then. He was brilliant. He said he wanted to sign me on earlier than expected because he knew that I'd become the new breadwinner in my family.

"If ever I needed to talk to Ron about anything, his door was always open. Perhaps he thought that more senior players should be adult enough to just get on with it, but in my case we're talking about a 17-year-old kid. I always found him excellent to deal with but, unfortunately, he wasn't manager for all that long while I was there.

"I had no idea I was about to make my debut. I'd played a couple or three reserve games and had gone on tour that summer with the first team. I started the following season well in the reserves but the chance only came when Bobby Ferguson's wife became ill while having their baby. Bobby was given special dispensation to miss the game but then the regular back-up keeper, Peter Grotier, turned up at the ground with a temperature of 104 degrees.

"I was actually walking along Green Street to the stadium, from Upton Park tube, to watch what was a night game, when I suddenly got the call to play against Ipswich. Someone from the club was waiting for me at the main gates and told me to get my arse in gear! It was about 50 minutes before kick-off – there wasn't enough time to feel too nervous.

"Ernie, who took me in the little gym underneath the main stand to warm me up, talked me through what I needed to do. 'If you get the chance to come for your first cross, make sure you come for it. Throw it out quickly. And whatever Bobby (Moore) says, do it'. Bobby just said to me: 'Good luck'. He was a man of few words.

"I then went back into the reserves but about six games later, Ron left out Bobby Ferguson and put me in the first team instead of Peter Grotier."

In fact, after his debut in the 3-3 draw against Ipswich Town on August 27, 1973, Day played another 32 games of that season. He played every match of the following 1974-75 campaign that culminated in an FA Cup winners' medal and personal glory as the PFA Young-Player-of-the-Year award recipient. Day was widely regarded as one of the outstanding prospects in a young team that was evolving following the departure of Moore in 1974. Ron Greenwood was not often moved to make boastful claims about any of his players but the manager didn't hold back when he declared to the press: 'Mervyn Day will be West Ham's goalkeeper

At full stretch to deny Arsenal at the Highbury Clock End.

for the next 10 years'.

Day admits the praise was flattering, though he joked: 'But Ron didn't offer me a 10-year contract, which is what the players of today would have been looking for if their manager had said such great things about them! Seriously, it's always nice to hear anyone say good things about you but Ron's words did become a bit of a millstone towards the end of my playing career at West Ham. When things didn't go as well as I hoped they would, people threw that comment about the 'next 10 years' back at me."

A 10-year contract? Not likely. Mervyn's 'reward' for his sensational first season form and regular acclaim as the 'next best thing' among English goalkeepers was a weekly pay rise of, wait for it . . . five pounds! "At the end of that second season, my deal got improved again, so they did look after me," he acknowledged.

Goalkeepers are a breed apart and tend to stick together, even when one is displaced by another. In Mervyn's time with the Hammers he faced competition from former Scottish international Ferguson and the very capable and often underrated Grotier.

"After initially being upset about being dropped, I think Bobby quickly accepted it. He got his head down, worked hard and responded very professionally. I never had a problem with either him or Peter. As all goalkeepers know, there's only one spot up for grabs and they tend to get on with it. Bobby stuck in there and was still at the club after I left."

Day's memory of the '75 Cup final is hazy – "I think I made a couple of fairly important, though not difficult, saves from John Mitchell and Viv Busby" – and he had some sympathy for his Fulham counterpart, Peter Mellor, who was criticised for conceding both goals by Alan Taylor's in Hammers' 2-0 victory.

"I was a blasé 19-year-old and remember Billy Bonds telling me not to let the

Kevin Lock and Billy Jennings, with Jimmy Greenhoff closing in, look on as Mervyn saves against Stoke City.

occasion pass me by. There were a few tears at the final whistle and I recall handing my medal to Ernie Gregory to look after while we did our lap of honour.

"The problem when you're a young player is that you tend to think that this is the norm, but it's not. It's a highlight, but you don't think that when you're 18-19. When I look back on my career, that's the biggest criticism I have of myself and, to some extent, probably the people here at the time.

"I don't think they quite helped me as much as perhaps people at a club help young players today. There weren't any psychologists at football clubs in those days – you tended to just get on with it. Nowadays, we understand that there are perhaps times when young players need a bit of help."

The support Mervyn believes he needed came in the latter part of his six seasons at the club. After the euphoria of his first two years had subsided, he had firmly established himself in the green jersey and missed just one game of the 1975-76 campaign, which climaxed with the European Cup Winners' Cup final, and he was ever-present again in 1976-77.

He maintains that he didn't think the penalty given against Pat Holland in the Heysel ECWC final should have been awarded. "We had just scored to equalise at 2-2 and they went ahead again from the penalty just a minute later. If only we could have held on longer . . . there was such a feeling of dejection at the end of the game, even though we'd been beaten by a good Anderlecht side.

"Those European home games under the lights had an absolutely fantastic atmosphere, especially the night we played the semi-final against Eintracht Frankfurt on a glue pot of a pitch and with rain tipping down. The crowd was a major reason why we got through to the final."

After just managing to survive a perennial struggle to avoid relegation from the old first division following finishes of 18th place, 13th, 18th and 17th in his previous four seasons, John Lyall's team finally slipped out of the top flight in May 1978. Mervyn had lost his place just before Christmas but, just like the decorations, Hammers still went down with 'Fergie' back between the sticks for the second half of a torrid campaign. This time they finished 20th, two off the bottom but a point from safety.

"In hindsight, it would have been better if I'd been taken out of the side, given a rest and then put back in after having regained my confidence. That might have prolonged my West Ham career, rather than taking the approach of 'we'll keep persevering with him', before then deciding: 'No, we can't do so any more'."

In football, it's an old cliché that you are only as good as your last game in the eyes of the media and the most fickle fans. While Day was being castigated for every error he made as the pressure piled up and West Ham continued their final descent towards the second division, few remembered his heroics on the final day of the 1973-74 season – when he saved Liverpool full-back Alec Lindsay's penalty to ensure a 2-2 draw and the point that guaranteed relegation was avoided for another year.

The unforgiving fans pointed instead to mistakes like the one that allowed Everton's Ronnie Goodlass to chip the ball over him, from almost the halfway line, in the 10th minute of the 2-2 draw at Upton Park in April '77. In the book, West Ham United: The Elite Era, a description of this match includes the comment: "Many supporters identify that goal as the beginning of the end for Day."

Mervyn didn't duck these issues when he spoke to *EX*. He talked with refreshing candour about his trials and tribulations, as well as the good times. He comes across as a man without ego, which is rare in a football environment, and when asked to revisit some of the less pleasing aspects of his playing career, he had no difficulty in doing so.

He continued: "The press could be pretty savage in those days and once they've got an agenda . . . I don't think that has changed, although they might be a bit more lurid these days and it's probably based more on a player's pop star lifestyle than his performance. A big difference between football then and now is the TV coverage – with so many cameras around the grounds, everything is magnified so much more today.

"My last couple of seasons at West Ham were very difficult for me. Once things start to go wrong and mistakes are made, you do tend to get paranoid about things."

Unfortunately, as Mervyn found to his cost, having a name like Day turned out to be a double-edged sword where unsympathetic headline writers were concerned. 'Brightest Day' and 'Day's Dream' were later replaced by less complimentary headings. "It became more like 'Day's a Nightmare' and that sort of thing – I was a cheap, easy headline I suppose. By the same token, at the start of my career I'd had positive headlines simply because my surname presented the newspaper sub-editors with an obvious play on words."

Despite a brief and unhappy return to the team at Ferguson's expense in October '78, Mervyn knew his time at Upton Park had finally come to an end after what turned out to be his final appearance – a 3-3 draw at home against promotion rivals Sunderland on February 10, 1979. He was blamed for the visitors' first two goals, received merciless stick from his home crowd for the rest of the game and ended up being booed off the pitch at the final whistle.

It was, literally, game over for Mervyn at West Ham.

Or, as one tabloid headline put it: 'End of the Day'.

Recalling his final game ordeal, Mervyn admits: "I received ironic 'cheers' every time I caught the ball or picked up a simple backpass, which hurt. It hit me even harder at the time, because I thought I'd had a really good rapport with the fans."

After the Sunderland debacle, manager John Lyall half attempted to defend his keeper with some typically well chosen words for the press, saying: "I feel very sorry for the lad. Our fans are a fantastic bunch and it is entirely out of character for them to be so cruel.

"Nobody is more upset about the mistakes than Mervyn himself. He has been coming in every day for extra training in an effort to battle his way through it. These are the things the fans don't see." (If only the current players were reading this!).

Before Lyall added, somewhat ominously: "I've got to decide in the next week about the goalkeeping situation."

A goalkeeper can easily feel as if he is the loneliest man on the planet when things are going against him. Unlike a midfielder who can 'lose himself' in the midst of the game, the 'invisible' winger who drifts infield rather than 'show' for the ball, or the striker who makes poor runs to ensure he is never likely to receive a pass from a team-mate, for the isolated keeper there is never any hiding place.

"No matter what any goalkeeper says about ignoring the fans behind the goal and staying focused on the game, that's not true. If you are stuck on your line or just six yards out, you can hear the crowd – every word they say.

"But that's the way it is. Fans have their particular favourites and it can be quite difficult for a player to handle when he is singled out for stick. In some cases it might be justified, but others times it's not. Football has changed, though, and I believe that when I played we were a lot more akin to the guy on the terraces than the players are now. Wages and lifestyle? Yes, we had nice wages and lifestyles, but these days they are virtually pop stars by comparison."

Day does not remember seeking out Lyall for a private chat when he was struggling to recapture his form, but says: "I always had a good relationship with John, although I didn't always agree with what he did with me. Then again, any player who is in and out of the side is not going to agree with the manager's decisions."

So how does Mervyn now think Lyall could possibly have handled him differently during his crisis of confidence? "I honestly believe I should have been taken out of the side a little bit earlier than I was, given a rest and then rebuilt my confidence that way. I needed a bit more moral support and a little bit more backing in the press, but what I keep coming back to is that that's the way people managed in those days. John wasn't any different to anybody else."

Who else was there for him to turn to for moral support? Maybe Ernie Gregory, the legendary keeper who was then the goalkeeping coach and a good ally. "Ernie was superb but he was old school too. That's how it was in those days – not just at West Ham, but at every club. All you could do to try and deal with it was work as hard as you can. When I lost form later in my career at different clubs, I could handle it because I'd been through it before."

Day didn't need to have any experience to realise that once Phil Parkes arrived from QPR for a fee of £565,000, there was no way back for him at Upton Park. "That signing came right out of the blue," says Day. "We'd literally moved into a new house at Danbury (Essex), with a bigger mortgage, the day before Phil signed. It was a total shock, but that's football. I knew then that I needed to move at the end of that season."

After a "sure move" to Watford fell through, Day was transferred to the Hammers' East London neighbours Leyton Orient in what was for them a club record £100,000 deal. "It shows you what a footballer's life was like in those days by the fact that my wife and I went away on holiday to the Isle of Wight that summer while I considered my next move. Honestly, the *Isle of Wight!*

"Bob Wilson was goalkeeping coach at Watford and he and their assistant manager, Bertie Mee, made it clear that I was definitely wanted there. But when I got back, the Watford manager, Graham Taylor, phoned me himself and said that he knew nothing about the negotiations and they he didn't want to sign me. Orient were always sure they wanted to

He didn't exactly sign for the second division O's in the happiest of circumstances, though, as he explained: "I was chatting to manager Jimmy Bloomfield in his office, about to sign, when Jimmy's assistant, Peter Angell, collapsed while taking the players on a pre-season run and sadly died of a heart attack."

The move to Brisbane Road restored Day's confidence. Apart from ex-Hammer Bloomfield (who died of cancer during Mervyn's four years at Orient) he also had two other fellow former Irons for company in Billy Jennings and Tommy Taylor. "With those two, plus Peter Taylor, Ralph Coates, Ian Moores, Bill Roffey and John Chiedozie, we had a decent side for the first two years I was there. Jimmy's footballing philosophy was the same as Ron's. Stan Bowles also played for us for a time, which was an interesting experience!"

In some respects Mervyn was surprised to find himself playing alongside Taylor again in a division below the top tier. He says: "Tommy Taylor should have been an England defender. He had everything – a bit of pace, decent in the air, very good on the ball and he was strong. I don't think he ever fulfilled his real potential – and the same can be said of Kevin Lock, who took Bobby Moore's place. He was a very cultured defender. Both Tommy and Kevin should have gone on to have enjoyed very long and successful careers."

Mervyn, who was appointed club captain at Orient in 1982, admits he found the prospect of his return to Upton Park as the O's keeper "quite intimidating". He says: "We once played against West Ham (New Year's Day, 1980), on a pitch of ice, and got beaten 4-0. I must admit, I probably threw two in!

"I can't remember getting a bad reception from the West Ham fans when I played against them for Orient but the reception I did remember from them was the one I got when I came back here with Leeds (October 7, 1989). Vinnie Jones scored the only goal of the game and I received a fabulous reception – well, I did until Vinnie's goal, and then I got slaughtered!" he laughs.

Mervyn under pressure from Billy Bonds on his return to Upton Park as a player for Leyton Orient in April 1980.

"It is always nice to be appreciated by the fans when you go back to a club that you thought you had served well for a period of time."

After 170 league appearances for Leyton Orient, Day left East London and started his move northwards by joining Aston Villa for a £15,000 fee in August 1983. He played 30 games for the Villains before moving on to Leeds 18 months later, in a £30,000 transfer.

He made more appearances for Leeds United (268 league) than any of his four other regular clubs, so does he perhaps look back on his eight-and-a-half seasons at Elland Road with more satisfaction than his mixed experiences at Upton Park?

"They were two different eras. In terms of footballing success, I had three of four unbelievable years at West Ham . . . winning the FA Cup, Young-Player-of-the-Year, Cup Winners' Cup final, four England under-23 caps and being in four different senior England squads (under Don Revie).

Although Mervyn has been frank here in reflecting on the more negative periods of his early career, the brilliance and maturity he showed at such a young age for a keeper in his first few seasons should not be underestimated.

"Leeds was also a good time for me because of the people involved and the fact that we achieved something by getting the club back up into the top division. I enjoyed playing and living in Leeds and I was their player-of-the-year a couple of times."

After leaving Leeds in the summer of 1993, brief loan spells at Luton Town (four league games) and Sheffield United (just one) followed and then it was on to Carlisle United in the summer of '93 for another 16 league outings to take his total tally to 683. A knee injury forced him to hang up his gloves at the age of 39 and concentrate fully on developing his coaching career that had been initiated by Howard Wilkinson at Elland Road.

"I have to say, John Lyall was an excellent coach and most of my philosophies have been based on what Ron and John taught me in my early playing days," says Mervyn.

"At West Ham – certainly when I played in the youth team under Bill Lansdowne – us keepers were always encouraged to play outfield, to actually use our feet. Some of the drills we did back then are still used today. The pass-and-move philosophy has always been part of West Ham."

Explaining his introduction to coaching, he continued: "In my last two years at Leeds, I'd been player-coach. Howard Wilkinson wanted me to coach the goalkeepers, as well as play, and in my last season there he asked me to come on the coaching side properly, although still play occasionally.

Mervyn with Alan Curbishley during their turbulent 20-month managerial return to the club between 2006-08.

"I then became assistant manager to Mick Wadsworth at Carlisle. A bad knee forced me to pack up playing after about 18 games and around two-and-a-half years after I went up there, I took over as manager.

"I had about 21 months as Carlisle manager and I'm glad I did it," said Mervyn, who won promotion from Division Three to the second tier at the first attempt and also claimed the 1997 Auto Windscreens Shield. "It was nice to lead the team out at Wembley," he added.

He was later dismissed in bizarre circumstances. While just about every manager goes into the job knowing they will inevitably be sacked one day in the future, not many find themselves replaced by . . . their chairman! But that's what happened to Mervyn when egocentric businessman Michael Knighton decided to put himself in charge of Carlisle in September 1997. Knighton had first entered football infamy earlier in the decade as the man who juggled a football across the turf at Old Trafford before admitting that he didn't have enough money to buy Manchester United.

"That was a very interesting experience," says a rueful Mervyn. "He sacked me six games into the season, appointed himself as manager . . . and managed to get the club relegated! When you own the club, you can do whatever you want. But it was a good learning experience for me in managing people.

Among the best known players under Mervyn's brief management tenure at Brunton Park were Matt Jansen and Rory Delap, who both progressed to the Premier League.

After Carlisle, Mervyn spent the next eight months as goalkeeping coach at Everton, under Howard Kendall, before joining Alan Curbishley at Charlton Athletic in 1998.

"I'd been offered the job as Alan's assistant at Charlton in 1995 but I think Richard Murray had just taken over as chairman and trying to finalise a contract with him was very hard work. They wanted me to come back down to London but didn't want to pay any of my removal costs from Leeds, so it didn't happen then and Les Reed joined Alan instead. It was three years later, when Les moved on to the FA, that I eventually went to Charlton."

Although Day and Curbishley were team-mates at West Ham in the early 70s, their friendship didn't really develop until they were reunited as players at Aston Villa in the early 80s "We didn't mix in the same social circles when we played for West Ham, because Alan is a little younger than me," says Mervyn. "We really got to know each other well at Villa, where we spent around 18 months together before I moved on to Leeds and he joined Charlton. Every time Alan was up north he'd come and stay with us, and vice-versa, so our wives got to know each other well."

Once managers have had a taste of going it alone, they are very reluctant to serve as a No.2 in an assistant role, but that has never concerned Mervyn. Explaining his decision to work with Curbs at The Valley for eight years, he said: "Charlton had just gone into the Premier League and that's the place to be. I wanted to see how Alan and I worked together and to be honest, it's gone very well."

Asked what different character traits he and Curbishley possess, Day added: "My wife would say the reason our working relationship has worked so well because Alan's a Scorpio – the same as her – and I'm a Cancerian.

"Alan can be quite fiery at times and very strong. I'm probably the one who is more for pouring oil on troubled waters, and try and work towards a more diplomatic solution to a problem."

Mervyn spoke to *EX* soon after he and Alan Curbishley returned to Upton Park in December 2006, following the sacking of Alan Pardew. The Irons old boys and their players pulled off a miraculous escape from relegation at the end of their first season and, despite a catalogue of injuries, guided the team to a respectable 10th place in the Premier League in their first full season back at the Boleyn in 2007-08.

But the new season was just four games old when Curbishley – and Mervyn – resigned after a dispute with the Hammers' board over the sale of players at the end of the August transfer window. If Curbs decides to return to management in the future, it's fair to assume that Mervyn will once again be by his friend's side . . .

In the meantime, Mervyn and his wife, former nurse Moira, live in a small village in Hertfordshire. They have a daughter, Rebecca, and sons Richard and James.

As with so many other former players we have interviewed for *EX*, and despite the circumstances surrounding his sudden departure from the club in September 2008, Mervyn will probably always have Hammers in his heart.

He says: "West Ham has always been my club. The way I was treated by the people here when my father died will always stay with me. Those sort of life-defining moments are always important, so wherever I was in football terms after that, West Ham's was always the result I looked for first."

Keith Robson, one of the most wholehearted characters to ever pull on the claret-and-blue, is seen (above) celebrating his goal in the ECWC final at Heysel and (left) in 2006 with an autographed programme from that classic match.

Chapter 14

HEYSEL REVISITED

To mark the 30th anniversary of West Ham's last major European final appearance, EX's Tim Crane sent a DVD recording of the ECWC final against Anderlecht to each of the Hammers' players. After viewing the 4-2 defeat for the first time since that thrilling night at the Heysel Stadium in Brussels, this is what they had to say . . .

What recollections do you have from the earlier rounds of the competition and the build up to the 1976 European Cup Winners' Cup final?

Keith Robson

Scored four goals during the campaign, including one in both the semi-final and final.

Even though I scored in the final, my greatest memory is of the goal against Eintracht Frankfurt in the semi-final, second leg. I remember the first leg of the semi in Frankfurt, because I missed a sitter on my right foot and Graham Paddon scored a 35-yarder – a great goal.

There were atrocious weather conditions the night of the return leg and we had our backs against the wall, having lost 2-1 in Germany. Eintracht were really the best side in the competition. Anyway, I was lucky enough to get a through ball from Trevor Brooking and as I was running towards the goal, the ball seemed to hit a divot and came behind me – and as it did I had to swivel round. I remember thinking, 'I've got nothing to lose'. I knew I had to get it out of the mud and I absolutely leathered it and it flew straight in the top corner. The pitch was so heavy that night but when I whacked it in the top corner I had never been so delighted in all my life. I think that beat the goal in the final for me. I was pleased for the supporters, because during that European run we had outstanding support all the way.

I used to room with Billy Jennings and we were all full of confidence, thinking we were going to win.

Tommy Taylor (left)

Centre-half who so nearly scored in the final.

In terms of preparation I seem to recall Bonzo coming over later because his mother-in-law had died and he arrived in a police wagon. After the game the police wagon took him back to the airport. We couldn't do anything for him, so we just had to do our best under the circumstances.

Alan Taylor (right)

Striker and second-half substitute for injured full-back Frank Lampard.

I had been very disappointed to miss out on both legs of the semi-final due to injury, which had probably cost me my place in the final. I was leading goalscorer that season so I was really despondent over not being picked for the final but, that said, I was probably not 100% fit. To be fair to John Lyall, it was a difficult decision because the boys had done ever so well in the semi-final against Eintracht Frankfurt and he probably wanted to stick by them in the final. However, I had scored twice against Ararat Erevan and again against Den Haag, and really wanted my place in the final.

Graham Paddon

Midfielder who scored one of the great forgotten West Ham goals against Eintracht Frankfurt in the semi final, first leg.

During that European campaign we turned Upton Park into a fortress. We intimidated people and sides like Ararat Erevan and Den Haag had never seen anything like it. Eintracht Frankfurt were the best team West Ham played while I was there and it was a real achievement to beat them. Ron Greenwood and John Lyall were great men and expected to be playing in European finals.

Pat Holland (right)

Selected instead of Alan Taylor to start the final and scored the opening goal.

I think there was a bit of conflict over my selection between Ron and John because John took me to one side before the away trip to Frankfurt and asked me if I was fit to play. I said I was and he told me not to go and let him down. So I think John fought my corner for both semi-final games and also the final, because Alan Taylor was back from injury by then and was telling John that he needed to know if he was playing. But John kept telling Alan that he didn't know yet and that's when I knew they were going to stick with me. You would never have got John to admit to this but that is my opinion.

I would say that I've never experienced an atmosphere in football like that during the Eintracht Frankfurt semi-final – and I include the FA Cup final in that.

Billy Jennings (left)

Striker who scored two goals in Den Haag to bring West Ham back from the brink of elimination.

The goals I scored against Den Haag were a personal highlight and I remember Ron saying at half-time that we needed to go out and put a bit of pride back into the club. It would have been easy to have rolled over in the second-half but we were a side that could always score goals and I got on the end of a couple of crosses to add respectability to the scoreline. I wasn't the biggest of players but I was sharp, with a decent first touch, and absolutely delighted to give the team a chance, which we took in the second leg.

Rob Jenkins

West Ham's physiotherapist for more than 20 years.

It's funny the little things you remember. I recall our game at Den Haag when the referee kept stopping play to tell our players to literally pull their socks up!

I would say the greatest contribution Billy Jennings ever made to the club came in the second-half at Den Haag. That brought us back into it and we beat them in the second leg. Now if you have got that home leg on tape you'll get something out of Frank Lampard (who has so far declined our request for an interview), because he scored an absolute humdinger from about 30 yards.

Graham Paddon's left foot in Frankfurt was sweet but the greatest goal in that campaign was Robbo's, when he swivelled and hit it. He'd done f***-all in the game 'til then and he absolutely belted it with his left. Well, he couldn't kick with his right foot!

How do you rate your own performance in the final?

Robson

From memory, we really dominated the game initially but having watched the tape, I must say that Anderlecht were also playing with all guns blazing. When you look at all their players, they had a really good side with the likes of Rensenbrink, Van der Elst and Haan.

But I really think we controlled the first-half and once we scored I thought things could only get better. Trevor (Brooking) hit the crossbar and Billy (Jennings) had a couple of good chances. Billy was spring-heeled and was really good in the air. Regarding my own performance, I think the occasion got the better of me and I probably wasn't as fit as I could've been.

On the night I came out fired up, because I had missed out on the FA Cup final, but in all seriousness I was a bit disappointed with myself – I'd had a serious injury which kept me out for three months. John Lyall said to me that if I came through a reserve game at Highbury, I'd have a good chance of playing. I loved playing with Billy – he was good at getting on the end of crosses and in the quarter-final in Den Haag he got on the end of my crosses to get us back into the tie at 4-2. Bill was a great player.

My goal in the final came after we swapped play from one side to the other. Trevor cut inside and whipped the ball over with his right foot – and I just ran near-post and flicked it in. Even though I scored a goal and ran my socks off, and didn't make any mistakes, I have to be hard on myself because I hate losing.

Tommy Taylor

I thought my performance on the night was all right. In fact, I didn't realise I touched the ball that many times until I watched the DVD. Another thing I'd forgotten was the amount of chances we had early on. I also kept thinking: 'Cor, wasn't I skinny!'

The chance I had in the second-half was hit as sweet as a nut and they usually go in or fly over the crossbar. A couple of feet either way and it would have just sailed in. The keeper did ever so well to get his hand to it. It's funny, I played with that same keeper for Beerscot, a club in Belgium. He always used to say: "I have the gold one, Tommy."

John McDowell

Utility man who only missed out on the Den Haag games throughout the whole campaign.

I've always held quite vivid recollections of the game and thought we played very well and were a tight unit in the first half. I felt comfortable and not under any pressure. Even when we conceded on half-time, we were still confident because Anderlecht had not carved out any chances of their own.

I felt my own performance was greatly affected by the half time substitutions. John asked me to switch to left-back from right-midfield and although I played in most positions during my time at West Ham, it is very difficult to switch from right-midfield to left-back. I felt that Pat Holland, Keith Coleman and myself had worked well together and nullified the threat of Rensenbrink and Van der Elst down our right side. I remember saying to John at half-time that I didn't want to play left-back and that I saw it as a straight swap with Kevin Lock replacing the injured Frank Lampard. Instead, I had to go left-back, Patsy was moved into the middle and Alan Taylor took Patsy's place on the right. With hindsight, this left us open in midfield and Rensenbrink and Van der Elst had the run of the park.

Paddon

On watching the performance for the first time in 30 years, I was struck by just how well we'd played. We were much better than I remember and for a side playing against a team who were, in effect, playing at home, I felt we deserved to win. Personally, I am happy with my performance.

Jennings

I didn't think I had that good a game before I saw the tape. But when I watched it, I was happy with my involvement in the match, although I would've loved to have scored a goal and was disappointed not to finish the early chances that came my way.

From my perspective, I'd only been at the club a year or so and had come from a lower level (Watford), so it was such a big thing for me to play in that European campaign.

Holland

I thought my performance in the first-half was disastrous. I was simply not with it and I was watching the DVD saying: 'Get your finger out!'. Even though I scored, there was just such a lack of confidence that I was getting angry watching it. I'd never been a confident player, or person for that matter. I wanted to be liked by the crowd so much but I never was and I remember Ron saying to me as a kid: "You'll have one enemy in your life and that is going to be you," because I had no self-belief whatsoever.

In the second half, with the changes John was forced to make, I moved into the centre of midfield and had a much better time of it, because: a) I'd scored; and b) I didn't have the crowd to worry about anymore. There is one instance where I chase back 80 yards to take the ball off their striker's foot and I thought to myself: 'You

Pat Holland latches on to a header by Billy Jennings, who watches the ball cross the line.

have done really well there but, overall, it wasn't a vintage Patsy Holland performance. In fact my dad, who was a lovely man, said to me after the game: "I've seen you play better." However, he was delighted with the goal which, as you know, came from a set piece – and that's something we never practiced. The philosophy was, the nearest player to the flag took the corner. Anyway, Billy Jennings got up and headed it and I finished it off with my left foot – a great finish.

But then a strange thing happened, Brooking, who was next to me, walked away – and I would love to know why he didn't come over and say 'well done'. I was the type of player who would celebrate any goal scored by my team-mates, regardless of how well I was playing, so it amazed me that Brooking didn't trot the few yards to pat me on the back. He'll probably say it was too far to go but I would love to know the truth . . .

Regarding the penalty, I came alongside Rensenbrink with the intention of hooking the ball and coming out with it. I was so confident I could do this. I get my toe on the ball, push it forward and then he topples over my toe. But if you look at the tape, he doesn't appeal for the penalty and tries to go on again. It wasn't a penalty, because I did actually win the ball.

Who do you think performed well among your team-mates?

Robson

I don't think we played to our full potential – we certainly didn't match the performance level of the semi-final against Eintracht. Ron Greenwood had watched Anderlecht play Wrexham in the quarter-final and before the game he said that if we performed to our best we would beat them. We had a good team, with excellent players, but I think a few of us went missing on the night.

Bonzo was a different class. He was taking the ball all the way through and opening up the play. If there was ever anybody you wanted behind you it would be Billy Bonds. He always gave 150% and he was the driving force behind the team that night.

Their keeper was exceptional in the second-half and thwarted the four good chances we had to go in front. As the game wore on we pushed further forward and left open spaces at the back for Van der Elst and Rensenbrink to exploit. It was make or break for us and the gamble didn't pay off.

I think Frank would be the first to say that he made a strange decision with the backpass that gifted Anderlecht their equaliser before half-time. It should have been a case of 'when in doubt, put it in row Z' but Frank knocked it short for Rensenbrink to pounce on. Soon after that Frank had to leave the game after pulling his groin and we had to change our whole system by bringing on Alan Taylor, which left us open at the back. It's easy to say now but I would have brought on Kevin Lock to keep it tight at the back.

It was two good football sides playing the game how it should be played. If we played each other 10 times we would probably have won five each – we were similar types of teams.

Tommy Taylor

Patsy Holland played hard. He did the full-back's job as well as going forward. We were a tight unit up until their equaliser. Frank just under-hit a backpass, that's all it was. Mervyn (Day) didn't stand a chance and apart from that moment, he hadn't had anything to do.

I still say to this day that we changed three people at half-time instead of just changing one.

Technically, they were very good but if we'd kept it to 1-0 at half-time, we would have beaten them.

The penalty was a bad decision – Patsy never touched him. I can accept it when a team is better than you and you get beat, but it wasn't the case against Anderlecht. They could've had no complaints if we'd won.

I loved Ron Greenwood and thought he was brilliant. Not taking anything away from John Lyall, he inherited a very good team with talented youngsters coming through. Ron knew everything about Anderlecht before we played them – what they ate, how they trained, absolutely everything. He'd got Bill Nicholson involved as well and I am fairly certain Bill Nick was in the dressing room with us as well. Everything was fine at half-time. We knew we were playing well and we just wanted to get out there and carry on playing the same way.

Paddon

I felt Billy Bonds had a good game and was the best of our lot, while Trevor didn't have one of his better days. Billy was the best I ever played with – I only played three times with Bobby Moore. I had 10 years at Norwich and was lucky enough to play alongside Martin Peters but West Ham are always number one in my heart.

They had some smashing players and to play with people like Bonds, Brooking and Lampard was a privilege.

Jennings

From the tape it's obvious that West Ham were equipped to play European football. We played from the back and it is noticeable how Tommy and Billy ran out from defence with the ball. Similarly, John McDowell and Frank Lampard were comfortable with the ball, running upfield and forcing the play. Anderlecht were one of the best teams around at the time and Belgian football was far superior then than it is today, but we took the game to them and the way we were playing we looked like scoring a second before Frank's injury.

Regarding the substitution at half time, I think John thought we could score goals against them and we certainly had our chances. John would have seen Alan Taylor as a catalyst for more attacking play.

Holland

I don't think there were any outstanding performances in our team but there was a lot of industry. Robbo had a bright start, while Paddon saw a lot of the ball, as did Bonzo. I thought Trevor didn't really get into the game like we know he could do.

On a separate matter, I would love to have seen Bonzo go up against Keane or Viera in their prime, because for me there would've been only one winner.

Do you have any memories of events immediately following the final?

McDowell

At the final whistle I was totally devastated and felt total disappointment. I didn't enjoy the reception as I really felt I deserved a winner's medal. I seem to recall a few high jinx on the coach back to the ground involving Tommy Taylor, Keith Robson and Graham Paddon but, to be fair, it was quite a low time for us all and any pick-me-up was welcome.

Jenkins

My recollections of the trip are more to do with the home-coming rather than going over to Belgium. British Airways gave us a champagne flight so we were all a bit tipsy by the time we got on the coach back to the ground – and my priority was to get Frank to Harley Street to see a specialist. Well, the directors and their wives were all on the coach as well as the players and their wives. Now, Tommy Taylor and Keith Robson put on a tape of Peter Cook and Dudley Moore's infamous Derek and Clive with the most disgusting language you could ever imagine. It caused quite a furore and I remember Ernie Gregory telling them to turn it off and that it was disgraceful. There was quite a to do over it – it was actually discussed at a board meeting, although nothing came of it. Tommy stayed at the club for another five years, so the directors weren't too upset with him.

Keith Robson and Pat Holland, our two goalscorers, embrace as John McDowell is about to join the party.

Robson

You don't realise just how upset you are until you come off at the end. You think about all those supporters that went over and you can't stop asking yourself: 'How did we lose?'. Then you have to shake hands with all the Anderlecht players even though you don't really feel like it. I was so low after the game that I wanted to give my medal away to Peter Brabrook's son, Wayne. I did give my shirt away but now I think I should have kept it and put it in a frame for my son, Thomas. But you can't turn the clock back. Tony McDonald always says I'm the last Hammer to score in a major European final and I'd never really thought of it like that.

Holland

I remember the wives coming in the shower area after the game, although I don't know why they were there!

Another thing I remember was the home-coming, which was in stark contrast to the FA Cup final a year earlier. After we returned to the ground following the defeat against Anderlecht, there were about 20 fans waiting for us. Nobody is interested in losers. I remember that distinctly, because my mum and dad were there, along with our dog, Patch, who rolled over when he saw me!

Would you like to recount any anecdotes from the 1975-76 European campaign?

Paddon

Before the first leg of the semi-final in Germany, Bobby Ferguson bet me a bottle of whisky that I wouldn't score. So after scoring after eight minutes, I went over to him and reminded him of the bet. To his credit, he paid up.

The finest goal of my career came at Molineux in the same season, when we beat Wolves 1-0. It was a blustery day and I remember taking the ball into their half and thinking I'm going to have a go – and the ball flew in the net. My good friend – and best man – Willie Carr was in the Wolves line-up that day, so it has kept me in good stead down the years.

Alan Taylor

I remember all the players' wives lost their bags on the way over and they weren't returned until much later.

Holland

I roomed with Johnny Ayris before the final and I said if I scored I was going to do an impression of Ken Dodd and his catchphrase, 'How Tickled I am'. When I scored, I ran over to the bench and I could see both Johnny and Kevin Lock laughing because they knew what it was all about.

Another thing I recall came during a lull in the game. I remember seeing a Ferris wheel outside the Heysel stadium, full of West Ham fans who couldn't get in. They were just going round and round on the wheel, watching the game in snatches.

Jenkins

The DVD reveals you wearing a shocking red tracksuit. Why?

That tracksuit was made by Gola. West Ham had overlooked me in their preparations for the trip and I didn't get a West Ham tracksuit. Gola rang me and asked me to wear their tracksuit, saying they would give me 200 pounds to wear it, so I smuggled it into the dressing room because I wasn't on any bonus for the game. I remember waiting until the last minute before putting it on and Ron Greenwood asked my why I was wearing it. I had to bluff my way through an excuse because, as you can see on the DVD, it's a ridiculous tracksuit.

Sadly, in November 2007, 18 months after these interviews were conducted, Graham Paddon died at his Norfolk home, aged 57.

Chapter 15

GEOFF**PIKE**

"If I'd scored it might have sent my wife into labour – she was sitting in the stands, eight months pregnant with our first child! We had a nice evening after the game and taking the Cup back to the town hall was fantastic"

EVERY successful team needs one – a hard-working, unselfish and determined midfielder who goes about his job with the minimum of fuss and always with the good of the team as his priority, content to allow more artistic team-mates to express themselves and grab the headlines.

The great Liverpool side of the 80s had Ronnie Whelan, Manchester United's dominance in the 90s was driven on by Roy Keane and Jose Mourinho's successful Chelsea team were hugely influenced by the barely-noticed Claude Makelele.

For West Ham United, in our hugely successful period of the early-80s, that role was filled by Geoff Pike – the archetypal 'local boy done good' who progressed through the youth ranks to become a vital influence in an era that generated an FA Cup final triumph, a second division title success, a League Cup final appearance, an impressive European campaign and then a highest-ever league placing for the club, all in the space of six years.

While the likes of Trevor Brooking, Alan Devonshire, David Cross, Paul Goddard, Tony Cottee and Frank McAvennie often earned the plaudits and the recognition for the victories that led to those memorable achievements, Pike's tireless commitment and willingness to sacrifice his own personal gain for the good of the team meant he was just as important a member of John Lyall's side.

However, that isn't to say the Clapton-born midfielder was nothing more than a 'water carrier' who simply won tackles in his own half and then gave the odd sideways pass. A top-class ball player in his own right, a record of 41 goals in 367 appearances proved that Geoff could also be relied on to weigh in with six or seven every season – many of which will be remembered by those who witnessed them as magnificent strikes that would grace any Premier League ground today.

And behind Pike, the player, was a genuine Hammers fan, born into an East London family, who grew up following the club as a football-mad youngster in Essex and saw his love for the claret and blue develop when he arrived at Upton Park as a schoolboy.

"I was born in Clapton but we moved out to South Ockendon in Essex when I was around nine-months-old," recalls Geoff. "Mum and Dad moved around in the area for the first few years but then settled in a house when I was around four or five and they are still there to this day.

The Birmingham City defender can't take it as jubilant Geoff (4) is about to jump into the arms of Billy Jennings and Alan Devonshire after scoring in the 2-2 draw against the Blues in April 1977.

"Everyone in the family were West Ham supporters – grandparents, aunts and uncles, cousins – and my association with the club goes back as far as I can remember. Supporting the Hammers was just the natural thing to do.

"I stood on the terraces as a kid with my dad, Alan, and I followed the team every week once I started training at the club. An abiding memory is the FA Cup replay against Hereford that was played on a Monday afternoon because of the power cuts at the time. I must admit, I bunked off school that day and went to the game with my dad, as did a lot of other kids!"

Having played local football for Rippleway Thurrock and Romford-based team Gidea Park Rangers, young Geoff was beginning to show outstanding promise, even playing in an age-group above himself and, thanks to the efforts of his dad and a school teacher, was given the chance to display his skills in front of John Lyall, the man who would eventually become his manager at the highest level.

"My old school teacher, Mr Davies, had got in touch with West Ham initially, because I was playing in the school team at the age of eight when most of the other boys were 10 and 11," he reveals. "Anyway, when I was 10, my dad just took me down to Chadwell Heath one evening and we were met by John Lyall, who coached the youngsters then. He said that I was actually a bit young but could join in anyway. So I did and it all went from there. I went back every Tuesday and Thursday night until I signed apprentice forms at 15.

"That was a dream come true but, for a time, I wasn't sure it was going to happen. The club had never made it obvious to me that I would be taken on and I'd gone down to Ipswich Town for a week's trial during one of the half-term holidays in my final year as a schoolboy. The following week, Bobby Robson phoned me three times telling me that he wanted me to sign and that he expected me to be playing in his first team within 18 months, so it was quite a carrot that was being dangled.

"My first love was West Ham, though, and I went back to the chief scout, Wally St Pier, and told him that Bobby Robson had been on the phone all week asking me to sign, and that I needed to know if West Ham were going to offer me an apprenticeship because otherwise I would go to Ipswich. That might have tipped the balance, because West Ham then decided they would take a chance on me and I started full-time at the club.

"Funnily enough, we played in the FA Youth Cup final a couple of years later and lost to Ipswich! They had the likes of Terry Butcher, Eric Gates and David Geddis, and I could well have been a part of that group had Bobby Robson got his way. For me, though, there was nowhere else I wanted to go, because West Ham was my club."

Having starred at youth team level and more than held his own playing for the reserves, it wasn't long before Geoff was knocking on the first team door. In the midst of an injury crisis at Upton Park in the spring of 1976, Geoff was handed his senior debut as a half-time substitute in a 2-1 defeat at Birmingham City, having already travelled with the squad to Den Haag for the European Cup Winners' Cup quarter-final, first leg.

Recalling his first experience in the claret and blue shirt, Geoff reveals: "I still haven't forgiven Yilmaz Orhan for denying me a full debut that day! Because of the injuries we had, it was between Yilmaz and me for the final place in the team. He was carrying an injury but told John Lyall he was fit to avoid missing out. Anyway, he limped around the pitch for the first 45 minutes and I had to come on at half-time.

"I didn't do badly, I came narrowly close to scoring, but my most vivid memory is being marked by big Kenny Burns. I actually caught him on the top of the foot as he cleared a ball on edge of box and thought to myself: 'Oh dear, here we go'.

"To Kenny's credit, though, he obviously knew I was just a young kid and took pity on me. If I'd been a seasoned pro, I would probably have had a few stud marks down the back of my legs!"

Having narrowly escaped a painful initiation at St. Andrew's, Geoff went on to make a further two substitute appearances before the end of the season, away at Leeds three days after his debut and then at Ipswich in a crushing 4-0 defeat. However, despite making the first team breakthrough, Geoff admits his Upton Park future was far from guaranteed and, when Ron Greenwood suggested he went to the USA that summer to gain further experience of first team football, it was seen by many at Upton Park as a make or break step.

"Although I'd made my debut, I wasn't progressing in the way I wanted to – wasn't pushing for a regular first team place," he says. "I knew the following season would be my last chance to prove myself and I needed something to give me that little boost.

"Ron asked me if I wanted to go over to the States for the summer to get some

Geoff celebrates a goal as Manchester City's Joe Corrigan and Mike Doyle (4) are both left grounded.

experience playing senior football in front of big crowds. It was around the time they were trying to get the North American Soccer League started up and a lot of star players were going over there on big contracts.

"I said I'd give it a go and went over to play for a team called Hertford Bicentennials. In my very first game we played against the New York Cosmos, who had Pele – and I managed to take the ball off him, so that's a nice little claim to fame!

"It turned out to be a great experience and I went on to play against people like Franz Beckenbauer and Eusebio, as well as Harry Redknapp and Geoff Hurst at Seattle Sounders.

"I actually went out there again the following summer (1977) and played for Connecticut Bicentennials this time. I was earning double the money that West Ham were paying me, the expenses were next to nothing because the house and car were provided, and that enabled me to save up the money for me and Pauline to put down a deposit on our first house the following year."

Upon Geoff's return from the States first time around, prior to the 1976-77 campaign, Lyall laid down the gauntlet for the 20-year-old to push on at senior level. And boosted by the experience on the other side of the Atlantic, he responded.

Handed his full debut in a memorable 5-3 win over Tottenham Hotspur in early November, Geoff went on to make 20 league appearances, scoring an impressive six goals along the way – the most important of which arrived on the final day of the campaign as Hammers, having been entrenched in a relegation battle for months, secured their top flight status at the eleventh hour with a 4-2 win over Manchester United.

Despite missing a penalty just before the break, Pike fired in a stunning strike just eight minutes after the restart to put Hammers in the driving seat in front of a packed Upton Park – a moment he admits "still makes the hairs on the back of my neck stand up when I think about it."

Sadly, the final-day rescue act turned out to be only a temporary reprieve, as Hammers failed to heed the warning signs and slipped out of the first division the following season for the first time since 1932. Having spent another three months playing in the States the previous summer, Geoff admits that the non-stop action eventually took its toll, making it a difficult year for both himself and the team.

"After two consecutive summers in America, tiredness really set in that year and it was hard going for me. I really needed a rest but things weren't going well for the team and it was a frustrating time all round. I was in and out of the team, not performing very well, and it all ended with relegation.

"Saying that, you can't even begin to compare relegation then with what it means now. The possibility of players leaving wasn't an issue – it was more a case of 'who are we going to get in?' rather than who would be going out.

"Of course, John made changes, shifted some players out and brought some in but that was just the natural rebuilding process. Despite going down, he still went out and spent big money to bring new players in. Alan Devonshire blossomed into a superb player, Ray Stewart, David Cross and Stuart Pearson all had a lot to offer and we paid a world record fee for a goalkeeper in Phil Parkes – who I really believe was the catalyst for our success that followed. Phil was a phenomenal goalkeeper, the players had complete confidence in him and he very rarely made a mistake."

Having been restricted to just 15 league and cup appearances in the 1978-79 campaign, Geoff bounced back to become a regular fixture on the right-hand side of midfield the following year and kept his place as Hammers progressed in the FA Cup to reach their second final in five years. Despite playing in the memorable semi-final replay win over Everton at Elland Road, though, he admits that, right up until the day before the final, he was never 100 per cent sure that he would be making his first-ever appearance at Wembley Stadium.

"No-one knew the team until the day before the game, but I hadn't done myself any harm by scoring in a 4-0 win against Charlton on the previous Monday night, and I think that might have tipped the scales in my favour," says Geoff.

"I was probably the last name on the team-sheet and it was unfortunate for Paul Brush, who had to miss out after playing in the semi-final, but the justification was that we won and it turned out to be a fantastic day, probably the most memorable of my career.

"I can remember coming out of the tunnel to hear the deafening roar of the crowd and I was also the first player to have a shot in the game – the ball was cut back from the left and I hit a left-foot effort that Pat Jennings saved.

"The other memorable incident, that still grinds at me now when I think about it, was when I had the chance to chip Jennings in the last 10 minutes. John had said beforehand that he often came a long way off his line and was vulnerable to the chip, but as I got to the ball some 20 yards out, I just whacked it and it flew wide for a goal-kick. As soon as I'd hit it, I remember John's words and looked up to see Pat eight yards off his line!

"Mind you, if I'd scored it might have sent my wife into labour – she was sitting in the stands, eight months pregnant with our first child! We had a nice evening after the game and taking the cup back to the town hall was fantastic. Two weeks later, our son Anthony was born and I've got some lovely pictures at home of him and our niece sitting in the cup. I don't know how, but I managed to take the trophy home for an evening and it was nice for the family to be able to enjoy the experience."

Despite playing his part during the triumphant conclusion to the 1979-80 campaign, Geoff certainly wasn't prepared for events that were to occur the following season, as a sudden change of position led to him enjoying the most successful and prolific season of his career.

"I'd played on the right-hand side of midfield in the FA Cup final but then, because of injuries, I played up front in the Charity Shield against Liverpool and didn't play particularly well – I got taken off with about 15 minutes remaining and didn't enjoy the experience at all.

"I thought it was going to be another one of those seasons and then came the turning point. We were playing a pre-season friendly against Charlton and Paul Allen was injured, so I went into the centre of midfield. John kept it like that for a few friendlies and, all of a sudden, it just seemed to click. We stuck by it, with me and Trevor in the middle, Dev on the left and Patsy Holland on the right, and I managed to find a new level of consistency because of it."

Even the word consistency doesn't quite do justice to his personal achievements during that record-breaking campaign. Geoff started EVERY single one of the 42 league, 12 domestic cup and six European matches played by the Hammers – an astonishing 60 games in total and a feat only matched by goalkeeper Phil Parkes. Indeed, long before compulsory squad numbers were issued, the claret and blue number 11 shirt could have had Pike written on it that season, such was his ever-present form.

Man-of-the-match in the eventful League Cup final against Liverpool in mid-March, Geoff then went on to be named runner-up behind Parkes in the Hammer of the Year award and finished the promotion-winning campaign with seven goals from his holding-role in midfield – a tally that some attacking midfielders would be happy with in the modern game.

Reflecting on that never-to-be-forgotten season, he is understandably proud of his contribution. "It was quite simply a fantastic season and it was a joy to play in that side. The key was that we had a settled team for virtually the entire season and everyone knew their jobs when we went out on the pitch.

"It was a case of 'how many we going to win by?' rather than 'are we going to win?' The confidence was fantastic and opposing teams came to Upton Park dreading the experience. That's not being big-headed, it just frightened the life out of them seeing what we had.

"It was capped off for me by being named runner-up in the Hammer of the Year award. To be recognised by the fans in that way was a wonderful honour considering some of the talent we had in the side that year, and it's something I've always been extremely proud of."

Buoyed by the confidence resulting from their promotion success, Hammers enjoyed a fantastic start to life back in the first division and were top of the league going into October. Although the 'title charge' fell away after Christmas, the team were well on their way to re-establishing themselves in the top flight and Geoff carried on his consistent form, making 34 league appearances that season.

With the likes of Trevor Brooking, Frank Lampard and Billy Bonds reaching the

Mark Ward, Tony Cottee and George Parris are the first to congratulate Geoff on his celebrated FA Cup goal at Old Trafford that helped defeat Manchester United in the quarter-final of that memorable 1985-86 season.

twilight years of their careers, Lyall faced a mini-rebuilding task in the early 80s that was boosted by the emergence of young talents such as Tony Cottee, Alan Dickens and George Parris.

The arrival of Frank McAvennie and Mark Ward in the summer of 1985 then provided the Hammers boss with the missing pieces in the jigsaw that was to fit together perfectly throughout that memorable campaign – although Geoff was to be denied a starring role after serious injury struck for the first time in his career.

"I missed the first half of the 1985-86 season because of a lower back problem that the doctors couldn't get to the bottom of," he recalls. "Eventually, they found a hole in my stomach muscle the size of 50 pence piece. They couldn't close it up because that would have restricted movement, so they put a piece of mesh in and I spent 12 weeks working the stomach muscles to build them up so they would grow around the mesh.

"I then picked up a knee injury towards end of season, so ended up playing only 10 league games. Neil Orr did very well in my place and it would have been difficult to dislodge him anyway."

Despite his lack of action, Geoff did manage to produce one personal highlight among the Boys of 86 – a memorable headed goal from the edge of the penalty area at Old Trafford to send Hammers on their way to a memorable 2-0 FA Cup fifth round replay victory over Manchester United.

"People still talk to me about that goal now," he smiles. "Lots of other incidents and memories from my time at the club stick in my mind but the fans seem to remember that more than anything else. I don't mind – it's not a bad thing to score at Old Trafford, is it!"

Having seen injury problems restrict his involvement that year, Geoff was pushed further down the pecking order by the arrival of Stewart Robson and the emergence of a young Paul Ince the following season.

Granted a testimonial after 10 years of unstinting service, a claret and blue association lasting 21 years finally came to an end in the summer of 1987, when John Lyall agreed to let his loyal midfielder leave the club for a minimal fee.

After initial interest from Birmingham City, Geoff eventually sealed a £35,000 switch to third division Notts County, managed then by John Barnwell, who is now chairman of the League Managers' Association.

Handed a more attacking midfield role, he hit 15 goals in his first season at the County Ground as the Magpies came within a whisker of winning promotion, but things turned sour the following year when Barnwell was replaced by the infamous Neil Warnock.

"It was a shame, because the first couple of years were very enjoyable and we came close to winning promotion. Then John Barnwell was sacked and Neil Warnock came in, and that was the beginning of the end," says Geoff.

"He wanted to do things his own way and his first task was to get rid of myself, Garry Birtles and Gary Mills, three experienced guys who I can only assume he considered as a threat. Worse than that, he did it through the media rather than face to face, something I was very disappointed about, and we ended up having a big row – the only time in my entire career that I had fallen out with a manager. If only he'd

Geoff at home with his treasured FA Cup winners' medal and the shirt he wore in the 1980 final.

got to know us as players and people first, he might have realised that we could help him."

After leaving the County Ground in the summer of 1989, Geoff returned home and agreed to join Leyton Orient. After making a handful of appearances for the Os, a pelvic injury forced him to finally hang up the boots at the age of 35, and he was offered the post of youth team coach by the club after John Gorman left to join Glenn Hoddle at Swindon Town.

Following two years in charge of the youngsters at Brisbane Road, Geoff was suddenly relieved of his duties by manager Peter Eustace in 1993, leaving him out of work and out of football for the first time in his adult life. It was a situation that eventually forced him to go back to school at the age of 40 and seek a new career away from the game in order to support his family.

"When you come out of a coaching job, you go home expecting the phone to ring, but it doesn't," he admits. "I was going to games to try and build some contacts and set myself up for another job but it just didn't happen and in the end I started up a family business with my brother, Richard, who was a floor-layer. That took off and is still going strong after 12 years but I soon realised it wasn't for me and I left him and my dad to run it while I searched for a way back into the game.

"A friend suggested I go over to America to get involved in the coaching schools out there, so I gave that a go and, while I was over there I bumped into a guy called Simon East, who was a lecturer at East Berkshire College in Slough. He basically offered me a menial job at the college but said that, through staff development, I could gain teaching qualifications that would allow me to go into any college of further education and become a lecturer, as long as I knew the subject matter.

"There was nothing else in the pipeline so, at the age of 40, I went back to school and worked for three years to gain my teaching qualifications. I knew I needed to have something to fall back on should I not get back into football."

Geoff briefly worked part-time for the FA as a monitor of the Academy Centres of Excellence in the mid-90s, a role that led to a sad falling-out with West Ham after his report forced the club's centre into temporary closure. Thankfully, the relationship was repaired over the course of time and he is now a welcome visitor to the Chadwell Heath training in his role as a South-East Regional Coach for the PFA – a position he has now held for almost eight years.

"I had just been offered a full-time lecturing post by the college when I got a call from Jimmy Armfield, who was Head of Coaching at the PFA. I had been for an interview for a job there a couple of years previously, but hadn't got it, and he asked me if I was still interested in the position. I said 'yes' and went to meet him at Lancaster Gate. He then told me to go to Manchester the following week to meet the rest of the staff, so I went up on the train and came back driving the company car, with a company mobile phone in my pocket! I've been doing it ever since."

Popular pundit Geoff during his days in the local Romford studios of TIME FM.

Geoff's role at the PFA is to liaise with 14 clubs in the south-east – ranging from the likes of West Ham, Tottenham and Norwich City to Fulham, Brighton and Southend United – and ensure that the young Academy trainees gain their UEFA Level 2 coaching qualifications as part of their Scholarships – a system that all Football League clubs are required to follow. He also works with senior and ex-professionals who want to gain coaching qualifications of their own.

As holder of a UEFA Pro-licence – the highest coaching qualification in the country – Geoff would automatically be able to take any coaching or managerial position offered to him at any level of the game and, although he admits to missing the day-to-day involvement at a football club, there is only one job that would tempt him away from his current role.

"It's a difficult one, because you never lose the football bug and I do miss the day-to-day involvement of working for a football club. The problem is, once you are out of the club environment, it becomes harder to get back in. I would probably have to take a job at a lower division club, maybe on a lower salary than I am earning now, and it would also be a 24-hours-a-day, seven-days-a-week role. In my present job, I work Monday-to-Friday and on Saturday I can go and play golf with my mates or spend time with my wife and family. I've built a new career for myself now and I enjoy what I do.

"There is only one thing that would tempt me back into club football and that is the chance to work for West Ham. I always look for the result of Notts County and Orient, but West Ham is my team. The club is in my blood and always will be."

In addition to his full-time work for the PFA, Geoff has also made his mark as a football radio pundit in recent years. He co-hosted Romford-based TIME FM's popular Friday night 'Hammertime' show for a couple of years until the station's bosses, in their wisdom, decided to pull the plug on their coverage of West Ham at the end of the 2005-06 season.

PONY
WEST HAM UNITED F.C.
DAGENHAM
MOTORS

Chapter 16

STEVE**POTTS**

"He gave me my chance and guided me as a young player, and the fact that I went on to enjoy a long career with West Ham has a lot to do with John Lyall. He also made sure all his young players behaved in the right way, and he taught me a lot of values as a person"

IT'S a sad reflection on the lack of loyalty in football today that the chance of a youngster progressing through the youth ranks and going on to spend all of his professional career at the same club is now virtually non-existent.

It's therefore fair to suggest that Steve Potts will go down in history as one of the last players to achieve such a feat. After making his debut under John Lyall as a 17-year-old on New Year's Day 1985, the loyal defender went on to make nearly 500 appearances for the Hammers during the next 17 years.

He played under a total of five managers, won two Hammer-of-the-Year awards, captained the side in our inaugural season in the Premier League and famously scored the only goal of his entire career in a 7-1 win over Hull City in October 1990 – the kind of unique feat that guarantees legendary status in itself!

For 'Pottsy', though, it was never about scoring goals – more about stopping them. One of Hammers' most consistent defenders throughout the 90s, he went about his job in a quiet, efficient manner, and won plenty of admirers for the way he conducted himself on and off the field.

Now retired from playing after spending a year with local neighbours Dagenham & Redbridge following his departure from Upton Park in May 2002, Steve is still a regular visitor to the Boleyn Ground and was only too happy to look back on his long and distinguished career in the claret-and-blue…

Despite growing up in Essex, Steve actually began life on the other side of the Atlantic. Born in Hartford, Connecticut, on May 7, 1967, after his parents had emigrated to the USA a few years earlier, he now holds both American and British passports.

Thankfully, John and Jean Potts had always intended to move back to England, though, and settled back in Dagenham when Steve and his elder brother, Dave, were just toddlers.

Being so young when his family returned home, Steve has no recollection of life in the States – but the connection almost handed him a dream opportunity during his playing career, when it was claimed that he might be subject to a call-up by the US national team prior to them hosting the 1994 World Cup finals.

"They did make enquiries," recalls Steve, "but it never went any further because

Bubbles time! Steve (front left) with fellow members of Hammers' successful youth team of the early-80s. Others in the picture who went on to make a splash in the first team at Upton Park are George Parris, Greg Campbell and Tony Cottee (far right).

I'd already played for England youth in a competitive game, which made me ineligible for any other nation. The rules have changed now and I would be able to play, but at the time it was just one of those things."

Back in Essex, he signed up for his local Sunday side – a team that included another future professional star.

"Dagenham United were holding trials when I was around seven-years-old and so I went along. The manager of the team was Alex Adams and his son, Tony, was captain of the side. You could always tell that he was going to go on to become a top class player. He showed the same qualities as a kid as he did much later on when playing for Arsenal and England – a born leader who got the best out of everybody around him.

"We had some fantastic players in that team – players who were better than myself and Tony as kids – but, for whatever reason, they didn't go on to make it at a higher level. I used to play on the right side of midfield, or at right-back, and later on I played alongside Tony in the centre of defence.

"I actually went along to Arsenal with him to train when we were youngsters but, for some reason, I just didn't feel comfortable there. I don't know why, but I had a gut feeling that it wasn't right for me. Luckily, the West Ham scout Ronnie Gale invited me to Chadwell Heath and as soon as I walked in the door, I felt comfortable. Whether it was because the training ground was only 10 minutes from my home, I don't know, but I knew it was the club I wanted to join. When it came down to choosing between Arsenal and West Ham, there was only one club I was going to sign for."

Having signed schoolboy forms with the club at the age of 13, Steve arrived at West Ham during a period of great success at all levels. The first team had just triumphed over Arsenal in the FA Cup final and were on the verge of winning promotion from Division Two in record style, while the kids were on their way to victory over Spurs in the FA Youth Cup final.

At the head of all this was hands-on manager John Lyall, who ran the club from top to bottom and knew the names of not only every young player at the club, but probably those of their parents, too. As a shy teenager trying to establish himself among more bullish team-mates, Pottsy was made to feel at ease and he admits that the experience of growing up under the guidance of Lyall and his staff played a huge part in helping him to develop both as a player and a person.

"John instilled a lot of discipline into every player at the club and, as a young lad trying to make your way in the game, it was an education to play for him. He had this aura about him – he would walk into the room and you would sit up immediately and listen to whatever he had to say.

"And the thing was, everything he said made sense. He could talk football all day long and, when you thought about what he'd said, it all seemed right. He never over-complicated things – they were just simple ideas that you could take on board.

"He gave me my chance and guided me as a young player, and the fact that I went on to enjoy a long career with West Ham has a lot to do with John Lyall. He also made sure all his young players behaved in the right way, and he taught me a lot of values as a person.

"He had absolutely everything, and it's not just me who says that. I don't think I've ever heard anyone say a bad word about him and that says a lot. As a manager, you can never keep everyone happy but John had this way of gaining respect even from those who weren't in the team.

"He knew how to deal with players individually and get the best out of them. He would handle someone like Paul Ince differently to how he would handle me, but he always got the right response. He was honest and loyal, and that rubbed off on everyone who played for him."

Just as he did with most young players at that time, Lyall handed Steve a taste of the big-time with a first team debut at a tender age before instantly withdrawing him from the spotlight in order to leave the player hungry and determined to earn another opportunity.

His initial chance came as a 17-year-old on New Year's Day in 1985, with QPR the visitors to Upton Park. Midfielder Paul Allen had initially been deployed as a makeshift right-back in place of the injured Ray Stewart. But having seen his team lifted by an impressive 2-2 draw at league leaders Tottenham on Boxing Day, Lyall handed the absence Stewart's No.2 shirt to Potts for the second London derby in a week. It was an experience he still remembers clearly.

"The team had spent New Year's Eve at a hotel in Epping and that was all new to me, because I'd been used to going out partying on New Year's Eve!" he recalls. "We got to the Boleyn Ground the following day and Geoff Pike failed a fitness test, which meant that Paul Allen had to move back into midfield.

"About an hour-and-a-half before kick-off, John called me out of the dressing-room and into his office and said: 'Do you fancy playing today?' I was a bit shocked and just mumbled: 'Yeah'. He told me to go and get ready and with that I walked back into the changing room. All the lads were in there, and they could probably tell by the look on my face what was happening.

"I can remember Tony Gale saying to me: 'The toilet is over there if you need it, Pottsy!' That was typical Galey and before I knew it, I was out there on the pitch with him. It all happened so quickly, which was just as well because it meant that I had no time to feel nervous.

"Things were going really well in the first half – Paul Brush gave us the lead after four minutes and I think Steve Whitton had a goal disallowed – but then it all went wrong and they scored three times in the space of 20 minutes. It was a disappointing finish but a great experience nonetheless, and I thought I'd played quite well.

"This will show you how much times have changed, though. After the game I had to walk past the Boleyn pub and along Barking Road to get to my mum and dad's car for a lift home. You can't imagine a 17-year-old Premier League player having to do that now!"

Another solitary appearance came the following year, during the record-breaking 1985-86 campaign, as the club reached its highest-ever league placing, and Steve was also a regular in Hammers' reserve team that romped to the Football Combination title that season.

His progress continued gradually over the next couple of years, with eight appearances in 1986-87 and 10 the following season but, although he was by then past his 20th birthday, Steve insists that there certainly wasn't any concern about his failure to make a greater impact at that stage of his career.

"That's how it was then – young players were given longer to develop and improve their game. For the vast majority of us, it was a case of playing youth team football, then going up into the reserves for a couple of years while making the odd first team appearance if and when needed. And then when you had reached, say, 20 or 21, they would look at you and weigh up whether you were going to make it in the first team.

"Nowadays, because there is so much money involved, clubs are looking at their young players at the age of 17 and asking if they are good enough to play in the first team. If they're not, then they are struggling. It's more cut-throat now, managers want instant results, so they often can't give their young players the time they might need to develop.

"The question now seems to be: 'Do we take a risk with an 18-year-old or do we sign an experienced foreign player instead?' Unfortunately, most clubs now take the second option.

"From that point of view, I was lucky in that I started out when youngsters were given more time to progress. Another factor was that, at that stage, I was looking at making right-back my position, and so I was behind Ray Stewart in the pecking order. Ray was a fantastic player, who very rarely missed matches. It wasn't until the late-80s and early-90s, when he suffered a serious knee injury, that I was given

The Reserves who won the Combination League in that memorable season of 1985-86. Steve has one hand on the trophy at front, with Eamonn Dolan and Paul Ince either side of him, Kevin Keen third from right in the standing row and coach Jimmy Frith on the far right.

the chance to play in his usual position more often."

Indeed, Steve became a regular during the 1988-89 season, a campaign that sadly ended with relegation and the departure of John Lyall after 15 years in the Hammers hotseat. And while the arrival of Lou Macari caused some consternation among senior members of the squad at the start of the following season, for young Steve it was simply a case of business of usual, as he made the right-back slot his own and began to establish himself as a steady and reliable replacement for the experienced international Stewart.

An injury sustained in January 1989 halted Steve's progress slightly and, by the time he returned to full fitness, Billy Bonds had replaced Macari in the dug-out. Steve began the 1990-91 promotion-winning campaign wearing the No.2 shirt and, in early October, he enjoyed a 'JFK' moment that no-one present at Upton Park that day will ever forget. It was his one and only first team goal for West Ham.

Mention of this landmark event brings a slightly embarrassed reaction from the ever-modest Pottsy, who says: "I tend not to talk about it, because one goal from 500 games isn't a particularly good record!"

When reminded that he spent his entire career as a defender and rarely ventured over the halfway line, even for attacking set-pieces, his response is just as humble…"It's still a bad record!

"I was playing at right-back that day and it just so happened that I had a fair bit of space on my side of the field and was able to get forward a bit. I'd had a shot saved earlier in the game and, when it all opened up for me again, I hit one from just outside the edge of the box.

"I'm not sure if it went through the keeper's legs or he just spilled it, but he should have saved it. It's a nice memory, though, and I certainly won't ever forget it.

"Funnily enough, although it was the only goal I ever got for the first team, I once scored a hat-trick for the reserves. Don't ask me how, but I was playing right-midfield and it was against Swindon. That was definitely a one-off, though!"

Just weeks after his goal against Hull, Pottsy was dealt a shock to the system when Bonzo made his first signing since taking over as manager, paying £600,000 to Luton Town for right-back Tim Breacker.

Steve faced the prospect of being frozen out but, rather than sulk or settle for reserve team football, he bounced back in typically cool fashion to become a pivotal part of the team in a new position.

"When Bill signed Tim Breacker, I was sitting at home thinking: 'Hang on a minute, that could be it for me. Maybe my career will be away from West Ham'.

"I found myself out of the team but then we had a few injuries to our centre-backs– Alvin Martin and Tony Gale had both picked up knocks – and Bill asked me if I'd play there. I filled in in the centre of defence and it just went from there.

"I'd always preferred centre-defence and had played there many times for the reserves. In fact, it was probably more of a shock to the supporters and press to see me there, because they wouldn't have been aware that I could play that role. Being shorter than your typical centre-half, it raised a few eyebrows. I knew the position, though, and in my own mind I was comfortable playing in the role."

Having proved his versatility during the relegation season of 1991-92, Steve began the following campaign firmly settled at the heart of the back four, as the good times returned.

With Mark Robson and Kevin Keen causing havoc on the wings and Trevor Morley and Clive Allen banging in 34 goals between them, Hammers won promotion to the newly-formed Premier League, finishing second above Portsmouth thanks to their superior goal difference.

However, when it came to handing out the end-of-season awards, it was ever-present Pottsy who came top in the Hammer-of-the-Year poll, recognised by the Upton Park crowd for his consistent and reliable performances at the heart of the defence.

"It was a massive honour for me to win it," he says. "Especially in a season like that, in which the whole team were fantastic and the attacking players performed so well. To be recognised by the supporters is a wonderful feeling, because they are the most important people at the club. I'll never forget that and the trophy they presented to me still takes pride of place at home."

It was the start of the prime years of his career, as Pottsy played an influential part in helping Hammers to retain their newly-acquired top flight status during a difficult couple of years. Handed the captaincy by Bonzo in 1993-94 following the departure of Julian Dicks to Liverpool, he missed just one game all season and was again an ever-present the following campaign, a feat that resulted in him being voted Hammer-of-the-Year for the second time.

The 1995-96 campaign provided Steve with another 34 league appearances, which meant that he had missed just five of 178 matches spread over the course of four seasons – a phenomenal figure for a central defender who was never found wanting in terms of bravery and commitment.

However, take a look through the press cuttings from that period and it's likely that you won't find a single headline dedicated to the talents of the long-serving Hammers defender. Not that Pottsy is bitter about the lack of a scrap-book detailing

One of the best man-markers in the game, Stevie gets tight to Manchester United's Mark Hughes in May 1995.

all his glories – on the contrary, the unsung hero preferred it that way.

Quiet and unassuming, he said: "I must admit, the fame and media side of football never appealed to me – I just didn't feel comfortable with it. I know it's part of the game and that a lot of players enjoy it, but I never craved it at all.

"I just wanted to play the game and then disappear. If I could see any of the club's press guys getting ready to approach me, I'd drop my shoulder and head off the other way! I'm a naturally shy and modest person and I was always much happier leaving the limelight to others.

"That's not to say I didn't want success on the pitch, though. When it comes to football, I've always been fairly single-minded and I believe that, if you want something, you should go and get it. So from that point of view, I worked hard to build myself a career in the game and play nearly 500 times for West Ham. It never came on a plate for me and I don't doubt that there were players with more ability than me who didn't enjoy such a long career, but I wanted it and I worked hard to stay at the level I reached."

The arrival of international overseas defenders, such as Croatian Slaven Bilic and Denmark's Marc Rieper, during Harry Redknapp's wheeler-dealer reign in the late-90s meant Steve could no longer count on a regular place in the starting line-up, while the emergence of the young Rio Ferdinand pushed him further down the pecking order.

But it was still no real surprise to see Pottsy called upon whenever injuries or suspensions created a gap in the team, whether at centre-half, right-back or even in the centre of midfield, where he stepped in to good effect on several occasions in the latter stages of Redknapp's reign.

However, with more than a year left on his Upton Park contract, Steve would never

have guessed that his appearance against Chelsea on March 7, 2001 would turn out to be his last in a claret-and-blue shirt. Following Redknapp's departure and the appointment in the summer of 2001 of Glenn Roeder, he was a regular squad member and occasional unused substitute, but never actually stepped out on to the field again at first team level.

It appeared that he would be handed the chance to say farewell to the Boleyn Ground faithful at the end of the 2001-02 campaign, when named as a substitute for a largely meaningless final game of the season against Bolton Wanderers. However, with 399 league appearances to his name, Steve was denied number 400 and walked out of Upton Park for the last time as a player that night with a touch of sadness in his heart.

"I'd be lying if I said it wasn't a big disappointment," Steve admitted. "I already knew that I'd be leaving the club and all I really wanted was the chance to run out there for one last time and say a proper farewell to the supporters.

"I just wanted a chance to say thanks and goodbye to them but I walked back to my car that night feeling . . . well, rather gutted. What should have been a really nice day turned a little bit sour in the end and I just felt a bit deflated when I got home.

"That's life, though, and I got over it. Worse things have happened and, if you look at some of the things that are going on in the world, not getting on the pitch for a couple of minutes is no big deal at all."

Following his departure from Upton Park, Steve spent a year playing for Dagenham & Redbridge in the Nationwide Conference. "I still felt fresh after not playing any football in my last season at West Ham and I wanted to play on for another year."

After leaving Victoria Road, Steve took a break from the game altogether, although he did briefly return to West Ham to host the corporate lounges at Upton Park.

Steve and his wife Joanne live at Gidea Park, Essex, and they have four children – Daniel, Georgina, Harry and Freddie.

Since retiring from football, Steve has embarked on a new career – as a London cab driver. His determination to pass The Knowledge was reminiscent of his dedication he showed in becoming a pro footballer.

It is anybody's guess just how much it would cost to navigate the London Marathon course in a taxi. But after running the circuit in 2008, black cabbie Steve was well on the way towards raising £20,000 for Children with Leukaemia after completing his first-ever marathon, on April 13.

"It was a great experience and such a good day," says proud Pottsy after taking a highly-respectable 4hr 4min 7sec, to run the 26 miles and 385-yards through the capital and generate that fantastic five-figure sum. "Everyone was pulling in the same direction and there were so many people watching, too.

"There were even a few shouts of 'C'mon Pottsy!' and that really helped me to get through it.

"I knew that I had to try to enjoy the day rather than get daunted by it all and despite trying to pace myself from the start, I just got carried along by a wave of people. All my pre-race plans soon went out of the window," laughs the former Upton Park defender, who had his own welcoming committee of 40 friends and

Steve relaxing at a Boys of 86 day out at Hunstanton races in 2006 with former team-mates Paul Hilton and Neil Orr, plus actor and West Ham fan Nick Berry for company.

family – including eldest son Daniel celebrating his 14th birthday – roaring him on at the 19-mile mark.

"That was a very special moment for me but it started to get harder towards the end. While I'd told myself right from the off that I was not going to stop, one bloke even coasted past me bouncing a basketball! It's difficult enough just getting around, so fair play to those runners who dress up, too," continued Pottsy, who finished in 10,478th place, but ahead of fellow ex-Hammers Kevin Keen (17,363rd in 4:43:33) and Paul Brush (18,081st in 4:48:25).

"Looking back, I really enjoyed the race in a peculiar sort of way. But no matter how many times I do it, I don't think I'll ever have that same feeling of elation as I did when I crossed the line to finish my first-ever marathon.

"Compared to the people who have dug deep into their pockets, I've done the easy bit," concludes the ever-modest 40-year-old. "And remember, the really hard work is done by all the doctors, nurses and patients, who have to deal with this terrible illness.

"Every penny counts in the battle against leukaemia and I'm really grateful to everyone who has sponsored me and helped me to raise so much money for such a good cause."

Reflecting on his long and distinguished career, Steve is understandably proud to be ranked ninth in the all-time list of Hammers' appearance makers.

"I've got so many good memories of my time at the club," he says, "and I feel genuinely honoured to have made so many appearances and ended up in the top 10 appearance holders. It's something that will always be with me and it will be the nice to tell the grandchildren in years to come that I played for West Ham so many times."

Chapter 17

BOBBY**BARNES**

"I was a young idiot, so I went to the front to lead out the lads, only to be greeted by lots of booing. I turned around to find that the rest of the lads were still hanging around in the tunnel! Typical Galey"

BOBBY Barnes was adored on the terraces. He could 'play a bit', as he says, but his cult status was brought about by his mop of dark locks and his alliterated name. And he was, as he remains, as likeable off the field as on it.

"Digger" – named after the character, Cliff Barnes, in the huge 80s American TV soap *Dallas* – stood out as different from the rest. His colour was one of the things that made him instantly conspicuous from his team-mates.

But there is a curious quirk of the football fan, Hammers followers in particular. He may be different, but he is one of us. If he was a black player on the other side, for some it would be a completely different story. That was the ugly side of football in the 70s and 80s.

Bobby, now 45 and an executive with the Professional Footballers' Association, told *EX*: "When I was playing in the 80s football was going through a particularly bad period with regards to hooliganism and racism. There were bad incidents going on, the most high profile being at St James' Park in 1984 with the banana-throwing.

"I remember it well. We were playing against Newcastle United and they pelted the pitch with bananas. They were bad days in football, and St. James' was one of the worst places to go, along with Elland Road.

"Tony Gale tells a good story about one of our visits to Leeds. We had been playing quite well but I was getting a lot of stick. Galey said to me at half-time: 'Bobby, you've been playing really well, first-half, so I want you to lead us out for the second'.

"I was a young idiot, so I went to the front to lead out the lads, only to be greeted by lots of booing. I turned around to find that the rest of the lads were still hanging around in the tunnel! Typical Galey.

"I didn't really experience any racism from West Ham fans, though. But they did give opposition players a bit, which I found strange as I was playing for their team at the time! I was okay but a black player on the other side would get some stick. I think I was seen by our fans as one of the lads, though."

Mercifully, football has changed for the best since then. In Bobby's first league game, against Watford on September 20, 1980, he was the only black player in Hammers' line-up.

Bobby on the attack against Arsenal, pursued by Paul Davis.

The lad from Leytonstone, east London, who now resides in Wanstead where he still runs regularly, says: "The players who came through in the early 70s and 80s have sown the seed for this generation to be able to play. I am a trustee of the Kick It Out campaign, the organisation that tackles racism in football.

"I think West Ham have been a credit to football by tackling the issue with banners and posters up, as well as dedicating a page in the programme. I am very proud of the fact that my club has taken such a positive step. You certainly don't get the chanting you used to and things have improved a lot. I don't think you can say it is eradicated – you still get the odd incident – but I consider Upton Park a place where racism is no more."

And the decline in racism isn't the only change. It is hard to believe that, around 28 years ago, when Bobby made his debut, West Ham were playing a European Cup Winners' Cup tie at Real Madrid's famous Bernabeu stadium.

Hammers fan Bobby recalls: "People always think my first game was against Watford but I actually made my debut at the Bernabeu against Castilla in the ECWC. It was a big stage – you could say it was all downhill from there!

"Years later, Billy Bonds told me that after that game in Madrid it was the one time he fell out with the West Ham supporters. There was a lot of trouble in the stadium and our fans did not behave well. I understand there was provocation – but there was trouble.

"We were forced to play the second leg at home in front of an empty stadium. Bill said after the game that the people who had forced that situation were 'Scum'. The fans turned on him for the first and only time over that incident.

"I came on with probably no more than half an hour to go. Although we lost, it was a magnificent experience playing for West Ham in Europe.

"I must have done reasonably well, because the following Saturday I made my first start. I even got a goal. I remember being 17-years-old, hoping to get a chance on the bench, but I started the game against Watford. I scored my debut goal and Trevor (Brooking) scored with a header in the last minute to win the game.

"We had a bit of a rough start in the old second division and I seem to remember that it was the game that kick-started our season and set us on our promotion run."

But Bobby made only seven appearances that season, which reduced to three the following campaign and then only one sub appearance in 1982-83. But in 1983-84 he was back on track, featuring in 17 matches, followed by his most active season, 24 outings in 1984-85.

Bobby attributes his lack of consistency to the same distractions young professionals face today.

"Socialising was probably the reason I didn't achieve as highly as I perhaps should have, given the promise I had as a youngster," he admits.

"As a 16-year-old I was well sought-after, I stood out. There were very few left-footed players, as is still the case now. I like to think I could play a bit, too. But after making my debut early and getting into the first team, I became the prime example of someone who thought he had achieved it all. At 17 or 18 I decided that I had made it.

"It is something I say to kids now – that your debut is only the first step. I should have got my head down and concentrated, stayed away from the social side of things. You speak to young players now and try to make them realise that they have to keep their feet on the ground. A couple of decent performances does not make you a superstar.

"I socialised with fellow players and other people away from the game. Older players – such as Parksey, Dev, Paul Allen and David Cross – who perhaps had more of an entitlement to go out. They'd go, and I'd join them. Perhaps I shouldn't have done," he says ruefully.

He certainly laid no blame for his lack of progress on his manager. Bobby said: "John Lyall was very much a father figure to all of us. He had a quiet authority and we respected him tremendously. We didn't always agree with him – but we respected him.

"It was a situation where you really didn't want to let him down. If you did so, he made you feel bad. He contributed to the fact that there was such a good atmosphere within the players. He was the head of that.

"John ran the club from top to bottom, which is quite rare. A manager doesn't have that sort of time or responsibility today. He used to go and watch the youth team play and I knew him from the age of 14. He was confident enough in his role as manager to know that he would still be boss in six years' time so that the kids who were 14 or 15 might well be the same players who would progress into his first team one day."

Strangely enough, Bobby also had spells as a player under two of Lyall's Upton Park successors – Lou Macari (at Swindon Town) and Harry Redknapp (AFC Bournemouth). He said of Macari: "Lou wanted to know every aspect of his players' lives – from what they were doing, where they went and who they were with. He had to know where they were drinking and what time they went to bed.

"He was very much a fitness man and was concerned with the physical demands of the game. I know he wasn't particularly well received by the lads at West Ham, though.

"They had been used to doing things a certain way, the West Ham Way. Lou's regime was in stark contrast to Harry Redknapp's methods at Bournemouth.

"While I was at Swindon, we went on a trip to Israel. Lou is very anti-alcohol and into clean living. But, for once in his life, he told us all to relax and have a drink. He told us it was okay to go out after training, as long as we didn't go silly. But he couldn't bear it and was soon sneaking around watching what we were up to.

"I was at a table with Jimmy Quinn. The next thing I knew, Lou sent over one of his coaches, who said to me: 'Lou wants to know why you have got two drinks in front of you?'.

"I turned around and said: 'Tell Lou it's Happy Hour!'. Lou wasn't very happy."

Of Redknapp, Bobby said: "Harry was manager when I was at Bournemouth, though the move didn't really work out for me. I'd been playing for Lou at Swindon under a regime completely different to what Harry allowed his team to get away with. It was much more relaxed and laid-back at Bournemouth, which I found difficult as I'd been used to the exact opposite and I found it hard to adapt.

"Lou and Harry were complete opposites as managers."

In his role at the PFA, Bobby is able to pass on his vast experience in the footballing arena as well as the financial sector to present professionals. Bobby himself was forced to find a second career, at Friends Provident after achieving a diploma in business, when he hung up his football boots at Hong Kong Rangers in 1995. He was not part of the Sky TV football revolution that sees many present day players, some with less than half his natural ability, retire at 35 with more than enough money to set themselves up for life.

Bobby continues: "The financial rewards for players are great these days. I am not at all envious, because I think they deserve it. Our generation were slightly short changed – the crowds were there, but we didn't see the great benefits. The clubs were run as much steadier ships in those days.

"But I've always felt that clubs are justified in paying players the sort of wages they do today. Entertainers deserve to be rewarded most. If you attend a pop concert, you pay the singer or band a proportion of the ticket sales. Footballers shouldn't be any different.

"With the average footballer's career lasting only eight years, a player will have to decide what he is going to do with the rest of his life. He'll have a very short time span to make his money, enough to set him up for the rest of his life.

"People have to remember that for every Michael Owen, there are 100 or 200 lower division lads who have their contracts up in the summer and don't know if they are going to get another. They have families and that uncertain situation reoccurs

Bobby, the office executive, working at the PFA but still keeping an eye on his old club.

annually for them. As a union, our role at the PFA is to look after the wellbeing of footballers."

Bobby still holds Hammers close to his heart. He was a fan first, before rising rapidly from the youth team, which is still evident today.

He adds: "The one thing that has always impressed me over the years about West Ham are the supporters. I left the club in 1986 but the fans don't forget and you remain a West Ham United player for life. Hammers fans still remember me.

"It is amazing when you think about it, because in those days, 22 years ago, I had all this hair and now I'm bald!

"West Ham fans stick with the club through think and thin. That's proven in the attendances they still pull in.

"I have very fond memories of West Ham. As a youngster, I was very much a Hammers supporter and it was a dream to go from the terraces on to the pitch. You are always conscious of the fact that you are a local lad and that your mates are out there watching you. I think a little bit of that has been lost these days. It is sad, but that is progress, and now there are not many people who play for their local club."

Chapter 18

FRANK McAVENNIE

"I think a lot of people who were at West Ham under John Lyall felt betrayed by the club over his sacking and the way he was treated"

JULY 13, 1985 and the eyes of the world are on the historic Live Aid rock concert – 'the Woodstock of the 80s' – instigated by Boomtown Rat Bob Geldof.

Some £1.5billion people watched the television pictures beamed to 160 different countries in the biggest broadcast ever known following Geldof's plea: "Don't go down the pub tonight. Please stay in and give us your money." Brits reportedly contributed around £1.1m of the £30m raised for famine relief in Africa on that momentous summer's day 23 years ago.

Among the 72,000 packed inside Wembley Stadium on that sunny Saturday afternoon were two lads who would otherwise have quite fancied a night down the pub. Frank McAvennie and his pal mingled completely unnoticed among the throng waiting expectantly to see Status Quo, David Bowie, Wham and Dire Straits perform on stage beneath the fabled Twin Towers.

"We made our way through the crowd and as we got onto the pitch, I came across a few West Ham fans – you could tell who they supported by the tattoos they had on their arms," recalls Frank, who had just completed his low profile £340,000 transfer from St Mirren to West Ham. Î was going: 'Excuse me, pal, can you let me through?' And they would say: 'Yeah, no problem Jock'.

"My mate pointed out to me: 'They're Hammers fans but they don't even know who you are!' I'd only just signed for West Ham and hadn't played a game for them at that point. We were about to start training on the Wednesday after Live Aid, so none of them knew who I was – they didn't have a clue.

"So I decided there and then to do something about it. At the start of the following week, I went back home for a couple of days and while I was in Glasgow I had my hair dyed really blond. I thought, they'll notice me now!

"My hair was blond anyway when I was at St Mirren but I had it bleached brighter because I wanted everybody at West Ham to notice me. It was something I did consciously, to try and make an impact on every one," he admits, "although it would obviously have rebounded on me if I hadn't produced the goods on the park."

Cockney actor and proper West Ham geezer Ray Winstone echoed the first impressions many Hammers' supporters had of John Lyall's mystery signing in his entertaining foreword to Frank's 2003 autobiography, *Scoring: An Expert's Guide*. He noted that we had signed a player from Scotland who didn't even play for either Celtic or Rangers. And when he first caught sight of that flash of peroxide emerging

West Ham's last great goalscoring duo – Frank and Tony Cottee in their 1985-86 vintage pomp.

from the players' tunnel, as bright as the Upton Park lights, he wondered if we'd signed a girl!

Voted Scotland's Young-Player-of-the-Year in 1981-82, Frank admits: "I'd always been a bit cocky and had confidence in my own ability. No matter how good or bad West Ham were going to be when I joined them, I knew I'd be playing with much better players than I'd been used to in Scotland."

Winstone was spot on in his assessment of Frank. One of the qualities that he and many others who have enjoyed Macca's company from time to time have appreciated about him is his lack of airs and graces. He might have looked a bit flash, but he never has been. He treats everyone the same.

All the fans loved McAvennie at West Ham. Most of the women who saw him perform his skills in those skimpy, silk thigh-hugging Adidas shorts the players wore back then wanted to be shagged by him – and some were. All the blokes on the terraces wanted to be him. He was West Ham's answer to George Best.

Essentially a man's man and at his happiest to be one of the lads, he smoked, drank champagne and occasionally snorted cocaine for a while after serious injury struck during his second spell with the Hammers. He doesn't womanise anymore, of course, because he has been happily married to Geordie lass Karen for the past seven years.

One of Frank's most endearing qualities is his ability to laugh at himself. Like most Glaswegians and Cockneys, he will find humour in even the most difficult situations, which is just as well given everything that he's been through.

"I was once asked if any of my former girlfriends ever had plastic surgery. 'Aye,' I replied. 'Jenny Blyth, when I took her gold credit cards off her!' She knew how to spend money," says Frank, roaring with laughter again.

He met Jenny, a former Page 3 stunner, and her model girlfriends on frequent nights out at the Phoenix Apollo restaurant favoured by not only the Boys of 86 but also showbiz stars, including some of the cast of *Eastenders* and boxer Nigel Benn. Gil and Panay, the two guys who ran this one-time in-place at Stratford Broadway, looked after their famous clientele very well. "I even had my own bed upstairs – and it wasn't for sleeping in!" recalls Frank with another typically cheeky ear-to-ear grin.

When he and his friends were not socialising at the Phoenix, Frank would more often than not be found enjoying himself 'up west', at Browns, Stringfellows or Blondes, the club owned by George Best. They were his 'locals', although he didn't go to those celebrity havens simply to be seen. Despite being a prominent figure on the celebrity scene in his West Ham days, he'd be equally happy engaging in patter with complete strangers than VIPs who craved the attention of the paparazzi.

It says plenty about his likeable personality that he always remained very popular in the West Ham dressing room, liked and respected by his peers but never envied, despite the blaze of publicity he attracted during the winter of 1985-86. He and strike partner Tony Cottee were scoring goals for fun all that season but a contract dispute between ITV and the Football League meant there was precious little television coverage of the game. It wasn't until the start of '86 that live matches returned to our screens and football supporters beyond Upton Park became fully

Frank celebrating one of his favourite goals in the 2-1 win against Everton on November 2, 1985.

aware of the new No.8's incredible impact in his first season in England. Until then, Frank was known to millions more people as football's new, big personality, a showman who got himself noticed off the field as well as on it.

He first entered the public consciousness following his appearance on *Wogan*, the then thrice weekly BBC chat show hosted by Terry Wogan that boasted a regular viewing audience of around 15 million. "That was the big turning point for me, the day my life changed forever," says Frank. "After my appearance on *Wogan* I got a lot of media attention and, I'll admit, I enjoyed it at the time," he continues. "I'd be sitting there with three Page 3 models on my arm and it meant I could get anything I wanted – girls or a table in any restaurant, that sort of thing – just by making a phone call.

"I just took every day as it came, because I thought it would all blow up in my face at some stage. I knew I was no oil painting and that the birds weren't after me for my charm and good looks. For them, it was the money and fame, so I knew it was never going to last with any of them. But I enjoyed myself at the time."

John Lyall didn't mind Frank's new-found celebrity status and the party lifestyle that went with it – not while his shrewd bargain buy was banging in the goals as he did throughout West Ham's best-ever league season. He top-scored with 26 in the league plus two more in the cup competitions, while Cottee matched him all the way with 20 plus six.

"The press tried to say that Tony and I didn't get on but that was all a load of rubbish. We have always got on really well," confirmed Frank, who was reunited with his old strike partner when they worked together for a season as co-hosts of the then new hospitality lounges in the Dr Martens Stand following its opening in 2001.

Cottee has always been quick to acknowledge Frank's unselfish attitude and, indeed, has gone on record as saying that he felt the fans should have voted McAvennie Hammer-of-the-Year at the end of 1985-86 instead of him. Frank and Mark Ward were voted runners-up to TC in the poll, but Cottee admits: "Frank deserved the award more than I did."

"I was always a team player and it wouldn't have bothered me if I hadn't scored all the goals that I did that first season," continues Frank. "No disrespect to Tony, but whereas he was an out and out striker, I was always a team man. If he was going through on goal and I was running beside him, he'd shoot. But if I was through on the goalkeeper and Tony was next to me, I'd draw the keeper out and give the ball to Tony. I suppose that's why we worked so well together as a partnership.

"The only issue was early on in the 1985-86 season, when the players all got together to discuss how we could improve as a team. I was running all over the place and shutting down defenders whenever they had possession, and it was generally felt that Tony could have been working a bit harder. For instance, if I closed down the opposition full-back, we didn't want them to use the keeper as their out ball, so Tony needed to close down people, too.

"We all had our say and Tony accepted it and took it on board, and we went on a tremendous run from that point. It wasn't John Lyall who called the meeting – it was our skipper, Alvin Martin. Everything was discussed and sorted between the players behind closed doors – as it should always be.

"We had a great team spirit and physio Rob Jenkins and coach Ronnie Boyce were a part of that, too. I'd call Boycey to the back of the bus to ponce fags of him! And if he said 'no', I'd threaten him that I'd tell John that he'd been supplying me!

"We did some funny things. Wardie and me would have stupid bets with each other on just about anything. Remember how Bryan Robson always seemed to get injured whenever Man United played at Upton Park? Well, one night they came down to our place and we had a bet on which of us would be standing nearest to Robbo the next time he went down injured! Remember when Wardie stuck Kevin Moran right into the wall!" Frank laughs again.

It was his honest endeavour and willingness to work hard for the team, as much as his phenomenal scoring rate in that first season, that made him such a huge crowd favourite, one of the most popular players to have ever worn claret-and-blue. Frank produced some brilliant individual performances, spectacular and audacious goals, but, first and foremost, he likes to be remembered as a good all round team player.

No-one could ever accuse him of lacking effort or shying away from the more physical aspects of the game. Within minutes of his home debut against QPR, he chased down Northern Ireland central defender Alan McDonald and sent him tumbling with the full force of a Chieftain tank.

Frank instantly recalled the incident. "McDonald had been bullying Tony. He'd smashed him twice early on in the game, so I called TC to come across and deal with him but he ignored me. So I went over to that side of the pitch myself and as the boy pushed the ball a little too far in front of him, I smashed him straight into the Chicken Run.

"I thought the crowd were going to kill him, because as McDonald was trying to pick himself up, the fans leaned over the wall and were giving him a slap! I couldn't stop laughing and thought, they'll do for me. It was my initiation with the West Ham fans, if you like, and I thought it was great.

"Fans are not stupid and the best advice I could give any young player now is to always give your best. Everyone's entitled to have a bad game but the fans know when you're not giving 100 per cent. And as far as I'm concerned if you're not giving that, you shouldn't be on the park. That's what disappoints me about the game today – when I see players, who are earning fortunes, just strolling around. I know when someone's not putting a shift in and so do the fans.

"Any defender can hit a 40-yard ball if they've got the time to do it but there aren't that many good players around today and when they are put under pressure, they often give the ball away.

"Bonzo gave me some good advice – yes, he did used to talk to me when he was a player, before he became the gaffer! He said, 'when you're having a bad game, you can still put people under pressure for the good of the team'. He told me that even when I was having a bad game, not to go into my shell and hide, and fortunately I never did that."

With two goals in that 3-1 victory against QPR, Frank had arrived as a Hammers hero and earned a permanent place in the hearts of his adoring fans. The soon to become familiar chant of 'One McAveneeeeee' reverberated around the Boleyn Ground as supporters rejoiced at the kind of free-flowing, one and two-touch football that was a purist's delight. "It was good to hear them chanting my name – especially after everyone had worked out how to pronounce it," he said, with another beaming smile. "At first, I think they called me MacCaverney, then MacaDougie and all that!"

In his still broad Glaswegian accent, Frank recalled that his team-mates had difficulty understanding him at first and, after just a couple of months at the club, he expressed feelings of homesickness. But once Macca embarked on his goalscoring spree, there was no way the boss was going to entertain any talk of him returning north. The fans would have been outraged.

"To hear them singing my name . . . I knew I was doing well," says Frank. "To me, football is all about the fans, it's an entertainment business. I hate going to see a boring game and it's down to the players on the park to entertain."

Ironically, Frank was originally signed as an attacking midfielder, to play 'in the hole' behind the front two of Cottee and the more experienced Paul Goddard. It was only after Goddard dislocated his shoulder in the opening game of the season at Birmingham that Macca was pushed up front alongside the pacy natural goal-poacher Cottee.

"It makes me laugh when I hear people talking now about all these magical formations that modern coaches use but the fact is that John Lyall bought me to play in the hole, as the withdrawn third striker, 23 years ago. I'd been top scorer for St Mirren playing in that position for two years. How far ahead of his time was John?

"I lived my life playing in the hole – it's something I'm very good at it!" he chuckles, unable to resist another one-liner.

But Frank's natural wit cannot disguise his serious love of football nor his understanding of how it should be played. Sure, he had the Midas touch in his first season as a Hammer but he worked hard for everything that he got. His intelligent running off the ball, positional sense and ability to augment the pass-and-move philosophy of Lyall, blending brilliantly with the accomplished ball player that was Alan Devonshire, earned him respect as much more than a one-season wonder.

"I wasn't a natural goalscorer," says Frank, "and I'd always played in midfield for St Mirren. I could hardly do anything wrong that season after moving up front with Tony but who's to say that we wouldn't have actually gone on to win the league if Paul Goddard hadn't got injured in the first game and missed so much of the season?

"Paul was a hell of a good player and if he hadn't got injured, I think it could have worked out really well with the three of us going forward. Paul was a bit like me in that he'd bring others into play and I can imagine that he would have set me up well coming from deep positions.

"I don't know what managers have seen in me when it comes to heading but I'm only 5 feet-10 inches tall and they bought a winger to play with me in Mark Ward. I thought you only ever signed a winger if you had a big, six-foot centre-forward but Wardie gave me superb service."

While reflecting on the club's highest-ever league position of third, Frank picked up on a contentious comment made by fellow former Hammer Brian Dear in volume one of *In My Day*, where Dear challenged Frank's previously perceived claims that the record achievement of the 1985-86 side exceeded those of the famous Cup-winning heroes of the 60s.

"I read what Brian said about me but I've never claimed that our team of '85-86 was the greatest-ever West Ham side or that it was in any way superior to the Hammers teams that won major trophies in the 60s. And I certainly wouldn't disrespect legends such as Bobby Moore, Geoff Hurst and Martin Peters and all that they did for the club either," he points out.

What is not open to debate is the fact that despite the status and undoubted skill of the much-celebrated World Cup trio of '66, none of Ron Greenwood's teams managed to finish higher than sixth in the top flight – three places behind the silky side of Devonshire, Martin, Gale, Ward, Cottee and McAvennie that played to Lyall's philosophy and came within a whisker of ending the Merseyside monopoly of the 80s. Liverpool finally clinched the first division championship on the last Saturday of the season at Chelsea, thanks to a goal by Kenny Dalglish – the former Scotland and Celtic legend Frank had idolised from the 'Jungle' section of the Parkhead terraces as a lad growing up in the east end of Glasgow.

When he considers the different central defensive partnerships he and Cottee played against together, Frank rates the Liverpool duo of Alan Hansen and Mark Lawrenson the highest. "They were very good but they also had their way of winding you up all the time. Liverpool were the biggest wind-up merchants in the world. I'd call them f****** arrogant b******s but Hansen and Lawrenson would talk to each other and make little comments about different opposing players. They would come out with things like: 'It's okay, let him have the ball, he'll give it to us anyway', and that sort of mickey-taking stuff. I used to get the hump with them.

"When I received the ball with my back to goal or a cross was on its way over to

Holding off Paul Davis of Arsenal – the other London club Frank could have joined in 1989.

me, I'd swing my elbows to try and keep Hansen away from me. But as I went to crack him, he'd already read the situation perfectly and would step back a few paces so that my arms were thrashing away in thin air. He'd make me look stupid, like a girl! You had to laugh, though. He was superb, as were Liverpool as a team."

Even so, Frank scored twice against the Hansen-Lawro combination in his first game against Liverpool at Upton Park and netted another brace against Everton, who finished runners-up to their local rivals that season. He rates the first of his two against Neville Southall that afternoon – a sublime chip – as probably his best West Ham goal. "And scoring against Millwall, and seeing the joy on the faces of our fans, also meant a lot to me," he added.

"Wardie told me that Mick McCarthy was going to break my leg when we played at Man City. I said, 'who's Mick McCarthy?'

"I always believed in getting my retaliation in first," says Frank. "so, as you do, I smashed McCarthy right in the nose in the first minute of the game at Maine Road. I thought, 'I've got him' – well, in those days you could tackle defenders and get away with it, not even get a booking. As I turned round, I said, 'oh, I'm sorry' with a big smile on my face.

"I saw blood all over his face – but he was still standing! I thought, 'shit!'. In his broad Yorkshire accent, McCarthy asked menacingly: 'Did you mean that?' and then he added: 'You might be a better player than I am but you'll never meet a harder player than me'. He then proceeded to kick the crap out of me for the next 89 minutes! Every time I stopped, he just punched me. So I just kept running – the only respite I got was at half-time. Even then, I thought he was going to come into our dressing room and punch me!

"I learned an invaluable lesson that day. Mick was hard but, at the same time, he respected me for the fact that I could give it as well as take it and, later on in my career, we became team-mates at Celtic. He was all for the way I played when we were in the same team at Celtic and he liked the way I always defended from the front.

"Even later in my career, Mick tried to sign me when he became manager of Millwall. But I could never have signed for Millwall on principle, because of what West Ham fans would have thought of me. I'm loyal like that. I was twice asked to sign for Rangers – I could have followed Mo Johnston, who went from Celtic to Ibrox – but I just couldn't do it. It has nothing to do with religion – it's just a personal thing. It would have hurt too many people. It's not right."

Frank continues to recall past opponents with big reputations and the battles he usually relished.

He says: "Although Tony (Cottee) didn't used to like playing against Tony Adams of Arsenal, I did. I smashed him as well and he reacted like a big baby. 'There's no need to do that?' he said to me once. I looked over to the Arsenal bench and saw my mate, Charlie Nicholas, laughing. He'd told me before the game that Tony Adams was going to smash me but I'd done the same to him – first. It turned out Tony had never said any such thing to Charlie, so I felt a bit sorry afterwards for what I did to Tony!

"But they were all good players and I liked playing against them. I enjoyed the banter with opponents – it was all good fun."

Frank starts to chuckle to himself again as more memories re-surface. "Terry Butcher was another who hated me. When Wardie got tripped up for that penalty against Ipswich, which should never have been given, but Ray Stewart scored it when we were still going for the title, Butcher was so angry that he kicked the dressing room door in.

"I liked to wind up Butcher and when we played against each other after I'd left West Ham to join Celtic and he'd moved to Glasgow Rangers, he delighted in reminding me that I'd never managed to score against him during my time in England.

"I told him during the game: 'No, I didn't, you stupid big p***k. But everyone else did!' I used to take him for a walk, to create space for others. I'd also tell Butcher to shut up and 'go and put a bandage on your head!" – a sarcastic reference to that famous early 90s image of England captain Butcher with his forehead swathed in a bloodstained bandage. "It was all good banter," says Frank.

"Mark Wright of Southampton was good, though. We were playing against each other in a meaningless end-of-season match once and we made a pact at the start that we wouldn't try to smash each other because we were both going on our summer holidays the following week! We tackled each other, of course, but we agreed that there would be no flying elbows from either of us that day.

"There was much more of a physical battle between strikers and defenders in my day. Some of the wimps playing today would be locked up in a mental home if players tackled the way we used to.

"I don't like to see diving but, having said that, when someone came near me in the box, I went down. It was part of the game. But you wouldn't dive and then roll over 13 times before looking up at the ref to see if he's going to give the penalty. I hate it when they do that. They don't book players enough for diving. They do when they go down in the box, but not enough when they deliberately dive outside the penalty area. It spoils the game."

Frank earned all six of his full Scotland caps during his first spell at West Ham. His debut goal in a 2-0 play-off win against Australia at Hampden Park in November 1985 helped to secure the Scots' ticket to the '86 World Cup finals in Mexico, where manager Alex Ferguson left a frustrated Frank kicking his heels on the subs' bench. Fergie's authoritarian approach was never going to make Frank and other free spirits like his old drinking pal Mo Johnston automatic choices, but canny John Lyall certainly knew how to handle McAvennie.

As word of his fantastic form spread and the Wogan TV appearance catapulted him into the national spotlight, the media clamoured for a bigger slice of the striker who stood out for much more than his dazzling hair. Lyall didn't mind Frank dominating most of the headlines but he never let him take liberties, as confirmed by a sequence of events that followed his triumphant Scotland debut. Frank relates a story that underlined Lyall's reputation as a brilliant man-manager who commanded the respect of his players by deeds, not only words.

"It was around the time of *Wogan* and I was suddenly getting a lot of press attention. Anyway, I'd agreed to do a TV interview at the training ground one morning but, in the meantime, I'd arranged to have some friends around to my flat in Brentwood for a few drinks the night after I'd scored my first goal for Scotland.

"We had a great time, plenty to drink and in the morning I had a big hangover. I thought I'd phone the training ground and say that I wasn't feeling too good. I'd expected Rob Jenkins or one of the coaches – Ronnie Boyce, Mick McGiven or Tony Carr – to answer it. I'd hoped to be speaking to Rob – you could always bribe him with a few cans of beer! – so I was a bit surprised when John Lyall picked up the receiver.

"I put on my best pitiful-sounding voice and said: 'John, I'm not feeling too well this morning, it must be a reaction from the game the other night or something. Is it okay if I give training a miss today and come in tomorrow?'

"He seemed genuinely concerned for my health and said something like: 'I'm sorry to hear that, son. It wouldn't be a problem to me if you have the day off except there are camera crews from ITV and BBC here and they're waiting to interview you'.

"I'd forgotten all about the interviews, to be honest, and so I asked John if he'd take care of it for me – make my apologies and explain to the television people that I wasn't feeling well and wouldn't be coming in to train that day. 'Okay son, leave it to me. No problem,' John reassured me.

"And with that I went back to bed to continue sleeping off my hangover.

"About 20 minutes later, there was a knock at my front door. John had sorted it for me, all right – he'd sent the camera crews up to my house! There were comatose bodies strewn all over my living room, so I quickly had to wake everyone up and bundled them upstairs to a bedroom, where they were piled up on top of each other. I got dressed and did the interview.

"I still had to make out to the interviewer that I wasn't feeling too well and afterwards they made a big thing on the telly about me possibly having to miss the trip to Australia for the second leg of our World Cup play-off qualifier. I was pissed, that's all it was, but the bloke interviewing me didn't seem to realise that. I've always said that I should always have been an actor!"

If Lyall did ever have reason to concern himself about what Frank might be getting up to off the field, he never had cause to doubt his commitment to West Ham on it. Especially after his in-form striker flew from the other side of the world on the morning of a game and insisted on playing for his club.

Frank explained: "I flew back from Australia, where we'd played that World Cup qualifier, and although John said I could take the day off, I told him that I wanted to play for West Ham at QPR. I don't think any other Scotland player on that long trip home played for their league club that day. We didn't fly into Heathrow until about nine o'clock on the morning of the game at QPR but I came through it and even scored our winner."

For all his sensational headline-making exploits through the years, Frank points out that his nocturnal off the field activities were exaggerated by tabloids waging a circulation war who saw him as an easy prime target. "I could never have played football if I did even half the things the papers claimed I was supposed to have done. I went out socialising up to Wednesday but on Thursdays and Fridays I was always chilled," he insists.

It was always going to be difficult, if not impossible, for West Ham – and Frank – to emulate 1985-86 and McAvennie, whose league goals tally dipped to just seven in 36 appearances in 1986-87, has his own theories on why Hammers were soon languishing back at the wrong end of the table.

"The board didn't give John the money to go out and buy the new players," he reflects. "We needed a bigger squad and to freshen it up. It was important to sign people while we were at the top and just about everyone would've wanted to play for us after the superb season we'd just had.

"It would have been hard for any new signing to have broken straight into the first team at that time, although I thought we only needed to strengthen the left-back position, where Steve Walford played and, later, (the right-footed) George Parris filled in.

"I'll tell you what, if we'd had Dicksy (Julian Dicks) in the team then, we would have won everything, because he could play. He could pass the ball 60 yards and he would have been great for Dev on the left-hand side. He'd have given the ball to Dev and then bombed on by him. And he would've looked after Dev, who used to take some stick from the opposition.

"We didn't need to bring in many new faces, because we already had Bonzo in our squad, an experienced player to come in as and when necessary once he was fit again. He was out injured all that season but we saw him in training every day and he was very good behind the scenes. We all respected him.

"But when John did buy, he bought mainly the wrong players," he said, recalling this period of decline.

"I hate to blame other people but Stewart Robson wasn't a West Ham player," says Frank, not the first of his team-mates from that period to be critical of Lyall's decision lavish £700,000 on the former Arsenal midfielder. Robust and wholehearted, Robson struggled to fit into a side whose attacking momentum was based on a slick passing game, intelligent movement and creative use of space.

"In my second season, I made my move as soon as the ball came out of defence – three steps ahead of the play. But the ball was going to Stewart and then it stopped. I was making my runs and getting caught offside. He didn't pass it when he should have done. I felt like I was behind Wardie and wasn't getting in the box when the crosses came in.

"I don't know whether Robson lacked vision or if he was just trying to prove what a good player he was? But, for me, good players can play one and two-touch, as we liked to do and that's how we played throughout my first season. It was beautiful to watch."

Frank revealed that he voiced his concerns to the manager. "I told him that I was having to change my game because of the way we were playing in my second season. I wasn't scoring enough goals but John tried to reassure me by saying: 'You're doing more work than anybody else'. He told me how much he appreciated what I was doing. He was happy with the way I was playing but I wasn't. I wasn't enjoying it like I had in my first season. It was becoming a chore, because I was changing my game for other people.

"It sounds strange, but I thought that I actually played better in my second season – without scoring the goals – than I did in my first. I developed into a better all round player but, too often, I was coming too deep in search of the ball. I was still working hard for the team but it wasn't doing my own form any good.

Eight games into the 1987-88 season, Frank suddenly found himself looking towards home and a dream move to Celtic.

It's well known that Lyall looked after West Ham's finances assiduously, as if it was his own money. Those who played under him talk of his tough, sometimes intimidating, negotiating tactics when it came to contracts. In September 1987, feeling a bit miffed when he discovered that he wasn't the highest paid player at Upton Park (Tony Cottee was), Frank approached the manager about a wage increase and it was agreed that he would be paid an extra £500 a week, raising his weekly basic to £1,500. In return, Lyall wanted McAvennie to commit to an extension of his contract – in the days when contracts still meant something.

But in fellow Scot and agent Bill McMurdo, Frank employed one of the most canny operators in the business, at a time when agents were still relatively new to football, and they requested an extra 50 grand signing-on fee that Lyall could not sanction. He pointed out that it was against club policy to pay any players a signing-on fee at that time, which, strange though it seems today, was true back then. Frank had more or less resigned himself to staying at Upton Park when he was informed by Lyall that the club had agreed to sell him for £750,000.

"I'm convinced that John set up the deal," he says. "It was Celtic's centenary year

On the ball at Upton Park at the start of the 1987-88 season. Within a month Frank left to join his boyhood idols Celtic in a shock £750,000 deal.

Showing he's still got it . . . Frank scoring against Chelsea in the 2002 London Masters five-a-side.

and he knew Big Jock (Stein) and the manager Billy McNeill. I think he only let me go because he knew it was my club and how much I'd always dreamed of playing for Celtic. But the fact is, I didn't really want to go.

"It's all about destiny and who knows what would have happened if I'd stayed at Upton Park. Maybe Macari would never have got the job there…?"

Within 18 months and his boyhood dreams fulfilled as one of the biggest stars of Celtic's 1987-88 Scottish League and Cup double-winning side (Macca scored 27 goals in 55 matches, including both goals in The Bhoys' 2-1 Cup final win over Dundee United), Frank was eager to escape the Glasgow goldfish bowl and return south of the border.

Arsenal, who were on the verge of winning the first division championship, offered him the same amount of money as John Lyall did to bring him back to Upton Park. Arsenal ultimately snatched the title from their main rivals Liverpool on dramatic Friday night at Anfield. West Ham were heading for relegation, their fate confirmed by a 5-1 thrashing by the Reds just five days before the Gunners' triumphed at the same ground.

"I could never have played for George Graham, although I did at least meet him to discuss the possible move," says Frank. "I took a couple of Page 3 girls with me to my meeting with him at the Holiday Inn in Mayfair, where I always stayed when I was visiting London. The two girls disappeared while George and I chatted. When we'd finished, they came back downstairs to join me and I said to George, 'we're going to a nightclub, are you sure you don't want to come with us?' He gave me one of those looks and we didn't speak for a couple of years, but he eventually signed Ian Wright instead.

"George offered me the same money that West Ham did but I spoke to Charlie Nicholas, Graeme Souness and Kenny Dalglish about him and while they all agreed that George and I would have got on okay for a couple of months, he would then have stamped his authority on me. They knew that I couldn't have played for him. John Lyall was strong, too, but he knew how to handle me."

A broken arm, sustained while playing for Celtic shortly before his then club record £1.2m return to Upton Park in March 1989, hampered Frank's contribution in the final two months of that depressing season. He failed to score in any of his eight appearances and, despite a spirited late rally from Hammers, they slipped out of the top flight. Worse still, the man who brought him back paid the ultimate price for relegation with the sack.

The board believed that Lyall was a spent force, that it was time for a long overdue shake-up. Most of the senior players, who considered John a father figure, rebelled.

"John was the reason I came back to West Ham," says Frank, "but even he admitted to me before I'd re-signed, 'we're going down and not even you can stop us'. I think he knew we didn't have a good enough team and that he was planning to make changes for the following year, but he never got the chance to. No disrespect, but when I went back, there were players at West Ham who shouldn't have been there – they couldn't trap a medicine ball in a phone box. I had the feeling of 'where did my club go to?' It was different.

"I remember saying to Alvin that I felt a big weight on my shoulders when I came back to the club, as if people were expecting great things of me."

Frank described the sacking of Lyall as "the worst thing I've ever seen in football." He says: "It was a horrible, horrible situation and I think John would still be alive now if it had all been done right. Getting the sack hurt him, big time.

"The ideal thing – and John would've accepted it – was to have appointed Bonzo as John's assistant for a year. I think John had primed Bonzo for his job anyway.

Frank and his wife Karen, who were married in 2001.

With John Lyall, the man who signed him twice for West Ham, at the Boys of 86 Dinner to honour the Cup-winning teams of 1975 and 1980 in September 2005. It was the last time they met before John's death the following April.

Possibly Alvin, too, would have had a future role to play in the management of West Ham if John had stayed at the club.

"Alvin had a bad experience at Southend but I honestly think he would have been an excellent manager. I could've played for Alvin. Would he have been strong enough? Yeah – have you never seen him after a glass of red wine!" Cue more laughter from Frank. "On the park, you didn't f*** about with Alvin.

"I lost a lot of respect for the club when John went. In hindsight, I wouldn't have gone back if I'd known that he would soon be gone. If it hadn't been for John, there's no way I would've wanted to go back there.

"But I'm also a realist and, at the time, I thought, 'b******s to this, let's get straight back up again'.

Lyall's successor, disciplinarian and long-ball advocate Lou Macari, immediately set about improving his players' fitness levels. He went down with most of the senior players like a lead balloon. There's the classic story about how the new boss, anxious to impose his healthy, clean-living philosophy on his new charges, bumped into McAvennie in the reception of the Swallow Hotel at Waltham Abbey – as well as being the usual meeting place prior to away games, it also became the temporary home of numerous new arrivals immediately after they joined the club.

It was close to midnight when Macari entered the hotel, only to find Frank suited and booted and obviously looking anything but about to retire to his bed. The conversation between the fellow Scots went something like this:

Lou: "Hello Frank, so where have you been tonight?"

Frank: "Nowhere . . . I'm just on my way out now."

To teetotal Macari, McAvennie's 'champagne lifestyle', as the tabloids liked to describe it, was anathema and they were never going to get on, although you would be hard pressed to find many Hammers players from that time who did have many good words to say about him. A scathing Frank said: "He almost ruined the club.

"Macari actually fined Ludo (Miklosko) for rolling the ball out, because he thought our keeper should be making the most of his big drop-kick. What kind of football is that?

"As soon as he arrived at the club, he told me, 'I'm gonna change you'. Why should he want to change me when I was doing well? Things were so bad, some of us actually talked about going on strike.

"I didn't want to play for him and the ironic thing is that he was one of my playing heroes when I was a kid growing up on the terraces at Celtic. I thought he was a great player . . . but he was the worst manager in the world.

"I know a lot of West Ham fans hated Incey (Paul Ince) but he would never have wanted to leave West Ham if John had stayed. The club could have become so big but Incey was another who didn't want to play for Macari.

"I think a lot of people who were at West Ham under John felt betrayed by the club over his sacking and the way he was treated."

Unfortunately, we will never know how McAvennie would have performed for West Ham under Macari. Just 55 minutes into the new season at Stoke, City's Chris Kamara – now much more well known for his excitable commentating style on Sky Sports than he ever was as a player – scythed through the back of Macca as he was about to receive a midfield pass. The heavy challenge left the Hammer in a crumpled heap, clutching his left leg that was broken just above the ankle and severely torn ankle ligaments. No-one realised the immediate extent of the damage – the ref actually waved play on and the game continued for a minute before Rob Jenkins came on to the field – but Frank left the old Victoria Ground on a stretcher.

Recalling the most agonising moment of his career, he says: "The tackle was a bit late but Kamara didn't realise how badly hurt I was. He said, 'get up you Scottish b******, it's a man's game,' and I called him everything in return.

"But it could have been much worse. Macari wanted them to operate on my leg, there and then in Stoke General Hospital, where the doctors said that I wouldn't even walk properly again, let alone be able to play football. They said my career was finished and I told them, 'f*** off, are you on drugs?'

"I said, 'strap it up. If you're saying my career's finished, then I'd rather hear it from one of the top surgeons in London'.

"So they strapped me up, gave me morphine to kill the pain and I travelled back to London with the other players – lying at the back of the team bus having a smoke! I was spaced out.

"I had the op' the next day at Roding Hospital in Redbridge. I was in plaster up to my arse, although the damage to my ligaments was worse. My left ankle still seizes up today when I'm walking and the weather gets a bit colder. I had an operation recently to clean it up and the surgeon who did it says he can't believe I'm still walking on that leg. Apart from the damage to my ligaments, arthritis has now set in.

"A lot of people don't know that I've broken just about ever bone in my body . . . my ankle, arms and my skull (at St Mirren, in the season before I joined West Ham) when I clashed heads in a cup quarter-final and was knocked out.

"But I don't bear a grudge towards Chris Kamara. Soon after the incident, Macari was quoted in the papers as saying that I possibly intended to sue Kamara but that was all nonsense – I didn't even know that I could've sued him and it never crossed my mind to do so. The first I knew about me supposedly suing him was when I woke up in hospital and read it in the papers.

"Kamara has never apologised to me for the tackle but we did speak years later, when I met him on an ex-pro's tour to Trinidad & Tobago and he asked me if we could have a picture taken together."

Frank admits: "I was never the same player after what was an horrific injury – only about 80 per cent of what I was before it. I've been taking anti-inflammatory tablets to keep the swelling down since 1990 and I still take them, twice a day, every day. I take more pills for my ankle now than when I was playing. Bonzo once said to me that I ran with a limp, but I'd never realised it.

"But having said that, when I went back to Celtic and Liam Brady was the gaffer there, before Macari turned up, he got me fit again. Liam had me training hard twice a day – with the other players in the mornings and then on my own in the afternoons. I look back now and think that perhaps Bonzo could have done more to have got me fitter.

"You need luck in football, too, and although I couldn't stand Macari, I would still have done it for the club on the park if I hadn't broke my leg in that first season we were in the second division. I'm convinced I would have scored the goals to have got us promotion at the first time of asking."

By the time Frank resumed to make just four sub appearances towards the end of the 1989-90 campaign, Macari had resigned and Billy Bonds stepped up from youth team coach to succeed him. The long, gruelling road back to fitness had taken its toll on Frank, though.

He admits he was never the greatest trainer and his increasingly indulgent lifestyle around this period didn't help his cause. During his near season-long absence, when Frank admits he stepped up his socialising and started dabbling in drugs, Bonzo had more strikers to choose from in Macari's winter signings Trevor Morley and Jimmy Quinn.

Even after scoring his first Hammers goal for three years and their first of the 1990-91 season, at home against Portsmouth, he was unable to command a regular place in the side. In 24 starts, he weighed in with 10 more than useful league goals as Bonzo's boys remained on course for promotion. But in 10 other matches he had to try and make his mark after coming on as a substitute. Mid-season signing Iain Dowie and rapidly emerging youngster Stuart Slater, though more of a wide man, were also vying for a place in attack as competition for places continued to hot up.

Frank's frustration boiled over when, in a midweek home game against Bristol City in March '91, he was sent off along with opponent Andy Llewellyn. Apart from ending a run of 10 consecutive league starts, suspension also ruled Frank out of the FA Cup semi-final defeat against Nottingham Forest at Villa Park.

"I'd just come back after injury and the boy was kicking lumps out of me. Obviously, I didn't realise when I hit the lad that I'd miss such a massive occasion as the FA Cup semi-final," he says.

Maybe Forest were happy not having to face McAvennie that day. The next time he played against Brian Clough's side, it was in his final appearance in a West Ham shirt – and he departed with a timely show of typical flamboyance that would have been too far fetched even by Roy of the Rovers heroics.

McAvennie had scored three goals in 16 previous starts and three sub outings on Hammers' return to the top flight but he doubled his league tally by grabbing an unlikely hat-trick on the last day of another dismal season. With Forest meandering in eighth place and West Ham already having fallen backwards through the relegation trap door, rooted to the foot of the table, McAvennie stepped forward to sign off in a style every bit as sensational as that with which he had announced himself seven years earlier.

After Mitchell Thomas feigned a hamstring pull during the half-time break to pave the way for McAvennie's last hurrah, Bonds had no option but to throw on Frank, who grabbed his chance with both hands to score on the hour and then again in the 81st and 85th minutes. The last was his 49th goal in 153 league appearances for Hammers (he also bagged eight in 33 cup-ties). Even allowing for the fact that Cloughie had his son, centre-forward Nigel, playing as a makeshift centre-back alongside Serie A-bound England defender Des Walker, it was some parting gesture.

"Who writes your scripts?" asked a bemused and slightly embarrassed Billy Bonds afterwards, the boss acknowledging the headline-grabbing departure of a man whose final three-and-a-half year contract had ended and who had just been given a free transfer by the club. By then Frank was earning £2,200 a week, the most he ever earned from football, and second tier-bound Hammers could hardly wait to get him off their wage bill.

Bonzo had younger legs than the then 31-year-old McAvennie to call upon as he began plotting West Ham's return to the top flight – in tandem with his new assistant Harry Redknapp – the following season, but Frank was nevertheless "gutted" to be on his way out through the Boleyn gates for the second time in less than five years.

In fact, he has accused the club of trying to retire him prematurely to cash in the insurance policy they had taken out on him, their most expensive £1.2m playing asset. Relegation then wasn't the financial disaster it can be today but, in 1992, the club was struggling to come to terms with the multi-million pound implementation of compulsory stadium redevelopment as dictated by the Taylor report into the Hillsborough Disaster of 1989. Bonds had a very limited transfer budget to work with because the club faced a battle to woo back the disgruntled fans who had turned their back on West Ham in the wake of the controversial bond scheme. It wasn't a good time to be a Hammers fan, or a player.

Frank says: "I was very unhappy when I found out that the club wanted to sign my insurance form to say that I wasn't considered to be fit enough to play again."

Even when reflecting on one of the most unhappy periods of his career, the cheeky grin returns to Macca's face as he admits: "I actually broke into the filing cabinet at Chadwell Heath and stole my file, where I found some medical correspondence about my injury. I knew something wasn't right.

"I went back to see the surgeon who had operated on me and it turned out that the injury the club thought had ended my career was, in fact, just an Achilles problem – and I was back training and playing again within two weeks.

"Now if they had come to me and said, 'look, here's four hundred grand and we'll take eight,' I might have agreed to the proposed insurance claim, but it was the way it was handled by the club that pissed me off.

"In the end, they didn't get anything for me, because I stayed on until the end of my contract.

"I'd like to have stayed at West Ham but, to be honest, I don't think Bonzo wanted me there. I was a lazy f****r in training but put a ball in front of me and I'd run all day long. I've never liked the running we had to do in training – and Dicksy was like me in that respect.

"When Bonzo was the gaffer, he sent us on a four-mile, pre-season run towards Romford, but me and Dicksy had other ideas. We started at the back of the group because we knew that's where we were going to end up! So, when all the others had gone off ahead of us, we jumped on the back of a passing milk float, hid among the crates and then got off again once we got close to the training ground, having passed most of the lads on the way.

"We had to tell the milkman to slow down, because it would've looked too suspicious if we'd got back first, ahead of Martin Allen, who was running like mad up front. We saw a gap between runners and came in about sixth and seventh but none of the coaches or the other players could believe how we'd finished the 'run' so quickly! Bonzo said: 'Different class, lads!'

"I think it was Paul Hilton and Tony Carr who were positioned on a couple of street corners en route, checking each player back in. After all the players had completed the run, they eventually arrived back at the training ground and told Bonzo that Dicksy and me must still be out there on the run somewhere. 'No, they're already back here and changed,' someone informed them. 'Well, they haven't f*****g passed me,' said Hilts! We had some fun.

"I never bore Bonzo any grudges, though. Managers have to make difficult decisions. I saw him later on at Celtic, when I was playing back there again and he'd come up to watch a game with Boycey and Tony Carr. Bonzo didn't have to come over to talk to me but I told him then that I held no grudges against him. I'd wanted him to take over from John Lyall as our manager and he should still be working at West Ham today."

After extending his eventful career – initially in Hong Kong with the South China team and then at Aston Villa and back in Scotland with Celtic (10 goals in 30 matches between 1992-94) and Falkirk – Frank's life after his playing days ended has been littered with, in the words of his own book, failed business ventures, court appearances and even imprisonment. Indeed, after kindly offering to collect me from Newcastle airport before this interview was conducted in September 2008, he

Frank pictured when EX interviewed him in September 2008.

spoke about an incident just a couple of months earlier, when he became embroiled in a bar skirmish with a local man while visiting the Isle of Man for a veterans' football match. Frank had been arrested after intervening when the man became aggressive towards his fellow former Scottish international Andy Goram but hopefully he will soon be cleared by the courts.

As he sipped afternoon coffee in the lounge of one of Newcastle's top hotels, Frank expressed the fervent hope that he had put all his past problems firmly behind him. He is upbeat and says his life is now on an upward curve again, with hopes for a much brighter future.

Married life has clearly been good for him – he and the beautiful Karen Lamberti, who live near Gateshead, were wed in September 2001 – and proud father Frank is also delighted to be in more regular contact again with his 12-year-old son Jake, from his first marriage, to Laura, in 1995.

And on the business front, he is looking to become an officially licenced football agent in the near future. He has gone into partnership with a friend in Scotland and their Calcio Promotions company already has some useful teenage prospects on their books. In fact, with the interview over, Frank set the Sat Nav in his new Audi to direct us to the Newcastle United's nearby Academy training ground, where we stood in the rain to watch the local team play Celtic in an under-17s friendly. Frank wanted to keep an eye on the promising Celtic striker who has already been signed to his company.

Although he enjoys being based in the North-East, 48-year-old Frank never misses the chance to return south and be among West Ham people who remember him as the unknown who turned into a golden boy. He has agreed to help launch our In My Day book in November and is still in big demand on the after-dinner circuit, too. And this adopted Geordie, with that mischievous grin as wide as the Tyne, is not yet about to join a monastery – he still likes the occasional night on the toon.

"The way my life's been, what I did for West Ham in my first season still seems like yesterday to me," he says. "My life's certainly not been dull and my football days have passed by a lot quicker than I expected.

"Maybe I could've done things a lot differently and maybe I should have, but I'm not one for regrets. I know I could have done a lot more as a player, though, if it hadn't been for the injury at Stoke, so I didn't fulfil my potential. My biggest regret in football was West Ham sacking John Lyall.

"I was at a Celtic dinner a couple of years ago and someone told me that Kenny Dalglish has said that I could've been the best player Scotland has ever produced. For Kenny to have said that about me to somebody else is a great compliment. Looking back, though, Andy Walker at Celtic and Tony Cottee at West Ham have both said that I was the best striker they've ever played with, so that's a nice compliment too."

Chapter 19

LIAM**BRADY**

"I don't think John was comfortable with the world of football that was beginning to emerge then. You know, players going to the papers and slagging the club off or saying they wanted to leave, agents making demands – he hadn't encountered any of that before and it was all so distasteful for him"

IT was on Friday, March 13, 1987 that Liam Brady became a West Ham player and the signing certainly wasn't an unlucky one for manager John Lyall, whose team had been in danger of slipping into the relegation zone until the talented Irish midfielder provided some much needed inspiration at a vital stage of the campaign.

Only months earlier, the Hammers boss had looked on with immense satisfaction as the club celebrated its highest-ever finish in the top flight of English football – third place behind Liverpool and Everton in the unforgettable 1985-86 season.

However, having failed to build on that success by not being able to strengthen his talented but small squad in the summer, Lyall was now under pressure as injuries and loss of form affected results, to the extent that Hammers had won just two league games since the turn of the year.

As the March transfer deadline loomed, the chequebook finally came out to snap up some new recruits. England under-21 midfielder Stewart Robson and young defenders Gary Strodder and Tommy McQueen added extra youth to the side, but it was the arrival of 31-year-old Brady that really perked up the frustrated Hammers fans and brought a touch of class to the side.

After enjoying a glittering career with Arsenal in the 70s, the Republic of Ireland international had left the English game in 1980 to move to Italy, where he had spells with Juventus, Inter Milan and Sampdoria, before ending up at Ascoli, with whom he spent just a few months before a return to London beckoned.

Reflecting on the sudden move back to England that caused some surprise at the time, Liam revealed: "My last move in Italy wasn't the best choice I ever made and I was pretty unhappy at Ascoli. I made it known that I would welcome a move and things began to happen after that.

"In those days, I didn't have an agent, so it happened in the way these things used to be done – I told a journalist my situation and he contacted a few people for me.

"West Ham came in and once I'd met John Lyall, I was really determined to make that my next move. I got out of my situation with Ascoli, everything went through, and I was delighted to come back to London.

"Celtic actually came in for me but by then I'd shaken hands with John. Celtic

Liam with John Lyall after signing for West Ham in March 1987.

would have been very attractive to me, because of the size of the club, their traditions and the Irish connection, but I was very impressed with John and I was never going to break my word."

As a member of the Arsenal side defeated by the Hammers in the 1980 FA Cup final, Liam had first-hand experience of the tactical victory Lyall achieved when he moved an extra man into midfield and played David Cross up front on his own to combat the attacking threat of the Gunners.

Trevor Brooking's famous headed winner saw second division Hammers triumph over their north London rivals and – in what was his last game on English soil before a big-money move to Juventus – Liam admits he was left with a permanent reminder of Lyall's qualities as a manager.

"John always came across as a real football person and a man of integrity – the sort of manager I was keen to get involved with," he says.

"I suppose the 1980 FA Cup final was when I realised how good a manager he was, because he got one over on Terry Neill with his tactics that day.

"Football is all about decisions and they either work for you or backfire on you. Had we got the first goal that day and gone on to win the game, people might have said that John set his team up the wrong way.

"But it worked for them, they got the early goal and held on, and we had a problem with it. They had an extra man in midfield and it stifled us. Paul Allen was man-marking me and Stuart Pearson had dropped back to help him, and it won the day for them.

"That's the West Ham perspective, though. From Arsenal's point of view, after a marathon semi-final against Liverpool that went to three replays and a monumental battle against Juventus in the ECWC semi-final, it was just one game too many for us and we were a little short of freshness that day.

"The truth, I suppose, is somewhere in between!"

The West Ham team that had denied Liam a second FA Cup winners' medal in the space of 12 months was a far cry from the somewhat dispirited one he found when he returned to England almost seven years later.

He says: "West Ham had finished third the previous season but it was a bit like after the Lord Mayor's show and they weren't doing very well. I came into a situation where the team was struggling but I knew they had a lot of good players and some very bright youngsters coming through.

"I knew the likes of Billy Bonds, Alvin Martin and Alan Devonshire, they were all great players and great blokes – real football people, so I was very comfortable about coming back to England at West Ham. My debut wasn't the greatest – we lost 2-0 at home to Norwich – and I could see that the players were low in confidence and a little bit worried about the situation we were in.

"Thankfully, things picked up and we secured the points we needed to make ourselves safe that season. I like to think I made a decent contribution in those last couple of months and I settled in at the club straight away," Liam recalled.

Indeed, it took only five games for Brady to establish himself as a true favourite at Upton Park, when he scored the goal that capped a magnificent 3-1 win over . . . Arsenal. In fact, what was described as an 'inflammatory gesture' while celebrating his strike led to a yellow card for the gifted Irishman – making him one of the first players to be booked for over-zealous celebrations.

"I think that win gave us the breathing space we needed," says Liam, "and we eventually finished well clear of the bottom three."

A key factor in securing our top flight status had been Tony Cottee's prolific haul of 22 league goals. However, after making his full England debut earlier in the season, the 21-year-old goal-poacher handed in a transfer request near the end of the campaign and Liam admits that it didn't take him long to realise that one or two other players at the club were also unsettled.

"I could tell that there were things that weren't right," he says. "There was a little bit of unrest. Because West Ham had done so well the year before, I think a few other clubs got into the players. Celtic were on to Frank (McAvennie) and Tony Cottee and Mark Ward were also being chased.

"I think it unsettled them, because they had their heads turned and knew that they would earn a lot more money if they moved. That went on for a couple of years and, when you look at it, West Ham are a club who have probably always had to face that kind of situation, which is a shame."

Having played his part in helping to steady the ship at Upton Park in the final two months of the 1986-87 campaign, Liam began the following season as a regular on the left side of midfield following injury to Alan Devonshire.

With Frank McAvennie soon departed to Celtic, the season turned into another struggle for Lyall's men and was compounded with personal misery for Liam, who sustained a cruciate knee ligament injury during a clash against Derby County in February 1988.

Not only did it end his season, it also ruled the proud Irishman out of his country's first-ever appearance at a major international tournament – the following summer's

European Championships in Germany.

"I'd played all eight games in the qualifiers and the injury more or less ended my Irish career," he admits, looking back on a fantastic haul of 72 full caps for the Republic of Ireland.

"In many ways, it probably ended my West Ham career, too. Had it not happened, I think I could have played on for longer and given greater service to the club.

"When I got back, I was never the same player again. I'd lost some pace and I seemed to suffer more from minor problems – back pain, aching joints, that sort of thing. I came back in the relegation season, which made things even worse, and I was just sad that my contribution was damaged by the injury I got."

Having spent more than nine months looking on from the sidelines, the experienced Brady could see the club was on a downward spiral and, after relegation at the end of the 1988-89 season signalled the end of John Lyall's 34-year association with the club, he believes the malaise surrounding West Ham was matched by the game itself.

"I don't think John was comfortable with the world of football that was beginning to emerge then," says Liam. "You know, players going to the papers and slagging the club off or saying they wanted to leave, agents making demands – he hadn't encountered any of that before and it was all so distasteful for him.

"If he'd been more of a ducker and diver, he might have been able to handle it better, but that wasn't John's style and maybe, in the end, he was too honest and genuine for his own good.

"Maybe he'd lost a bit of enthusiasm because of the way it was going but the situation was never arrested and it ended in major disappointment."

The summer of 1989 appeared to herald a brand new era at West Ham United, with the appointment of Lou Macari as Lyall's successor marking a completely new direction and style of management for the club. However, the change simply led to even greater disruption in east London and, although he wasn't absolutely sure of it at the time, the 1989-90 campaign turned out to be Liam Brady's last as a professional footballer.

He reveals: "I'd been having doubts about my future at West Ham and then, when I saw Lou's management style, I knew things were going to get worse before they got better.

"Lou had this way of being confrontational all the time – he used to do things to upset players and that was his style. A lot of the West Ham lads were set in their ways and didn't take too kindly to the way he treated them.

"I think it needed someone to come in, sit them down and say: 'You lot are all coming to the end here if you're not careful, so realise that you can only improve your careers by being good professionals and getting results. That way you can prolong your time here.'

"But Lou didn't approach it that way, he confronted them with aggression and it just went from bad to worse. There was all sorts going on and I think, to be honest, he lost interest in the whole thing after a couple of months. His antagonistic approach hadn't got the reaction he wanted from a lot of the players, and it's a pity they didn't give the job to Billy Bonds in the first place."

Hammers legend Bonzo was eventually handed the task of picking up the pieces following Macari's controversial departure in February 1990 but, by then, Liam had already decided that his boots would be going away for good at the end of the season – even the sudden change of personnel at management level wasn't going to change his mind.

"I didn't say anything publicly at the time, but I kind of made my mind up that it was going to be my last season. I think I told Billy and a few of the players, my contract was up anyway and I began making other plans.

"I don't know, maybe if Billy had asked me to stay another year and perhaps help with some coaching, I might have considered it. But I think he probably realised he could do with saving on my wages to bring someone else in and add some younger blood to the squad."

So with his departure confirmed, and the likes of young Kevin Keen and Stuart Slater beginning to emerge as long-term contenders for the wide left position, Liam prepared to see out his final season having, ironically, at last found some relative peace and calm at club level.

However, in typical Brady style, his farewell was anything but mediocre. With Wolverhampton Wanderers the visitors in a final day fixture that meant nothing to either side following the end of their play-off aspirations weeks earlier, the relaxed atmosphere enabled Bonds to send on his veteran substitute late in the game with three points already in the bag.

And the Irishman responded by rounding off a glittering 17-year professional career with a stunning 25-yarder that sparked a mini pitch invasion and prompted referee David Allison to blow his full-time whistle two minutes early in order to avoid further mayhem!

"I don't think many people have retired by scoring a goal with the last kick of the game – it was a bit extraordinary to say the least," smiles Liam.

"Billy had asked me if I wanted to play from the start. I said no, because I was going and it was a chance to give a young lad like Kevin Keen a go, to stand him in good stead for the following season.

"I told Billy that I'd come on in the second half, to either win it for him or enjoy the victory! He just chuckled, but that was more or less how it happened. We were 3-0 up and I just said: 'I'll come on now, Bill.'

"The goal was a lovely way to end it all, and I'll never forget turning away to see the fans running towards me! That was the Chicken Run, who were great towards you if you were having a good game, but not so friendly if you were having a poor one!

"They were on my side that day, though, and it was a nice way to go out. I enjoyed my time at West Ham, I got to know what the club was all about and what the fans want – football played the right way, a bit of flair thrown in and plenty of commitment, too."

After using that magical left foot for the very last time in spectacular style, a surprising lack of coaching offers meant that Liam didn't take the usual route favoured by retired players. Having seen the growing influence of agents in the game, he used his sharp brain to create a new career for himself.

AVCO

"I started a sports management company because I could see it was going to be big, big business," he says. "I thought there was a place for people to do it properly – to give players good advice, keep them out of the papers and teach them how to look after their money.

"I could see there was all sorts going on. Agents were coming in from everywhere, not necessarily with the best interests of the players and clubs at heart, and I could see a niche for representing people in the right way.

"I set up with a guy called Fintan Drury, who was based in Dublin and has since gone on to bigger and better things, and we named the company Brady Drury Sports Management. Fintan had the business expertise, while I was the one on the ground, dealing closely with the players and clubs. We had the likes of Julian Dicks and Stuart Slater on the books, and it was going very well to begin with, but then I got the chance to manage Celtic in 1991 and the whole thing fizzled out.

"Even after being involved for just a little while, though, I could see the life of an agent wasn't really for me. I only scratched the surface, to be honest, but I could see there was a lot of ducking and diving going on – and it's only got worse really."

It was the unexpected offer to begin his managerial career with Celtic, in July 1991, that rescued Liam from the murky world of agents and handed him a deserved return to the game.

Having turned down the Scottish giants as a player just before signing for West Ham, he wasn't going to say no a second time, although one of the biggest jobs in football turned out to be slightly less prestigious than he had imagined it would be.

"It was a dream job that in some ways turned into a nightmare," admits Liam. "We'd signed Pat Bonner on to our books at the management company and he'd asked me to speak at his testimonial dinner, which I did.

"On the evening, I just got vibes from some people at Celtic that there was going to be change at the club and that perhaps I should be interested.

"In many ways, it was a great opportunity, but I was too inexperienced and I probably went into it with my eyes closed a little bit.

"With any football club, you've got to know the background and make sure you know exactly what you're taking on, and I was perhaps a little naive there. I think I kept up the footballing standards that the club and the fans demanded but, when it came to the crunch, I didn't really get the breaks or handle it correctly.

"It was also very results-driven. Second or third place was never good enough for Celtic and it was at a time when Rangers were dominating, throwing money at players whenever they needed them.

"I went two years without winning anything and in my third season it didn't look as though things were going to improve, so I decided it was time to go.

"I didn't get the sack, although I felt it was probably on the way, but I looked at the situation and thought I wasn't doing the job properly because of the pressure, and not handling the pressure in the way an experienced manager would.

"There were other factors, though, most notably the club's financial position. There were EGM's virtually every couple of months and it was unbelievable. There were people outside the club trying to get rid of the board, the board were hanging on, there was no money to bring the stadium up to date with the Taylor Report, the media were having a field day . . . and I was the manager in among it all. It was just the wrong place to be."

After resigning at Celtic in November 1993, Liam then stepped into a slightly less glamorous role as manager of struggling Brighton and Hove Albion. Despite guiding the Seagulls away from the second division relegation zone, though, he again found himself battling amidst boardroom wrangles and crippling financial restraints.

"I thought I had to salvage my managerial credentials somehow and beggars can't be choosers, so I went to Brighton," he explains. "I actually did quite well there – got them out of relegation trouble and brought the crowds back – but I was surrounded by financial issues. I had no resources whatsoever and, instead of realising after my second year that I'd done what I could there and should move on to a better job, I hung on at Brighton for another year.

"The last season left me so pissed off, though, that I said: 'That's it, I've had enough of management!' We had a board of directors who wanted to sell the stadium from under the fans' noses and just pocket the money – it was like a Carry On film at times.

"So I had five years or so in management, and that was long enough to get it out of my system completely!"

After his experiences as an agent and then manager, it must have come as something of a relief to Liam when his next job involved a return to his spiritual home, Highbury, to take on the responsibility of producing Arsenal's next generation of Premier League stars.

It was in August 1996 that he was offered the job as the club's Head of Youth Development and Academy Director and, more than 11 years later, he is still enjoying the role at the club he originally joined as a 15-year-old apprentice in the summer of 1971 before going on to play 307 games for them.

"I'm very pleased I got the job. The club wanted someone to oversee the youth development, but not be attached to the first team manager, so that if the manager left, they would keep the stability at youth level.

"The role has its pressures, and youth football does have its unsavoury aspects. The worst part is having to tell a young lad that he is no longer wanted by the club. Nowadays, you have to tell them at the age of nine, 10, 11 – every year you have decisions to make – and it's heartbreaking for me as well as the kids.

"That's the big down side of it but there are many other rewarding aspects and, generally, it is a job I love doing. Having been at Celtic and Brighton, I certainly appreciate the fact that I am now involved with a club like Arsenal.

"To get the support and backing when you have an idea or a plan, and being allowed to carry it through on your terms, is something I wasn't used to, and the 12 years here have been great."

As for the future, he have no plans to eventually succeed Arsene Wenger as the main man at Highbury or, indeed, suffer any more stress at a senior level in the game. In March 2008, however, he did accept the part-time position as coaching assistant to the then newly-appointed Republic of Ireland manager, the Italian Giovanni Trapattoni, who was Liam's boss at Juventus in the early 80s.

“But no, there won’t be any return to full-time management,” he smiles. “I’m happy with my lot and the next thing on my list will be retirement,” adds Liam, now 52, who combines his roles with Arsenal and his country with regular punditry appearances for the RTE Irish television network.

Looking back on his brief but eventful spell at Upton Park, how would he reflect on his time as a Hammer?

“I suppose I’d say I was at the right club at the wrong time,” he admits. “And because of my injury, the fans never really got to see the best of me, which was a disappointment.

“But it was a great club to play for and I made some great friends there. I’m still always pleased to see the likes of Bonzo, Alvin, Dev, Galey and Parkesy, and John Lyall was a great manager for whom I had a lot of respect.”

WEST HAM UNITED F.C.
AVCO

Chapter 20

JULIAN**DICKS**

"When you have the assistant England manager telling me that I'd play if only I grew my hair longer, it's a bit of a joke really. Especially when you had people like Ian Wright and others with skinhead haircuts. I'd rather they had told me the truth"

WHEN Gianfranco Zola prepares his team for their next match, you can bet that he wishes he could count on the same kind of wholehearted performance from his players that four different former West Ham managers knew they would get from Julian Dicks every time he stepped onto the field.

Arguably the finest left-back in the club's history along with Frank Lampard, Julian first witnessed the passion of Hammers' fans when he played for Birmingham City at Upton Park in December 1985. "Going up and down in front of the Chicken Run as a 17-year-old was scary," he recalls.

Julian revealed that two months before John Lyall signed him for £300,000 in March 1988, Birmingham had turned down a slightly better offer from Glasgow Rangers boss Graeme Souness.

"John and his chief scout, Eddie Baily, met me in the office at Birmingham City. I was earning £140 per week, which was good money then, but John told me that I'd be on £650 a week basic at West Ham, plus £100 a match appearance money and bonuses depending on the team's league position.

"He asked me if I needed five minutes to think about it. I spoke to my then wife, who was a Birmingham girl, and after three or four minutes I said 'yes'."

Not that money was ever the be all and end all for Dicks, who was 19 when he left Birmingham and his old Polonez car for the bright lights of . . . Billericay.

He made his Hammers debut in a 2-1 defeat against Sheffield Wednesday at Hillsborough on April 2, 1988. He looked almost angelic, as if butter wouldn't melt in his mouth, when we saw him in the car park after the game, chatting to his parents. Their choice of names for their two sons – the eldest Grantley and then Julian – was a curious one. Grantley and Julian sounds more like a couple of yuppie accountants or IT geeks than no-nonsense footballers. (Grantley played non-league for Bath City). Mrs Carol Dicks explained that she wanted her sons to be "different" – and she certainly got her wish where Julian was concerned!

At West Ham, where he became an immediate hit with the fans, Julian was different class. He would prove to be one of Lyall's shrewdest signings and it was just as well for the club that he never considered leaving in the summer of 1989, after the Hammers had just been relegated and Lyall was sacked.

The arrival of Lou Macari was a culture shock to most of the players and no-one was more rebellious against the new manager and his methods than the man he appointed as his captain. Health-conscious Macari was perhaps a bit ahead of his time in banning high calorie foods from the training ground menu and refusing to allow his men to eat chips the night before a game.

Defiant Dicks would blatantly ignore tee-total Macari's rules, taking great delight in piling his plate sky high with chips as the team sat down for their evening meal in the hotel the night before an away game. Like a headmaster who had given up on his most troublesome pupil, Macari soon just shrugged his shoulders with an air of weary resignation.

"Lou and I got off on the wrong foot but he wanted me to calm down and play for England," recalls Julian. "That's why he took the captaincy away from Alvin Martin and gave it to me. He thought that by making me captain, I'd calm down. Alvin was fine about it, and it was a great feeling to be captain of such a great club. What an honour it was."

But, as Julian admits, the extra responsibility on his young shoulders did nothing to temper his conduct on the field. "It didn't work," he agrees.

"The worst thing about Lou is that he came in and tried to change the philosophy of how West Ham played football. He wanted the long-ball game and that wasn't for me. I wanted the ball on the floor. If a long ball was what was needed, then it had to be a quality pass. To me, just getting a ball and smashing it up the field, that just wasn't right, not with the class of players we had at West Ham then."

Despite failing to tame Dicks, the manager maintained a grudging respect for his best player and relished sparring with him. During training sessions in the gym, Macari liked to join in the five-a-side matches and his no-holds barred 50-50 tackles with his skipper were not for the faint hearted. Although Dicks irritated Macari with his undisciplined approach, the Scot knew he could always count on his Captain Courageous to go into battle for him throughout his seven months in charge.

Billy Bonds was universally welcomed as Macari's replacement in February 1990. Julian agreed: "The majority of the players wanted him to take over – he was the obvious choice."

But if Bonzo had any preconceived thoughts of taming Dicks in a way that Macari never did, those slim hopes were quickly dashed. The rebel player didn't share his new manager's enjoyment of punishing cross-country runs through the forest or even laps around the training pitches. "It used to take me and Frank McAvennie 13 minutes to complete a mile! I hated running – but come the game on Saturday, Bill knew I'd give him 95 minutes every time, whereas so-called 'fit' players didn't give him that same commitment," Julian points out.

Dicks and Bonds were united on one thing, though. When the club introduced its controversial bond scheme in 1992, neither manager nor captain would have much to do with trying to convince disgruntled supporters that it was worth buying into. When the West Ham 'hard man' spoke out publicly against the bond issue, it only enhanced his cult status among the fans who already idolised him anyway. If Dicksy hated the bond scheme and the ill conceived plan to extract upfront money from long-suffering fans, then what chance did the club have of supporters buying into their ambitious plan?

Julian Dicks has always been a non-conformist. His pre-match 'warm up' consisted of nothing more than thumping a ball against the wall of the small gymnasium under the main stand – he never went out onto the field with his team-mates to do loosen up muscles. "Timmy Breacker would be out there doing his stretches for what seemed like hours before a game, but I was lucky in that I didn't need to do all that," he explained.

While the other players were consuming recommended energy drinks in the final minutes before leaving the dressing room, Dicksy would guzzle down a can of Coca-Cola. The fact that he enjoyed a few pints of beer on nights out was irrelevant. Most of his team-mates around that time did, too!

On the team bus coming home from an away game, and unbeknown to the manager at the time, Dicks – the captain – and one or two others, would occasionally liven up the journey by 'mooning' out of the window at passing motorists! It wasn't the best example to be setting to younger team-mates but Julian, still displaying a stubborn streak, remains unrepentant.

"I know I got sent off and booked a lot of times, but I never let any manager down in a football sense," he protests.

Sure, he never gave less than total effort and, to the shame of some of his team-mates, would run through bricks walls in the cause. You could guarantee that he would always give as much against Farnborough as he did against Manchester United. He didn't need to rise to the occasion – to Dicks, *every* match was worth winning.

"It used to wind me up when I saw players around me not caring. I always wanted to win at all costs, but I never went out to deliberately hurt anyone," says Julian, trying to justify his natural aggression. He now admits, though, that his only regret of his career was the right elbow he thrust into the face of Newcastle United's Franz Carr at St James' Park in August 1992.

But he was no use to anyone when he was getting himself sent off for wild and reckless challenges and some skirmishes that bordered on outright thuggery (take a look at an action sequence from a game at Wolves in 1992, which now looks shocking on his *Terminator* DVD, and see if you can tell whether he's acting out a violent scene from the film *Green Street* or playing a football match!).

The statistical evidence, which reads more like a crime sheet, is both irrefutable and damning. He was at his most reckless during the 1992-93 season, when he made history by becoming the first, and only, West Ham player to be sent off *three times* in one season and missed 13 matches through suspension. In all, he was dismissed five times while playing for the Hammers.

It was his abrasive approach and poor reputation that cost him the senior England cap his ability in the early-90s surely merited. Although Graham Taylor did award Julian two England 'B' caps (v Czechoslovakia and the CIS), both Taylor and his successor Terry Venables admitted that the West Ham No.3 missed out on elevation to the main international stage due to his abysmal disciplinary record and an

Captain Courageous (ahead of Ludo Miklosko) leads out Hammers against Manchester United in 1992.

uncompromising persona that he just refused to change – for anyone.

Even now, Julian expresses no regrets that he didn't receive the England caps his skill warranted. "When I was younger, I would've loved to have played for England. I'm not being big-headed but I know I was good enough to play for my country.

"Graham Taylor took me to Russia with the senior squad but even though I was the only left-back he had available, he still played Andy Sinton – a left-winger – at left-back instead of me. I think it was my sendings-off and bookings that cost me the chance to play for the senior England team.

"But when you have the assistant England manager telling me that I'd play if only I grew my hair longer, it's a bit of a joke really. Especially when you had people like

Ian Wright and others with skinhead haircuts. I'd rather they had told me the truth."

The two international managers clearly considered him a liability, a ticking tomb-bomb easily capable of embarrassing the FA. Then again, a string of managers and players who were given the honour of representing England between then and now have done a very good job themselves of inflicting embarrassment upon the national football team, without any help from the risky former West Ham defender.

England has been bereft of genuine left-footed players for many years but Julian Dicks, in vintage form and even on an off-day, would walk into the national side these days. He was 10 times the player of left-footers Ashley Cole, Wayne Bridge and Stewart Downing combined.

What has to be given full acknowledgement, however, is that despite his rebellious nature, non-conformist attitude and innumerable over-aggressive challenges on the field, Julian was still a very skilful footballer. One of the most accomplished West Ham defenders – ever – when it came to distributing the football.

In stark contrast to his confrontational on-field image . . . the ripped shirt collar to free him of restrictions, baggy shorts and socks around his ankles, all topped off with the fearsome shaven-head look he favoured in his second spell with the club . . . there was also a subtlety to Julian that few people outside West Ham and its supporters could fully appreciate. Amid the flailing arms, elbows and boots, the eyeball-to-eyeball confrontations with opponents and referees, and the venomous penalties that were very rarely struck with anything less than brute force, it was easy to overlook the fact that he possessed one of the sweetest left foots in the game. He displayed a deftness of touch any midfielder would have cherished.

To Dicks, a long ball didn't mean an aimless punt in the vague direction of forward runners, as we've seen in recent seasons from defenders lacking the imagination and skill to deliver from the back line. When Julian struck a 60-yard crossfield pass, it reached the feet of his waiting team-mate with unerring pinpoint accuracy. It was a pass, not an ugly, hopeful hoof.

In his prime, and free of the terrible knee injuries that so blighted his career, Julian would have been the perfect wing-back, long before they became fashionable. His fitness levels were unquestionable, his shooting ability top class. He would cleverly chip balls onto the chest of target men like Leroy Rosenior and John Hartson and delivered consistently accurate crosses. And, of course, he tackled with all the tenacity of one of the Pit Bull Terriers he used to breed.

And considering his size, Julian was also one of the best headers of a ball – effective in either penalty area – and, for that reason, would also have made a strong left-sided centre-back.

I was treated to a classic example of Dicksy's skill and precision accuracy one afternoon while visiting the training ground to carry out some interviews. I had entered the gym area just as the players were finishing and making their way to the dressing rooms. Dicks was the last to leave. He was barefooted and there were still three or four discarded footballs around at one end of the large hall at Chadwell Heath. High on the wall at the opposite end of the brick building was a clock with a metal grill protecting it.

What happened next was unforgettable. I was amazed as Julian strode nonchalantly over to the balls and, even without teeing them up, thumped one after the other against its intended target – the clock face. His ferocious, yet bewildering accurate, strikes flew through the air over a distance of some 50 or 60 yards, rising all the time, until crashing against the metal frame of the clock. He wasn't showing off – there was no-one apart from myself looking on – and you couldn't help but admire the feat.

However, there were devilish days when he would childishly whack a stray football or two over the perimeter fence and onto the railway line, for some poor groundsman to try and retrieve. Billy Bonds would be there cursing him again.

When his transfer to Liverpool in September 1993 was imminent, if not quite signed and sealed, Julian once declined a polite approach for an interview with a little less than good grace. Ronnie Boyce, who was still coaching there at the time, turned to me with the consoling words: 'Don't take it personally, he talks to all of us like that sometimes!' I must add that it was a rare rebuff from Dicksy, who has otherwise always been helpful and willing to talk, providing many press men with a wealth of juicy quotes throughout his controversial and turbulent career.

That career was severely interrupted, and ultimately brought to a premature end, by a very bad knee injury he first suffered at Bristol City in October 1990. John Green, one of the new breed of qualified physiotherapists in football at the time, had not been employed by West Ham long before he found himself nurturing Julian through his long-term rehab programme. The single-minded determination Dicks showed during those dark and lonely periods are a great testament to his character.

But while Julian has always appreciated Green's dedicated help and encouragement throughout his injury ordeal, he has much less pleasant memories of Brian Roper, the club surgeon who performed the initial operation on his battered left knee.

He says: "After the first operation on my knee, the surgeon said he'd removed my cartilage, which was fair enough – I didn't know anything about what was wrong. He then also told me that I'd torn my posterior, lateral and meniscus ligaments . . . but that he'd left them in because he said they were from an old injury.

"I think I was out for about six weeks but when I came back, I lasted only about 10 minutes before my knee just gave way on me. It wasn't painful but it had locked and it swelled up like a balloon – and that's when John Green told me that there was more to it than that. I told Billy that I didn't care who the club surgeon was, I wasn't going back to see him again.

"John took me to see an independent consultant, John King, who was very honest and direct with me. 'You're f****d!' he said after examining me. I was 22-years-old and it wasn't what I wanted to hear. He added that it was 50/50 whether I'd ever play again. He said my ligaments were knackered and that I needed a complete reconstruction. I felt sick.

"He told me I'd be out for 14 months but that, touch-wood, I might play again. I was told that the original injury had nothing to do with my cartilage.

"I regularly visited John King in Harley Street where I'd pedal away on a special machine to build up strength in the muscles supporting my knee. Charlie, the security man at the training ground, would drive me there in his old Ford Fiesta.

Before settling in Spain, Julian was landlord of the Shepherd and Dog pub near Colchester, Essex.

"This was after I'd had a row with Billy, when I presented him with a taxi bill for £220, the cost of taking me from my home in Billericay to Harley Street and back again. He said the club wouldn't pay it and that I should go up to London by tube. But I was on crutches and had a brace round my knee. In the end I think Bill asked Charlie if he'd drive me to Harley Street.

"Charlie and me would be in the car together for two hours each time, and we did this for a year. His driving was that bad, we nearly crashed the Fiesta regularly! But he'd stop off on the way so that I could buy a kebab, and we'd usually have fish and chips on the way home. Charlie was a lovely old boy. He's dead now, God bless him."

Dicks confounded the odds by making another comeback in the winter of 1991-92 and he credits John Green and John King with extending his career by a further six seasons. It was the orthopaedic surgeon King who also guided Julian on a future career path.

"For a month, I used to go down the pub and get absolutely smashed out of my head," admits Julian. "But I went back to see John King one day and he advised me to give up booze and take up golf instead."

A first round of 116 didn't deter Dicks, who got beyond the snapping-of-clubs stage and developed into an accomplished golfer who once pursued his ambition to become a professional sportsman again before he had to accept that his dodgy knee could no longer take the strain.

Dicks marked his long-awaited return to the West Ham first team, after an absence of 14 months, by scoring against Sheffield United at Upton Park in December 1991. It spoke volumes for his outstanding displays in the second half of that depressing relegation season that he missed half the games yet still won the fans' vote for Hammer-of-the-Year.

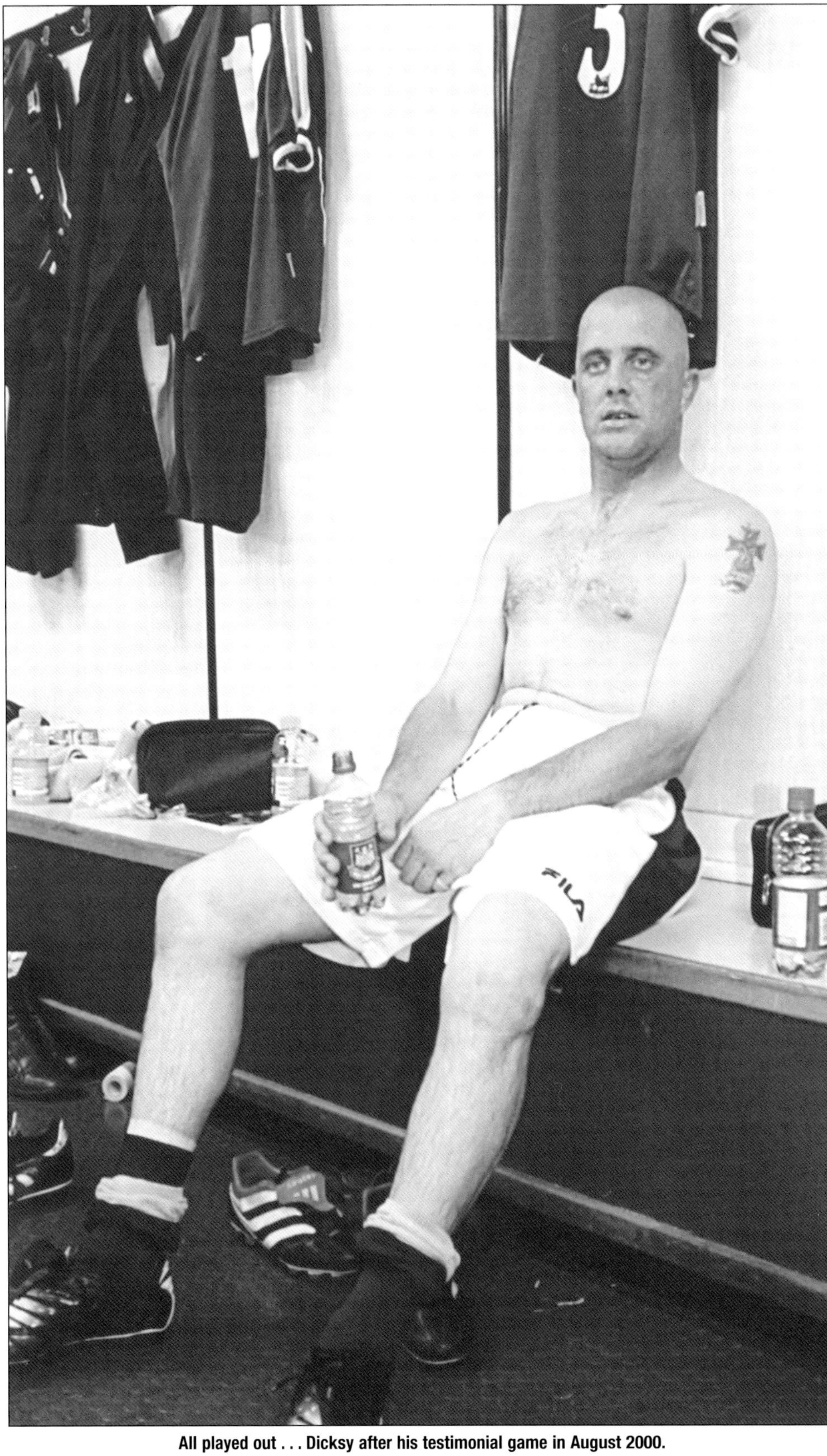

All played out . . . Dicksy after his testimonial game in August 2000.

With 11 goals in 1992-93, Dicksy – who immediately reclaimed the captaincy from Ian Bishop – led Hammers back to the top flight at the first attempt. But when the Hammers were languishing near the bottom of the division seven games into the 1993-94 campaign, there was an inevitability about the departure of the club's most saleable asset.

It was Liverpool manager Graeme Souness, denied the chance to sign Dicks for Rangers some six years earlier, who got his man at the second time of asking. Although gutted to see their big favourite on his way, the fans accepted the reasoning of Billy Bonds and his No.2 Harry Redknapp that the £2.5m deal – involving two players from Liverpool – was in everybody's best interests. The experienced David Burrows was a competent direct replacement at left-back, while Mike Marsh brought creative spark to midfield and Lee Chapman – for all the cruel 'donkey' taunts – contributed enough goals in his first season to ensure Hammers avoided relegation for the second time in two years.

The prospect of winning trophies at Anfield must have been a big pull to Julian but his career finished trophy-less. Having struggled to win over the scouse fans, his Anfield days were definitely numbered when Souness left and Roy Evans stepped up from assistant coach to become first team manager. In the following close season he told Dicks he was unfit and overweight. Instead of joining the first team squad on their tour of Germany, Julian was left behind and would later train with the youth team. In playing terms, he was banished to Liverpool's reserves. Recurring knee trouble – he had more pieces of cartilage removed – clearly affected his general fitness and the ability to show his true worth.

The best thing you can say about Julian's brief time on Merseyside, apart from the lucrative financial deal negotiated by his female agent Rachel Anderson, was the fact that his penalty strike against Ipswich Town, on April 9, 1994, was the last goal ever scored in front of the famous Kop terrace before the stadium became all-seater.

Redknapp had happily washed his hands of Dicks when he was No.2 to Bonzo but barely a year on, once he'd taken over the top job himself, he was in the mood to welcome back the Prodigal Son. Redknapp admits that no-one at West Ham – not even the dinner lady – wanted to see him again. "Everybody was opposed to it – they thought I was off my rocker," Harry said.

Naturally, Dicks was booked on his return game against Southampton, although he quickly points out that he'd just played 28 matches for Liverpool and received just the one yellow card in his nine months at Anfield.

More would inevitably follow. Julian saw red again when he was sent-off for stamping on Chelsea's John Spencer, an incident that earned him another three-match ban and Spencer eight stitches in a head wound. "I swear on my girls' lives that I didn't mean to stamp on him," he pleaded. MP David Mellor branded Dicks an "Animal" in the papers. A less than convinced Redknapp had called him "a liar" in the dressing room.

But Julian was too good a footballer to be remembered for his litany of on-field misdemeanours. He deserved his status as a Hammers hero and the passing years haven't diminished the memories of his wholehearted performances and that lethal left foot.

Twin strikers John Hartson and Paul Kitson got most of the credit for keeping Redknapp's team in the top flight after they arrived in 1997, but it was Dicks who drove that team on when the spectre of relegation reared its ugly head again. Check out his *Terminator* DVD, released in November 2006, and purr with delight as you watch him score twice and then deliver a wonderfully precise cross for Hartson to head home in an epic 4-3 home win over Spurs at rain-ravaged Upton Park.

The West Ham fans, unlike England managers, were never slow to appreciate Julian's value and named him their player-of-the-season for a fourth time.

But the knee problems kept recurring and Julian had to go back under the knife again in another bid to save his career. He missed the whole of the 1997-98 season and, for the second time in his career, many doubted whether he would ever play again. Dicksy recalls those dark days in the summer of '97: "My surgeon said I could end up a cripple later in life, so he didn't really want to do the operation. I took a 13-hour flight to Alabama with John Green and saw Jim Canon, a friend of John King's, who said he'd do the op' but he warned me I had a one-in-10 chance of playing again. I signed a waiver to the effect that would clear the medical people of any blame if it didn't work out.

"The operation in America went well but I had to build the knee up even more than I did after the first op'. People, including ex-players, wrote me off again, and it was hard, but I gave it a go. I played about another 12 games for West Ham."

After two major operations and seven more in between, Dicks' Hammers' career effectively ended one grey afternoon at The Valley in October 1998, when West Ham were badly beaten 2-4 by Charlton Athletic. Asked by Redknapp to adapt to an unfamiliar and demanding left wing-back role, to accommodate a new back three of Neil Ruddock, Rio Ferdinand and Ian Pearce, the tactical change pushed Julian's suspect fitness levels to the brink. He struggled to cope with the surging runs of Danny Mills and admitted he played poorly.

"I'd never played as a wing-back before and I wasn't happy about it. I knew the writing was on the wall when Harry told me the day before the game that he'd be playing only three at the back at Charlton."

More cynical observers could argue that Dicks was hung out to dry that day. If Redknapp genuinely believed Julian was fit enough to cope with such an unfamiliar and demanding role, then he grossly under-estimated the size of the task. The manager regained the moral high ground the following week, though, when Dicks refused to travel to Newcastle after being told that he would only be among the substitutes. He had effectively signed his own West Ham death certificate.

"There were players who didn't give a toss about West Ham or whose shirt they were wearing, so there was no way I was prepared to go all the way up to Newcastle just to sit on the subs' bench," says Julian.

It wasn't quite the end. His last appearance in the claret-and-blue came in a dismal 4-0 home defeat by Arsenal on February 6, 1999. The London derby marked a lamentable home debut for Paolo Di Canio and Marc-Vivien Foé and it was a sad day to call time on Dicks' professional career.

The constant swelling of his badly damaged left knee meant he could hardly train between games and as the Premier League continued to evolve into a league

Julian was forced to abandon hopes of becoming a golf pro due to recurring knee problems.

dominated by a new breed of highly-efficient (if not necessarily skilful) athletes, Julian knew his time was up.

"It was hard to accept having been with the club for 11 years, especially as I was still only 29, but I'd had nine operations on my knee by then. I knew the end was coming," he admits.

After 326 league and cup matches and 65 goals, the club rewarded him with a testimonial match against Athletic Bilbao in August '99 but it didn't provide security for life. He says: "I remember Harry sorting my (severance) pay out with the chairman and it still hurts me as much to think about it today as it did back then. The testimonial was when it did finally hit me that my career was over.

"Although I was covered by insurance, I didn't receive an insurance pay out because the injury that caused me to stop playing was my left knee – and that was excluded in the policy I had at the time. All I had for security was my pension.

"Even my testimonial wasn't as financially rewarding as it might have been – I had to pay Athletic Bilbao 35 grand to play in it! Don't get me wrong, I did OK from it, though."

A restless man at the best of times, Julian was tempted out of retirement in 2001 to play for his local non-league team, Canvey Island. Playing in the same side as fellow former Hammer Lee Boylan, he helped them reach the third round of the FA Cup for the first time in their history in January 2002, although injury ruled him out of the glamour tie at Burnley, which Canvey lost 4-1.

Despite enjoying the less glamorous life of a part-time Ryman Premier League footballer, his knee problems finally took their toll. As well as causing him to quit football completely, he was also forced to abandon initial hopes of making it as a professional golfer.

"I'd played in a couple of big junior tournaments but when my knee went again it put a block on my golfing career. But I don't regret playing for Canvey – I enjoyed my short time with them and I'd do it again if I had the chance, because I just loved playing. I'd even turn out now for a local side in Spain if I had the chance.

"I still miss playing. For me, it's not about money or fame, it's about playing football. All I ever knew was football. No matter who I played for – Birmingham, West Ham, Liverpool or Canvey – I always gave 110 percent. When I played, a lot of footballers were like that.

"Despite the injuries, the sendings-off and all the bookings I've had, and there were too many of them, I wouldn't change anything about my career. Even my injuries, I wouldn't change them. Those experiences have made me the person I am today," says Julian, 40, and now living in Spain.

Frank Lampard gave West Ham great service from the full-back positions for more than 17 years but few would disagree with Harry Redknapp's view that Julian Dicks is the best left-back ever to pull on a Hammers shirt. And West Ham still haven't found a better left-back to replace him, either in footballing terms or in the hearts of the supporters who worshipped him.

Chapter 21

TIM**BREACKER**

" It was an honour to play for Bill – all the players looked up to him and it's not surprising that you never hear a bad word said about him. I respected him as a manager – he was straight-forward, honest and up front with you – but I respected him just as much as a person. He was an example of how you would want to live your life, professionally and personally, and I like to think I did a good job for him"

HE will go down in the history books as Billy Bonds' first signing as West Ham manager back in October 1990 but, had things turned out differently, Tim Breacker may well have already been at Upton Park by the time Bonzo took over – as the first signing of his predecessor, Lou Macari!

The former Luton Town defender had been out of contract at Kenilworth Road in the summer of 1989 – just months after helping the Hatters to a convincing win over West Ham in the League Cup semi-finals and around the same time that Macari arrived in east London to take over from John Lyall.

When the beleaguered Scot expressed an interest in signing the twice-capped England under-21 international, it seemed Breacker's Luton days were over. But, for reasons that still elude Tim to this day, Macari's interest suddenly cooled and the deal was off. However, it wasn't long before a change of personnel at the Boleyn Ground eventually signalled the switch he had been preparing for…

"I really thought West Ham were going to sign me at the start of the 1989-90 season," recalls Tim. "Lou Macari had spoken to me just after taking over at West Ham and I actually met him in Swindon.

"I was out of contract at Luton and we had a chat about the possibility of a move. Everything seemed fine and he said he would phone me. He called once when I was out and spoke to my wife, but that was it – I didn't hear another thing from him.

"I presumed he had looked elsewhere but, as far as I can recall, he didn't sign another right-back and, to this day, I don't know why he backed off so suddenly. At the time, I couldn't wait around forever, so I went back to Luton for pre-season and signed a new contract. They said they would sell me anyway if an offer came in, because of the financial situation they were in. I think Aston Villa might have shown an interest, when Josef Venglos was in charge, but nothing came of it and I ended up staying there for the entire season.

"We escaped relegation on the final day but the team was gradually disbanding. They had sold Kingsley Black on deadline day to Nottingham Forest, and it looked

PONY
DAGENHAM
MOTORS
PONY

as though it would be difficult for the club to survive much longer in the top flight.

"I began the following season at Luton but got the tap on the shoulder at the end of September and was told that West Ham were in for me again. By then Billy Bonds was the manager and, once I'd spoken to him, I knew I was on my way."

Despite the fact that swapping Luton for London meant dropping out of the top flight and into the old second division, Tim made his decision back in the days when clubs in the second tier still had realistic hopes of winning promotion and immediately establishing themselves among the elite.

West Ham were only too willing to underline their ambitions and a fee of £600,000 was paid to secure the services of the blond-haired right-back, who insists he had no reservations about the move.

"I didn't see it as a step down, because West Ham was a massive club and it was only a matter of time before they would be back up in the top flight," he says. "I'd always admired the way they played and the set-up at Upton Park had been very impressive. For me, it was just about the chance to join a big club who had the ambition and support to be successful.

"I spoke to Billy Bonds in early October and he gave me the weekend to think about their offer. That Saturday, they beat Hull City 7-1 and my mind was made up!"

After making his debut as a 37th minute substitute for Julian Dicks in a 1-0 win at Swindon Town on October 20, Tim followed that with a first start four days later, against Blackburn Rovers in another 1-0 victory, as Bonzo's side stretched an unbeaten run that had begun at Middlesbrough on the opening day of the season and would continue for 21 matches, leaving them perfectly placed to achieve their dream of promotion back to the big time.

It didn't take long for Breacker to realise he had made the right decision in signing up for Bonzo's brigade – a belief that was cemented when he appeared in the Upton Park legend's second testimonial match, against Tottenham Hotspur, just a few weeks after his arrival.

"I'll never forget playing in Bill's testimonial match. It was a Monday night yet there were still 20,000 fans there and the atmosphere was amazing," he recalls. "I thought to myself: 'If it's like this for a testimonial match, what must it be like for an important league game?'

"There was a tremendous atmosphere all around the club and it turned out to be a great season. The fans were brilliant, home and away, and we had some real characters in the squad. It was also an honour to play for Bill – all the players looked up to him and it's not surprising that you never hear a bad word said about him.

"I respected him as a manager – he was straight-forward, honest and up front with you – but I respected him just as much as a person. He was an example of how you would want to live your life, professionally and personally, and I like to think I did a good job for him."

After making the right-back spot his own within weeks of arriving – a switch that saw Steve Potts inadvertently embark upon a new role in the centre of defence – Tim established himself as a model of consistency and a firm favourite among the Upton Park faithful. They appreciated his willingness to get forward and support the attack as often as possible, as well as his defensive strengths.

In early March, he claimed his first goal in a claret-and-blue shirt – a 25-yard cracker in a 2-2 draw against Plymouth Argyle – before playing his part six days later in one of the most memorable nights in recent Upton Park history – the FA Cup quarter-final victory over Everton.

However, just as the season reached an important climax in both the league and cup, Tim's progress was halted by the cruel hand of fate, with injury forcing him on to the sidelines for longer than originally expected.

"I'd been struggling with a niggly knee injury," he recalls, "and after we'd beaten Everton in the quarter-final, I was advised to have an operation to trim the cartilage. I was told that if I'd it done straight away, it would be healed in time for me to play in the semi-final, and would eliminate the risk of the knee going completely if I continued playing.

"So I had the operation but, typically, it took longer to heal and I wasn't ready in time for the semi-final against Nottingham Forest. That was a major disappointment – the reason you become a footballer is to experience matches like that and they don't come along very often.

"I'd played in two FA Cup semi-finals with Luton and lost them both so, looking back, maybe it wasn't my lucky competition!"

After returning to action for the final three games of the season with promotion already secured, more disappointment was to follow for Tim as Hammers were pipped to the second division title by Oldham Athletic on the final day.

A return to the top flight helped to soften the blow but the feel-good factor didn't last for long – the 1991-92 campaign turned into a living nightmare. Rooted to the foot of the table for the entire season, the club's misery was compounded by the controversy generated by the ill-fated bond scheme, and Breacker was by now familiar with an Upton Park rollercoaster ride in full flow.

"That season was certainly one to forget," he says. "The situation with the bond scheme certainly didn't help us but, from a playing point of view, it seemed that we had a poorer side than the previous year – despite the fact that we were in a higher division.

"We also had problems with injuries – I remember having to play at centre-half on a few occasions – and things just went from bad to worse as the season went on."

Along with Tim's former club Luton, Hammers fell through the relegation trap-door and were faced with another mountain to climb in the newly-formed 'First Division' following the advent of the FA Premier League. The arrival of Harry Redknapp as assistant to Bonds signalled a new era at Upton Park and, with the club's off-field problems behind them, a second promotion success in the space of three years set them back on the right track again.

As an integral part of both successes, Tim is well qualified to comment on any differences between the classes of '91 and '93, and admits that the maverick style of Redknapp was clearly in evidence as Hammers made an instant return to the top flight.

"I think the side of 1990-91 was a lot more settled," he says, "and we found a high level of consistency. We were going out there every week knowing exactly what we

DAGENHAM
MOTORS

had to do and, more often than not, we did it. There were a lot of 1-0 wins, especially away from home, and I think promotion was cut and dried with six or seven matches left to play.

"In 1992-93, things were a bit more erratic and we had to chop and change a lot more. Harry had come in alongside Bill and there was a lot of movement in the transfer market, so things weren't as settled as they had been two years earlier. I remember we had to go to Swindon and win our penultimate game because

Portsmouth had come on strong, and in the end we just scraped our way up. It was still a fantastic achievement, though, and the perfect way for the club to bounce back after the previous year's disappointment."

As Hammers battled to bring some stability to their league status following the yo-yo years, it was the defensive consistency provided by Ludek Miklosko, Steve Potts, Tony Gale and Breacker – who missed just two league matches in 1993-94 – that ultimately proved the key factor in our inaugural Premier League campaign.

Following Redknapp's controversial elevation to manager at the start of the following season, the make-up of the squad underwent drastic changes. Although he remained steadfastly loyal and committed to the cause throughout the early years of Harry's reign, Tim admits that it became difficult when the playing squad began to develop a foreign feel.

"I think we had it just right in the 1993-94 season," he says. "Bill and Harry seemed to have the perfect partnership – Bill was the front man, a great man-manager who knew how to motivate and get the best out of his players, while Harry was in the background, wheeling and dealing in the transfer market and taking care of the bits that perhaps Bill wasn't so comfortable with.

"Then Harry took over and we started to see the foreign influence. The problems with Boogers, Raducioiu and Dumitrescu are well-documented and, as Harry admitted at the time, those signings were always going to be gambles.

"Looking back, now that I am on the other side of it, I can understand the situation a bit better. When you are working on a limited budget, you often have to take gambles and, at the time, the foreign market was much cheaper than going for British options.

"The thing was, when the going got tough, it was the English lads who were called in to dig the team out of a hole and put up a bit of a fight. It wasn't until Harry was able to bring in the likes of John Hartson, Paul Kitson and Steve Lomas that things really began to improve and, with youngsters like Rio Ferdinand and Frank Lampard coming through at the time, Harry was then able to take it on another level."

With Hammers' boss favouring a modern wing-back system and bringing in the likes of Andy Impey and Trevor Sinclair to fill the position on the right-hand side in the late-90s, Tim's first team opportunities were becoming increasingly limited, although he still managed to stay involved and provided typically reliable and determined service whenever called upon.

A loan spell at QPR in October 1998 provided him with a brief spell of action and, despite West Ham's offer of a contract extension to take him up to a testimonial at Upton Park, Tim turned it down in favour of joining Rangers on a free transfer in February 1999.

"It would have been nice to have had a testimonial," he admits, "but the opportunity to play regular first team football, with a club in London, was more attractive. I had just started a degree in sports science while at West Ham, so staying in the capital enabled me to continue with that. Gerry Francis offered me a two-year contract, so I took the plunge and, looking back, I think I made the right decision."

A troublesome ankle injury forced Tim to hang up his boots in February 2001 – just as Francis was preparing to make way at Loftus Road for Ian Holloway – but

Tim in his coaching days at QPR.

with Rangers crippled by financial problems and on the verge of administration, he was asked to stay on and help the new manager.

"Ian Holloway had been unable to bring his own staff in and so asked me to help him for the rest of the season. We just seemed to click and he offered me a permanent job," Tim explained.

Tim also has his sports science qualifications – a first class honours degree from Roehampton University – to fall back on.

Hammers fans will no doubt remember the right-back's energetic and lengthy pre-match warm-ups back in the days when Dicksy used to make do with a can of Coke and the rest of the team didn't appear until five minutes before kick-off! The Bicester-born defender with the powerful thighs was clearly ahead of his time when it came to matters of fitness and thorough pre-match preparation.

"I'd always been interested in the fitness side of things and used to discuss it quite a lot with John Green, the physio at West Ham. I began the sports science degree in 1998 and graduated with first class honours in 2001."

Tim left QPR, along with coaching colleague Gary Penrice, in a clear-out by the chairman when Ian Holloway departed Loftus Road to join Plymouth at the start of the 2006-07 season. Tim followed Holloway to Home Park and then on to Leicester City, but left the Walker's Stadium with Holloway in the summer of 2008.

Now 43, he lives in St. Neots, Cambridgeshire with wife Jane and their three children, Jamie, Sam and Amelia.

Chapter 22

MARK**ROBSON**

"Someone spotted me and, all of a sudden, all these fellas came steaming over to the car, cheering and singing and wanting to shake my hand. It was unbelievable, a great moment, and just summed up the West Ham fans"

Mark Robson may have only spent just over a year as a West Ham United player...but what a year it was. Few Hammers fans had heard of the Stratford-born winger when he arrived on a free transfer from arch-rivals Tottenham Hotspur in the summer of 1992, yet just a matter of months later he had secured his place in Upton Park folklore as an influential member of the team that won promotion to the Premier League at the end of the 1992-93 campaign.

For a local lad who had been born just a goal-kick away from the Boleyn Ground and followed the likes of Alan Devonshire and Trevor Brooking as a youngster, it was the stuff that dreams are made of.

And although his Hammers career ended on a rather sour note just a few months after he had helped the club into the top flight, the former Spurs and Charlton Athletic winger has nothing but happy memories from one of the most thrilling campaigns in the club's history.

"I was only at West Ham for one full season but, for me, it was fantastic," says Mark. "It was the club I had supported as a boy, growing up just around the corner to the Boleyn Ground, and to play for them was one thing, but to win promotion to the Premier League in that season was something else.

"It was an absolute dream to pull on a West Ham shirt. Before I joined the club, I used to drive past the ground every day when dropping my wife off at Upton Park station, where she caught the train to work. I used to say to her: 'I'm gonna play there one day.'

"It was a bit tongue-in-cheek, but it was something I really wanted to do and for it to come true was fantastic."

The obvious question is how an avid West Ham fan, living just minutes from the ground, managed to slip through the club's scouting network as a talented boy?

In fact, Mark did actually start out as a young hopeful at Upton Park, before spending trial periods at a number of other local rivals and finally ending up far from home in his quest to make it as a professional.

"I was actually at West Ham as a schoolboy – I think they were my first club at the age of nine – but then I moved on and did the rounds," he recalls. "I went to Arsenal, Spurs, Watford and a couple of others, before I left home at 16 and signed apprenticeship forms with Exeter City, who were in the old fourth division then.

"There was a scout called Lenny Harvey, who did a bit of work for Exeter covering the London area, and he invited me down there. It was a bit unusual for a young lad to uproot and head off to Devon but I felt it was the right decision. My mum and dad (Jean and Bill) were very supportive, and things worked out well for me.

"I got into the first team at the age of 17 and, the following year, Spurs came in and brought me back to London. It took me a while to settle in at Tottenham and I went out on loan for a couple of months to Plymouth Argyle, where ex-Hammer Ken Brown was manager.

"I had a great time there and, when I came back to Spurs, I got my chance and made it into the first team."

Having made the breakthrough under Terry Venables at White Hart Lane, Mark looked set for a glittering career alongside superstars such as Paul Gascoigne and Gary Lineker.

However, the cruel hand of fate conspired to deny him the chance to establish himself in north London, as a horrific knee injury suddenly halted his progress and ultimately signalled the end of his first team days at the club.

"I'd only played around six games when I tweaked the ligaments in my knee and was out for around five weeks," remembers Mark. "I got back in the frame, though, and things were looking good again.

"Then I suffered an injury that was a lot worse. We were playing against Crystal Palace at White Hart Lane, and I went in for a challenge with their keeper, Nigel Martyn. I snapped both the cruciate and medial ligaments in my knee, which basically needed a complete reconstruction.

"I was out for an entire year and I never really got back in the side after that. I was playing reserve team football and had a couple of loan spells at Watford and back at Exeter, just to get some games under my belt. I couldn't make the breakthrough again at White Hart Lane, though, and they let me go at the end of the 1991-92 season."

Without a club and still fighting his way back to full match fitness after his career-threatening injury, Mark was all set to pack his bags and head off to the continent in search of a boost.

He certainly wasn't expecting the last-minute call that offered him the opportunity to fulfil a lifelong ambition…

"I actually went over to Holland that summer, for a trial with De Graafschap. I was only there for four days – just so that they could have a look at me – but I played two matches and did really well.

"They offered me a contract just before I was due to fly home and I more or less agreed to go back and sign it a couple of days later.

"But the night before I came back to England, my wife rang and said that Harry Redknapp had phoned and wanted me to call him back. I'd spoken to Harry a few weeks earlier, told him that I'd left Spurs and wondered if he and Billy Bonds would be able to fix me up with anything.

"So I called Harry back – I think West Ham were on a pre-season tour in Scotland at the time – and he said they'd like to have a look at me. There was no way I could

You can see how much playing for West Ham meant to popular winger Mark Robson.

turn down that opportunity, so I put off signing for the Dutch side and came to West Ham for a couple of weeks instead.

"I played in a few friendlies – I remember having a good game against Leyton Orient – and I must have done okay because Bill and Harry offered me a one-year deal.

"I liked Harry. He just used to make you feel like a million dollars, always praising you if you did something well. At the time, it seemed like a real good partnership between him and Bill."

With the club still coming to terms with relegation from the top flight a few months earlier amid the fall-out from the bond scheme protests, the mood at Upton Park was one of apprehension as the new campaign got underway, but a winning start relieved the tension and Mark soon made his impact.

"I started on the bench – I came on at Barnsley on the opening day and then against Charlton in our first home game, and did really well – but then I didn't even get changed for the next game up at Newcastle. Bill and Harry said it wouldn't really be my type of game!

"I started the next match, though, against Watford at home, and that was it, I stayed in the side for the rest of the season."

The chirpy Cockney had made an instant impression on the Upton Park faithful, who were full of admiration for his skillful and tricky wing-play, ability to cross and shoot with either foot and obvious commitment to the cause.

He was one of them, a local boy made good, and the type of character always guaranteed to be a crowd favourite at the Boleyn Ground.

Reflecting on that memorable campaign in which he appeared in all but two of Hammers' 50 league and cup outings and hit an impressive nine goals from the wing, Mark is understandably proud of his contribution to the success that provided the platform for Hammers to enjoy life among the elite for the next 10 years.

"It couldn't have gone better for me, really," he smiles. "I scored nine goals and, being part of a winning team, my confidence grew and the whole season was a fantastic experience.

"We had a really settled side – Kevin Keen and I were the wingers and we both contributed a lot. I played on the right and he played on the left but we used to switch over sometimes to confuse the full-backs and it worked well.

"I had Tim Breacker behind me at right-back, and he was fantastic to play with. He used to just run all day and always gave you an option when you were on the ball. Then we had Dicksy at left-back and I used to combine well with him, too, because he would send 70-yard crossfield passes right on to my toe. I used to tell him before the games to hit the space behind the opposition left-back whenever he could, and we created a lot of goals that way.

"I remember we went on a run of about 15 matches without losing and the confidence was just sky high. Clive Allen and Trevor Morley were scoring regularly up front, Martin Allen used to chip in with a few, and me and Keeny were also on the scoresheet fairly often.

"My first goal in a West Ham shirt will always be memorable – away at Bristol City in a 5-1 win early in the season, although my best was probably at Millwall. We lost 2-1 and, unfortunately, I gave away a penalty. But I scored our goal and also got the man-of-the-match award and had to give my first ever interview live on TV after the game."

As well as adjusting well to life on the pitch, Mark naturally found it easy to settle in off the field, too. A popular figure in the dressing room, he admits that the atmosphere and spirit among the players played a huge role in their promotion triumph.

"It was great, we had a magnificent team spirit and that certainly played a part in our success. The lads all got on, we used to socialise together and enjoy each other's company and there was a brilliant atmosphere around the place.

"There was a mixture of backgrounds. We had a few local lads, a bit of Yorkshire grit with Peter Butler and a couple of Scousers in Bish and Alvin. I got on really well with Alvin – a very funny guy and great to have as a team-mate.

"I remember him telling me when we won promotion to make sure I took it all in and enjoyed the celebrations, because you don't get many moments like that in football. He was 100 per cent right and I still have great memories of that time."

Recalling those famous scenes after the 2-0 final-day victory over Cambridge United that sealed Hammers' return to the big-time in May 1993, Mark admits he savoured memories that will never fade.

"The scenes in the dressing room afterwards were fantastic, everyone was on cloud nine, the champagne was flowing freely and it was a great way to round off a fantastic season.

"Then I remember driving home afterwards and, because I had to drop someone off, I ended up coming through East Ham. I had my wife with me in the car and we were at the lights by the Town Hall, and there were a load of West Ham fans outside the Denmark Arms pub.

"Someone spotted me and, all of a sudden, all these fellas came steaming over to the car, cheering and singing and wanting to shake my hand. It was unbelievable, a great moment, and just summed up the West Ham fans.

"It was, without doubt, the highlight of my career. Not just for the fact that we won promotion to the Premier League, but also because the club was so close to my heart and it was my lifelong dream to play in a West Ham shirt. It's something that I am very, very proud of and I'll never forget it."

Sadly for Mark, those final-day celebrations turned out to be the pinnacle of his Upton Park career. Despite putting pen to paper on a new contract soon after the end of the season, he found himself out of the starting line-up by the time Hammers kicked off their inaugural campaign in the Premier League and, just weeks later, heading out of the club altogether.

"They offered me a new two-year deal in the summer and, as you can imagine, I was delighted to sign it," he recalls. "Then they brought in Dale Gordon for big money and I was the first one to get the chop. Kevin Keen had left the club but Matty Holmes was signed and he fitted in on the left, with Dale on the right.

"I was obviously a bit disappointed but I got on with it and just told myself that I'd keep working hard in the hope of getting back in. I played in the home game against QPR, which we lost 4-0. That was my first full game in the Premier League and I actually did all right – I think I even got the man-of-the-match award.

"I was back out the side again for the following game, though, and I never really got the opportunity to prove that I could do it in the top flight. That was the disappointing thing – that I didn't even get the chance.

"They probably didn't fancy me in the Premier League. They never actually said to me that I wasn't strong enough or quick enough but when Keith Rowland played on the left-wing in front of me, I knew things weren't going to improve.

"At the time, I was obviously a little bitter about it but, looking back now, perhaps they were right. It just would've been nice to have found out if they were!"

Robbo was left distraught when Bonzo informed him that the club had accepted a bid from Charlton Athletic for his services in early September 1993, and he reluctantly dropped back down to the first division after just one start and two substitute appearances in the top flight.

Mark went on to spend four seasons at The Valley, before leaving on a free transfer in May 1997 – just 12 months before Alan Curbishley's men secured promotion. He headed to second division Notts County soon after and spent two years at Meadow Lane while also enjoying a short loan spell at Wycombe Wanderers as he wound down a 12-year professional career.

He hung up his boots in October 1999 but renewed his connection with the Hammers soon after his playing days ended when he returned to the club to coach the youngest of our Academy hopefuls, before heading back to Charlton Athletic when a full-time role became available.

However, his early steps as a youth coach didn't take him into unfamiliar territory – Mark had entered the field many years before.

"I'd actually been coaching throughout my playing career," he says. "I ran one of the local Senrab teams when I was still quite young, so I already had the experience of coaching young lads.

"Then when I retired from playing, I went over to West Ham to coach the babies, the six and seven year-olds, and I really enjoyed that. I was obviously looking for a full-time coaching role and a job came up at Charlton, who offered me a role overseeing the nine to 16-year-olds.

"Within a few months, they wanted me to look after the under-19s, which was great for me – it was the next step after working with the younger kids."

Since then, Mark has continued to progress up the coaching ranks at Charlton. The the 2008-09 campaign marks his second season as first team coach at The Valley under former Hammers boss Alan Pardew, who returned south of the Thames himself in December 2006 just days after being sacked by West Ham.

"Pards told me he was going to bring in Phil Parkinson when he arrived, but that he wanted me to stay on as first team coach, and I was delighted by that," said Robbo.

"I'd been the Development Coach the previous summer, basically looking after the 17-21 year-olds and the reserve team progress. Then Iain Dowie left and I was assisting Les Reed, before things changed again when Pards came in.

"I thought I might be back in my old role with the youngsters and reserves, but he kept me involved with the first team, which was fantastic for me."

Chapter 23

JOHN**MONCUR**

"It became a standing joke among the English lads – you didn't know which ones were going to turn up each day. The trouble was, most of them were earning more money than us!"

ADMIRED for his determined, never-say-die attitude and intelligent, silky skills on the ball, and loved for his cheeky sense of humour and legendary practical jokes, Stepney-born midfielder John Moncur certainly gave value for money as Hammers established themselves in the Premier League throughout the mid-to-late 90s.

Having left the club on a free transfer in the wake of our relegation from the top flight in May 2003, John disappeared from the football scene, but *EX* caught up with the chirpy Cockney to reflect on his Hammers career.

Given the choice between a move to West Ham or Chelsea nowadays, it's sadly a fact of life that the vast majority of players wouldn't think twice before heading off to Stamford Bridge and the lure of Abramovich's riches.

The west London club not only contain a large wedge of talent nurtured in the Upton Park academy, they also have the power of persuasion to sign virtually any star name in the current game, safe in the knowledge they can provide a financial package to outbid just about every other club in the world these days.

However, not so long ago, things were quite different, for it was the unfashionable Hammers who were gazumping their west London rivals in the transfer market.

Moncur was a cultured, hard working mid-fielder who had begun his career with Tottenham Hotspur but failed to make the grade at White Hart Lane behind the likes of Glenn Hoddle, Ossie Ardiles and Paul Gascoigne in the mid-to-late 80s. A cluster of brief loan spells around the country followed before he eventually settled down at Swindon Town in the early 90s – then managed by his boyhood hero, Hoddle.

In the summer of 1994, after the Robins had been relegated at the end of their one and only season in the Premier League, the impressive Moncur was widely tipped to remain in the top flight. Coveted by both West Ham and Chelsea – by then managed by Hoddle and on the verge of a European Cup Winners' Cup campaign after losing to double winners Manchester United in the previous campaign's FA Cup final – he faced a straight choice between east and west London . . . and surprised many people by eventually agreeing to an £800,000 move to Upton Park.

"I knew I was leaving Swindon and it basically came down to a choice between Chelsea and West Ham," he recalls, "I'd known Glenn Hoddle since I was a kid, I

Moncs – a good ball player who also relished a tough midfield battle.

grew up with his brother and he was my idol, and obviously I'd played under him at Swindon, so I knew that the opportunity was there for me and I think a lot of people expected me to follow him to Chelsea.

"There was just something about West Ham that grabbed me, though. I was a local boy anyway – both my Mum and Dad were from the East End – and that was a big factor. My Granddad had died a couple of years earlier, he was a massive West Ham fan, and I just thought how proud he'd have been to see me run out in the claret-and-blue shirt.

"I was also attracted by the tradition at West Ham and the style of football they were famous for. I thought that would suit me and I felt I could be a big player for the club.

"I spoke to both clubs but made my mind up it would be West Ham and, once I'd done that, there was no going back. I've always been the type of bloke who lives and dies by his decision, and I don't look back at what might have been.

"Glenn obviously wasn't too happy – I think he was a bit shocked that I chose West Ham over Chelsea – but that was my decision. It changed our relationship a bit and I knew I'd never get to play for England once he took over as manager!"

While the move back to his roots seemed like a perfect opportunity, little did John realise that he was about to become embroiled in one of the most turbulent periods in West Ham history. Just weeks after putting pen to paper at Upton Park, he was stunned to see Billy Bonds, the manager who signed him, controversially leave the club in the wake of the board's ill-judged attempt to rearrange the coaching set-up and replace him with Harry Redknapp. Moncs also watched in amazement as the club's other major summer signing disappeared soon after he arrived.

"It was a bit of a mad time, I must admit," he says. "I'd only been there two weeks when it all kicked off with Bill and Harry, which was a bit of a shock to say the least. Then there was the Joey Beauchamp thing, which I'll never forget.

"We'd signed at the same time, so I got to know him early on, and I remember we were on the coach going down to Eastbourne for a week of pre-season training when he turned to me and said: 'I can't have it here.'

"I asked him what he meant and he told me that he thought it would only take him an hour or so to get to training every day from where he lived in Oxford, yet it was taking him two-and-a-half hours, and he didn't think he could cope with it.

"At first, I was waiting for him to smile and make a joke, but then I realised he was deadly serious. I just said: 'You're having a laugh?' It was unbelievable and I knew at that point he'd never play for the club.

"I knew what the fans were like and I knew he'd get slaughtered. We had a friendly at Southend and he just couldn't wait to get off the pitch.

"It was a couple of strange weeks, that's for sure, but I didn't get too worried about my own position. Harry took over and in the end I had a great season. We just avoided relegation and I really enjoyed my football."

Having arrived right at the start of Redknapp's long and eventful seven-year reign, John soon became a regular fixture in the centre of midfield, admired by fans and team-mates alike for his wholehearted approach, attractive style of play and colourful personality, as well as the legendary practical jokes that were regularly played on his unsuspecting colleagues.

With the lucrative Premier League still in its infancy, he was reaching his prime just as the financial rewards for top flight footballers were beginning to escalate, while still enjoying the relatively relaxed and fun atmosphere of what he describes as the 'old school' era of the English game. That mindset gradually started to change with the arrival of foreign players and coaches, who brought with them a new, ultra-professional way of thinking.

With Redknapp settled in the Upton Park hot-seat, his wheeling and dealing created a strong foreign influence during the mid-90s – a change of policy that created an interesting environment for Moncur and his English team-mates.

"It was an enjoyable time and, for a lad of 26-27, it was a great club to be at," says John. "There was a group of us who would go out socialising together – me, Dicksy, Hutch, Bish and Kenny Brown – and we were all good mates who would stick together.

"Things started to change when Harry moved into the foreign market, because all of a sudden there was a new mentality coming to the club and it didn't mix too well with what we were used to.

"It's well documented that Harry signed some good ones and some bad ones, but it's only when I look back now that I realise how amazing it all was. Like I say, there were some good foreign signings – the likes of Marc Rieper, Slaven Bilic and Paolo Di Canio all did the business on the pitch, but then you had Boogers, Dumitrescu, Raducioiu, Futre, Porfirio and many others on loan and on trial whose names I can't even remember!

"I mean, really, what was going on there? There was no doubting their talent but, for whatever reason, they just didn't fancy it when the going got tough.

"To be honest, most of them were good lads, they just didn't know how to deal with the whole situation. I think one of the problems was that the right structure just wasn't in place for the foreigners to feel settled. Most of them were just stuck in a big house out in Essex, not knowing anyone or how to integrate into society.

"As a footballer, there are times when things aren't going well for you and it's all going a bit wobbly on the pitch. It's hard enough, even when you have your family around you and are living in your local area, so imagine what it's like if you are in a different country, with no-one to talk to? All you'd want to do is go home.

"A few of them were strong enough characters to see it through, but so many of them just couldn't hack it. It eventually became a standing joke among the English lads – you didn't know which ones were going to turn up each day. The trouble was, most of them were earning more money than us!

"One thing's for sure, it was never dull under Harry, and whatever you say, he kept us in the Premier League for seven years. The fans saw some great football and I think it was the sort of environment that suited me, because it was never boring."

Having seen Redknapp's reign come to an end in May 2001, Moncur wasn't unhappy to see rank outsider Glenn Roeder succeed him. The pair had known each other for many years through England star Paul Gascoigne, whom John befriended during their Tottenham days and Roeder knew having acted as Gazza's 'minder' at Newcastle and then Lazio.

One to delight the fans, as John gives ex-Hammer Paul Ince the slip during a game against Manchester United.

In Roeder's first season in charge, Moncur made a worthwhile contribution to the cause, making 20 league appearances at the age of 35 and providing a protective influence on young midfield starlets Joe Cole and Michael Carrick. But despite signing a new one-year deal, things turned sour the following season for the loyal veteran, as he was cast aside by the under-fire Hammers boss during a traumatic campaign that eventually ended in relegation.

"I'd had a decent season in Glenn's first year – played 20-odd games and made a contribution that I was happy with," he says. "The following season, though, he just made his mind up that I wasn't part of his plans and that was it.

"I was basically told that my age was against me and that he didn't think I could do a job for the team. Personally, I thought that was a poor decision. I had consciously worked hard to change my game as I got older. I realised I couldn't tear around the park like I used to, so I became more of a holding midfielder who put his foot in and showed commitment to the team.

"I was disappointed Glenn didn't even use me as a substitute, because I think I could've helped the team. Harry used to tell me to go on and change the game if we were struggling – and I felt I could still have done that during my last season.

"I'm not saying I would have saved us from relegation, but I felt that I could spark

FILA
FILA

a reaction among some of the other players who were finding it tough and lacking in confidence. I confronted Glenn about it and asked him to give me a chance, but he'd made his mind up and that was it.

"It was a shame because I had no personal problem with Glenn. I'd known him for a long time through Gazza, and I considered us to be friends, but he had his opinion and there was nothing I could do about it. I carried on training as hard as I could and kept trying to get in the team, but the door wasn't open for me. That's football, I suppose, and I just had to get on with it."

Moncur admits there was a lack of authority and that Roeder failed to gain the respect of all his players. However, he also insists that the blame for relegation in 2003 should have been shared more collectively rather than laid solely at the door of the beleaguered Roeder.

"As the season went on, it was obvious that there was a serious problem," he says. "Certain players were being allowed to get away with more than others and I'd have to say that Glenn lost the respect of some of the squad.

"I remember once in training, we were playing a practice match and, all of a sudden, Sebastien Schemmel got the hump about something and just sat down on the grass while the game was going on. I couldn't believe it, and in the end I said something to Glenn about it. He sent Schemmel to get changed, but I got the feeling it was only because I'd spoken up about it.

"It was sad the way everything turned out, but I wouldn't lay the blame entirely on Glenn's shoulders. I've always been the type of bloke who blames himself when things go wrong, and I think the players that year had a lot to answer for. We let ourselves down, individually and as a team, and there were certain players who let the manager down, too.

"That team that got relegated was probably the most talented bunch of players in West Ham's history. But they were lacking the commitment and desire you need to go with it.

"It's something I tell my boys now – ability gets you to the door, but attitude gets you through it."

Following confirmation of our relegation, and as one of several squad members out of contract that summer, Moncur was informed that he would not be offered another one-year deal that would have secured him a deserved testimonial at Upton Park.

The then 36-year-old slipped quietly out of the exit door as the fire-sale of our talented young stars grabbed all the publicity, and that was the last the football world heard of John Moncur. Although linked with a host of clubs in the lower divisions and presented with an opportunity to start a new life on the other side of the Atlantic, he admits that no offer was attractive enough to persuade him to uproot his young family. In fact, the only deal he would have been interested in was the one that sadly wasn't forthcoming from Upton Park.

"Once we had been relegated, I half hoped that the club would turn round and offer me a new deal, because I felt sure I could offer something in the first division," he says. "I was told that there was no new contract for me, though, and that was it. Personally, I thought the fact that they let me, Nigel Winterburn and Paolo Di Canio go was criminal, because we were the sort of senior players who would've done a good job for the club at that level.

"The thing that upset me was that they said I was too old . . . and then they signed the likes of Rob Lee and Kevin Horlock. Don't get me wrong, Rob Lee had been a great player, but he was the same age as me and I felt I could have done just as good a job as him.

"That proved to me that it wasn't really about age, which was a bit hurtful. Still, I didn't let it bother me. I'd had nine years at the club and although it would have been nice to end with a testimonial, I was grateful that I'd spent that long at the club.

"Although I didn't know it at the time, my last game as a professional was against Arsenal at Highbury, chasing around after Thierry Henry. I suppose that's enough to make anyone want to retire!

"I had a few different offers when I left West Ham but none were attractive enough to take me away from my regular way of life. I had the chance to go to both Coventry and Cardiff, and the former Liverpool defender, Steve Nicol, asked me to go out to America to play for his team in the MLS.

"After thinking it all over, though, I decided to finish at the top and now I'm glad that I did – it was the right decision. I do miss it, of course, when you've spent 20 years as a pro you do miss the everyday banter and laugh with your mates – it's a way of life.

"I've got mates, the likes of Gazza and Razor (Neil Ruddock) who have struggled since packing up, and I'm grateful that my life has been good since I stopped playing. It's a void in your life, and you miss running out in front of a crowd and tasting the atmosphere, but I've managed to cope and get on with my life."

Just before he had departed Upton Park in May 2003, John surprised many people by speaking publicly about his Christian faith – a part of his life that, up until then, had been kept completely private, not only from West Ham fans but also from some of his team-mates and colleagues.

As someone who was always well known for his mischievous sense of humour and love of a good night out and a few beers, and given that pro footballers of his era were meant to inhabit a stereotypical world of birds, booze and boorish behaviour, it was viewed as something of a shock that he should admit to his religious beliefs.

However, as he explains in a revealing insight, it's his faith that has enabled him to turn his life around for the sake of his family, without having to sacrifice the cheeky personality and love of a good time that endeared him to those who encountered him in his playing days.

"It's something I've always believed in and it's been good for me," he says. "It was around 1999 that I started to show more of an interest, and I think I needed something like that to change my ways and give me a bit of a wake-up call.

"I've always been quite an emotional person, living on the edge slightly, and when I was younger that got me into trouble. I had quite a tough time at Spurs – there were times when I couldn't see my career heading anywhere and I dealt with that in the wrong way.

"I got into a few scrapes, in nightclubs and that sort of thing, and just generally got myself into bother that I didn't need. Basically, my social life took control of me. I

PONY
Dr. Martens
PONY
ULTIMO
PUMA

PONY
Dr. Martens

was getting into a lot of aggro, and I was at a stage where it could have gone either way for me.

"Thankfully, I had a couple of wake-up calls and, most of all, my faith and my family gave me the strength to change my life. I'm proud that I'm not doing drugs anymore, or not in jail, because that's the kind of life that I was looking at.

"I know there is a stigma attached to the Christian thing, especially in football, but it doesn't bother me. I'm proud that I believe in Jesus Christ and that's the end of it. I've always been able to take a bit of stick – I love it really. The boys down at the golf club call me 'Johnny the Christian' but it doesn't bother me one little bit.

"At the end of the day, I know what my priorities are now. I have a lovely family and the most important thing to me are my three boys. That is my responsibility and I'm glad that I'm around now to see them grow up. I just want to do the best job I can as a dad, and we'll see what happens."

Living in Loughton, Essex, with wife Kerry and their three sons, George, Freddie and Timmy, John is no longer involved with the game professionally. Having moved into property development towards the end of his playing days, he still retains an interest in that field and is investing in a separate private venture.

Most of his time is spent looking after his three boys and indulging in his other sporting love – golf. With two older brothers who both earn a living from the game – Terry, who works as the Head Pro at Langdon Hills Golf Club in Brentwood, and Nick, who runs a golfing academy in Spain – John has always had an interest and was indeed renowned for his prowess on the course during his playing days.

Now playing three or four times a week, he currently plays to a handicap of 1.1 and is aiming towards reaching 'scratch', which would enable him to follow his former team-mate Julian Dicks into the professional game if he so wished.

"At the moment, I'm enjoying watching my kids grow up and I don't think I could give that up. They are more important than anything else I could consider doing. Who knows what will happen in the next five or 10 years? I may have to go out and start working again, but I've made my decision to devote myself to my family now and, as I said earlier, once I've made a decision, that's it.

"As for getting back into the game, again, who knows? It's hard to get back in at a senior level if you have been out of it for a couple of years, but maybe there will be the chance to work with the youngsters. West Ham did ask me to get involved with the Youth Academy but for now I'm just happy as I am."

Whatever route he decides to take in life, 42-year-old Moncs will always have the support and admiration of a West Ham following who remember him as one of the last great characters to grace Upton Park.

The last word goes to John: "The fans have always been quite a hard crowd to win over, but I think I earned their respect. They always seemed to love players who would give 100 per cent every week and also be able to put their foot on the ball and show a bit of skill. That was all I ever tried to do."

From those who feature at the start of this book, Bill Lansdowne and Ken Brown in the late-50s to Johnny Moncur in the new millennium, that is all West Ham United supporters have any right to expect from all the players who have been fortunate enough to pull on the claret-and-blue.

INDEX